THE SECOND
Bill of Rights
&
THE NEW FEDERALIST PAPERS

Eleven Amendments to the United States Constitution
and Fifty Papers that Present Them.

EDITED BY
JOHN B. MILLER

ANONYMOUS CONTRIBUTING AUTHORS:
Amicus
Atticus
Prosperus
Valerius

Published by The New Federalism, LLC

ISBN: 0984876405
ISBN-13: 9780984876402
Library of Congress Control Number: 2011944344

TheNewFederalisam LLC, Arlington, MA

Contents

Introduction

One of the remarkable things about America's Founding Fathers is that so many of them were practical men and tinkerers. Washington himself, though famously a statesman, was, by trade, a surveyor and engineer. Benjamin Franklin may have been a master diplomat, but by trade he was a printer, inventor, and scientist. Benjamin Rush was a physician by trade, and father of American psychiatry. Samuel Adams was a brewer, and his cousin, John, a lawyer. There were land speculators, such as Robert Morris, merchants, soldiers, and farmers.

The editor and creator of the present volume, Dr. John B. Miller, began his career studying soil mechanics at the Massachusetts Institute of Technology, and was only laterally drawn into law. No doubt the two impulses combined in his instinct to tinker with the greatest of all secular laws, the Constitution of the United States, and shore it up with a *Second Bill of Rights*. Fifty supporting essays from four anonymous contributors, the undersigned not among them, make up what Dr. Miller calls *The New Federalist Papers*.

It's not unusual, in and of itself, for an American to offer amendments to the Constitution. Thousands of proposals have been made over the years, and many are under consideration. They often focus on narrow gripes—a plan to repeal the Second Amendment on the right to bear arms, for example, or to disallow the desecration of the flag, or to protect abortions or to prohibit them, or to permit prayer at school meetings and ceremonies, to cite but a few of the scores of amendments that have been proposed in recent congresses.

What makes Dr. Miller's *Second Bill of Rights* and *The New Federalist Papers* different is that they are a holistic attempt to repair what he and his co-authors perceive as flaws revealed by two centuries of experience. Dr. Miller makes a point of retaining the Founders' masterful structure and their commitment to individual freedom and liberty. He starts not with any narrow problem but with an effort to find a balance among the enumerated powers of the national government, the police power of States, and the day-to-day exercise of liberty rights by citizens. The first four amendments and the first thirty-one essays offer what Dr. Miller calls "a practical way to 'reboot' the constitutional computer back to the Founders' vision—citizens blessed with freedom and liberty in the midst of defined federal and state power." The amendments are bound together with practical definitions of the rule of law and the meaning of words in the Constitution.

In its fifth and six amendments, *The Second Bill of Rights* moves to federal finance and revenue. The fifth amendment would impose the same annual financial accounting and reporting requirements on the federal government that the federal government imposes on publicly held corporations. The fiscal year end would be moved to April 30 and public delivery of financial information is required by October 1. This timing—five weeks before federal elections in even years—finally favors voters. Managing the value of the currency would be brought back into the sunshine. Specie would be restored to the dollar, and Congress alone would be empowered to establish (and adjust) the quantity of gold that defines our national unit of account. Proposals are offered to replace (or simplify) the income tax.

In its seventh and eighth amendments, the *Second Bill of Rights* moves to the controversies over citizenship and representation. The changes would require Congress to establish a process for dealing with immigration, residence, and naturalization. Limitations would be placed on the Congress in respect of what it can do with the decennial census. Gerrymandering would be ended, and—here one senses the master of soil mechanics at his most imaginative—the Columbia District reduced in size to little more than the Federal Mall.

In the remaining amendments, *The Second Bill of Rights* turns to other issues that have arisen from the Founders' notions of federalism. It would narrow federal power to regulate commerce among the States and confirm that Congress has no power over any citizen's choices relating to retirement, health care, or financial security. The duty of the Judiciary to preserve liberty rights, the rule of law, the police power of States, and the republican form of government would be confirmed. Other provisions would ensure judicial nominees are experienced in the common law and reduce burdens on federal dockets from certain non-federal civil actions and from actions relating to the uniform services. The roles of Congress, the President, and the Court in respect of the war on terror would be clarified. Re-codification of the statutes of the United States during a period of transition is set forth.

The Second Bill of Rights and the New Federalist Papers couldn't come at a more opportune time. America turns out to be in what I have called a "constitutional moment." No doubt many will cavil that such a sweeping revision of the Constitution as Dr. Miller is proposing is unlikely in a fell swoop. But it is hard to imagine a time when constitutional questions are so much a part of the national debate. Even as I was writing this introduction, the news wires were reporting that the Occupy Wall Street movement was preparing its own set of constitutional amendments.

History shows that the instinct to improve upon the original Constitution erupted even as it was ratified, animated by concerns very much like those that are expressed here, animated by a quarter of a millennium of experience with the first written constitution. If one can imagine the Constitution as a sprawling home, here is a master of soil mechanics and law with a plan to shore up the foundation. A reading of these essays will repay the effort.

—Seth Lipsky
Author of
"The Citizen's Constitution: An Annotated Guide"
New York City
January 2012

Editor's Note

On November 10, 1787, several weeks after returning to Mount Vernon from the Constitutional Convention in Philadelphia, George Washington wrote to his nephew, Bushrod Washington, about the draft constitution and the amendment process it contained. The draft had been transmitted to the States for review and ratification. Bushrod Washington had served in the Continental Army and was present at the surrender of Cornwallis at Yorktown.[1] Nominated by President John Adams in 1798, he served on the Supreme Court for thirty (30) years.[2]

George Washington's letter to his nephew is a humble yet inspiring view of the Constitution, its imperfections, the remedy to fix them, and the faith our first President had in generations of Americans who would come after him:[3]

> The warmest friends and the best supporters the Constitution has do not contend that it is free from imperfections; but they found them unavoidable . . . [The friends of the Constitution] are [aware], if evil is likely to arise therefrom, the remedy must come hereafter; for in the present moment, it is not to be ob-

---

1   After the war, Bushrod Washington studied law in the Philadelphia office of James Wilson. James Wilson's arguments in favor of the draft constitution before the Pennsylvania ratification convention are described in Number 14, below.

2   Bushrod Washington authored the opinion in *Corfield v. Coryell*, which defined the "privileges and immunities" of American citizens. This description is a primary source for the definition of "liberty rights" in *The Second Bill of Rights*, at Amendment 2, Sections 2 and 3. See, Numbers 5, 8, and 17, below.

3   *George Washington's Sacred Fire*, Peter A. Lillback, Appendix 8, at p. 875 (Providence Forum Press, 2006).

tained; . . . [A]s there is a Constitutional door open for it, I think the People (for it is with them to Judge) can[,] as they will have the advantage of experience on their Side, decide[,]with as much propriety on the alterations and amendments which are necessary as [we can] ourselves. *I do not think we are more inspired, have more wisdom, or possess more virtue, than those who will come after us.*[4]

George Washington gently reminds us that although the structure of the Constitution was sound, actual experience might reveal faults that would require careful consideration. While individual freedom and liberty would always be synonymous with the word American, Washington expected that those who would come after him might need to tinker with details of the Constitution—based on experience.

The Second Bill of Rights and the New Federalist Papers are intended to encourage the kind of careful thought Washington expected. To preserve the republic they created—one based on individual freedom and liberty—those who came after the Founders would need to consider the faults that experience would reveal. The "tinkering" proposed in *The Second Bill of Rights*, and described in *The New Federalist Papers*, suggests the kind of improvements Washington anticipated when he wrote to his nephew.

Like the Founders, we may not agree on every issue, and will not find angels among us to decide every issue for us. But, surely, with humility, mutual respect, honesty, and some wisdom, we can find a way forward that is worthy of Washington's confidence. The amendments we suggest will again fall short of perfection. And, like Washington, we trust those who come after us, based on experience, to tinker again.

John B. Miller

---

4   Unless otherwise noted, words have been italicized by the authors or the editor for emphasis.

Foreword

Two hundred and twenty-five years ago, on May 25, 1787, the Founders assembled in Philadelphia to prepare, debate, and transmit a draft Constitution to the Continental Congress. Participation in the Constitutional Convention carried risk. What if those in attendance could not agree? What if the Convention produced active disagreement? The most beloved American of his day—George Washington—agreed to attend, and to preside over the Convention. The delegates met continuously until September 17, 1787, when the draft Constitution was transmitted to the Continental Congress. The same draft was subsequently ratified by constitutional conventions in each of the thirteen states.

The republic they established was the world's first free-trade zone. By every measure, the republic is the most fabulous success in history.[1] Why did it succeed so well? And, looking back over the last 225 years, why didn't it fail like the French Revolution of 1789, the Soviet Revolution of 1917, and so many other *revolutions* on the ash heap of history? Mark David Ledbetter, an American-born teacher, who has lived in Japan for more than 30 years, provides a simple answer that rings true:[2]

---

1 *Monitoring the World Economy, 1820-1992*, by Angus Maddison (OECD Development Centre, 1995, Paris, France). Population grew from under 10 million in 1820 to more than 255 million in 1992. GDP grew from $12 million in 1820 to $5.6 trillion in 1992. Between 1820 and 1992, US GDP per person multiplied by a factor of 16.7, at the top of all countries, along with Canada, Australia, and New Zealand. In these same four countries, national GDP grew by a factor of 464 over the same period, again at the top of all countries. Figures are in 1990 dollars.
2 *America's Forgotten History, Part One, Foundations*, by Mark David Ledbetter, 2011, available at Smashwords.com.

Revolutions have a poor track record. Failure is common and success is normally followed by blood, terror, and repression worse than what came before it. So why was the American Revolution different?

The key point may be this: it was not a sudden explosion of pent-up rage in the masses. Such explosions normally either die out or come to be controlled and directed by a small cadre of (self-defined) indispensable leaders with a (self-defined) superior understanding of the progression of history and needs of the people. Rather, America's was an evolutionary revolution with both leadership and intellectual underpinnings diffused throughout society.
. . . . .
The people already had a sense of personal power because of well and long established traditions of self-government in the North American colonies. The leaders did not cry "power to the people" as much as leaders of later revolutions, but in fact *the people already accepted power as their due.* Leaders of later revolutions, though, led people who were not accustomed to power. The leaders held power in trust for the not-yet-ready people. This means, of course, they held it for themselves and soon became very comfortable holding it. Those later revolutions lived on slogans of people power but America's lived on the reality. . . .

Revolutions are sudden things but the evolution behind America's that let it succeed was the work of centuries. It was, in truth, not only an American work but an English one. Englishmen in a new world continued what they had begun in the old. The waves of immigrants through the 17th century brought with them the developing ideas of individual rights, representative and constitutional government, and government by consent of the governed. The ideas were familiar in England. But in America, without a long entrenched power structure or aristocracy, or an immutable division between landowners and non-landowners, the ideas were more easily translated into reality.

Three of these points are particularly useful in reading this book:
- At the time of the revolution, Americans already accepted power as their due.

- The revolution was not only an American work but also an English one.
- Waves of immigrants (before the revolution) brought the emerging ideas of individual rights, representative and constitutional government, and government by consent of the governed.

Madison, Washington, Franklin, Adams—all of the Founders—accepted the assignment of establishing a republic in which each citizen already accepted power as his due; in which individual rights prevailed, and representative and constitutional government was preserved, with the consent of the governed. They did not cry "power to the people;" they gave it. They did not think of themselves as indispensable; they assured regular transition of power. They did not presume to know what was best for their fellow citizens; they encouraged individual choice and responsibility.

The Founders established a republic that did not hold power in trust for others who were not yet ready. They knew their fellow citizens already accepted power over their own lives—the power of individual freedom and liberty—with respect for their fellow citizens under the common law.

Against the backdrop of freedom and liberty established by the Founders, consider the question asked by Sen. Burke (D-Neb) of then Asst. Atty. Gen. Robert Jackson in 1937 hearings before the Senate Judiciary Committee. Jackson was later appointed to the Supreme Court and authored *Wickard v. Filburn.*[3]

> Do you not recognize that there is a vast power that does not lie in either the federal government or any state government, but has been reserved so far by the people themselves, and they have not yet been willing to turn over to any government, no matter how beneficial its purpose may be?

Sen. Burke asks the question addressed throughout this book—the same question that has faced Americans since the Boston Tea Party. Do we still accept power over ourselves as our due, as Americans did in 1787? Or, are we willing to turn [power] over to government?

---

3   More about Burke, Jackson, and Wickard in Numbers 19 and 20, below.

Americans again live in interesting times. Actual experience with the hard face of totalitarianism, communism, and national socialism—*collectivism*—has confirmed that extensive central planning cannot co-exist with individual freedom and liberty. Their sibling, the soft face of collectivism, approaches its financial and political end.

Americans may soon need to reach again for the limited government the Founders envisioned in 1787, with a few of its imperfections fixed and a few more controls incorporated. We hope to advance the discussion of how the Founders' vision might be most conveniently restored.

Amicus, Atticus, Prosperus, Valerius, and the Editor

The Thesis, the Remedy, and an Admission

The Thesis

A humble thesis, with three parts, led to this effort:

The Founders succeeded, with intellect, wisdom and humility, in establishing a limited government under a written constitution—*flexible* in structure and words, but *inflexible* in protecting individual freedom in the exercise of liberty rights (in common with other citizens).

The Founders correctly predicted that factions within a free society would periodically threaten what the Founders most valued—individual freedom in the exercise of liberty rights—an inevitable risk in *any* government administered by some over others.

Decades of flirtation with "expert central planning" as the excuse for government interference with individual freedom and liberty approach inevitable financial and political failure.

The Remedy

The remedy we propose is a package of eleven (11) interrelated amendments to the U.S. Constitution, designed to restore and strengthen the internal and external controls, and add to the auxiliary precautions that Madison, Washington, Adams, et al. placed in the Constitution *to protect individual freedom and liberty rights from the self-interest of factions and from government administered by [some] over [others].* The *Second Bill of Rights* is focused on principles established by the Founders.

The Second Bill of Rights will disrupt the vicious struggle amongst factions to use the coercive power of government in pursuit of competing self-interests. But, the content of the *Second Bill of Rights* is focused quite simply upon enduring principles the Founders named—limited government, individual freedom, liberty—principles of general application that transcend the factional politics of the moment.

The eleven amendments in *The Second Bill of Rights* fall naturally into four groupings—and range from the most general in the first group to the most specific in the fourth group. The first group, *The Liberty Rights Amendments (1—4)* relate to principled allocation of rights and powers between governments (national and state) and citizens. *The Finance and Revenue Amendments (5 and 6),* provide for financial transparency and equal treatment in revenue collection. *The Citizenship and Representation Amendments (7 and 8)* add "controls" that: regularize naturalization, curb factions in federal elections, and restore representation of citizens in Washington to Maryland. The fourth group, *The Federalism Amendments (9—11),* makes technical amendments in jurisdiction and provides for transition.

An Admission

We are the first to admit the Second Bill of Rights is not perfect. No human effort has been, or ever will be. But, perfect is often the enemy of good. Despite its flaws, the *Second Bill of Rights* is a package upon which the Founding principles can once again comfortably rest. The failure of "expert central planning" should mark the return to the Founders logic of individual freedom and liberty. The *Second Bill of Rights* is offered to achieve this result, "with malice toward none, with charity for all" and in the hope of a "new birth of freedom" across the United States.[1]

---

1   The Founders provided for an amendment process in the Constitution, and used it eleven times in the first five years: ten amendments in the first Bill of Rights, plus the Eleventh Amendment, a technical correction in federal court jurisdiction.

Executive Summary of the Second Bill of Rights

The *Liberty Rights Amendments* (1—4) restore the default settings for individual freedom under law that were established by the Founders in 1789, through a mandatory "reboot" of the Constitution. The *Liberty Rights Amendments* restore the original balance among the people, the States, and the national government. Amendment 2 declares a single category of citizenship, confirms that the freedoms, privileges, and immunities—the substantive liberty rights—held by citizens at the time of the Founding are natural rights (not rights bestowed by government), furnishes a broad written definition of liberty rights, and establishes a rebuttable presumption in favor of a citizen's exercise of such rights in the face of federal government power. Amendment 3 resets the due process and equal protection clauses to once again be a durable package of procedural protections for citizens against *both* the federal and state governments, and makes clear that discrimination by government *in favor of* or *against* protected classes is impermissible. Amendment 4 resets the police power of the States, a power that is to be exercised through laws of general application that preserve the common exercise of liberty rights. Amendment 4 also establishes a similar presumption in favor of the exercise of a citizen's liberty rights against state government power, voids federal legislative and regulatory action aimed at interfering with a state's police power, and directs cases and controversies involving the police power to state courts, with discretionary appeal to the US Supreme Court. Amendment 1 ties this all together through the addition of a constitutional definition of the Rule of Law.

The *Finance and Revenue Amendments* (5 and 6) restore the original balance between taxing and spending. Amendment 5 requires the federal government to adopt accounting practices and reporting practices similar to those imposed upon States and private companies, and to complete such reporting on a schedule designed to favor the electorate. The amendment also precludes Congress from delegating decisions regarding the value of the currency to any other segment of government. Amendment 6 abolishes the entire federal income tax structure in favor of a consumption tax that dramatically reduces the cost of compliance, eliminates traps for the unwary, reduces overhead to American businesses and citizens, and substantially eliminates the underground economy. Alternative Amendment 6 provides protections against misuse by the federal government of the federal income tax as a vehicle for micro-managing the economy and arbitrarily favoring some factions over other factions.

The *Citizenship and Representation Amendments* (7 and 8) require Congress to establish a legislative process for gaining residence and citizenship by which foreign persons and their children shall become subject to the jurisdiction of the United States; eliminate gerrymandering in the creation of House district boundaries through technological innovation; and restore virtually all current residents of Washington DC to the state of Maryland.

The *Federalism Amendments* (9, 10, and 11) move us back toward the Founders' vision of federalism. Amendment 9 restores the limits on Congress's power to regulate commerce among the States to transportation, trade, or exchange of goods and services in such commerce; and confirms that Congress has no power over any citizen's choices relating to retirement, health care, or financial security. Amendment 10 makes adjustments in the Judiciary to restore its position as bulwark of liberty rights. Amendment 11 requires a re-codification consistent with these amendments, and authorizes Congress to enact transition legislation with respect to retirees and persons approaching retirement.

The *Constitution of the United States*, including *The Second Bill of Rights*, is set forth in the Appendix.

The Second Bill of Rights

The Liberty Rights Amendments (1—4)

THE SECOND BILL OF RIGHTS 1. [28. THE RULE OF LAW IN THE UNITED STATES]

1. The Rule of Law in the United States shall forever be comprised of: allocated powers among the people, the states, and the national government under this Constitution; broad liberty rights retained by the people; the police power retained by each State to preserve the common exercise of liberty rights; limited, enumerated legislative powers vested in and exercisable only by an elected Congress; separation of national powers among Congress, the Executive, and the Judiciary; and development of the common law consistent therewith by an independent state and federal judiciary.

2. The Preamble to this Constitution is a statement of general purpose, and not a grant of powers to the government. The language in Article I, Section 8 "to pay the Debts and provide for the common Defence and general Welfare of the United States" is a limitation on the power of Congress to lay and collect taxes, duties, imposts, and excises, not an independent grant of power in addition to those otherwise set forth in Section 8. The Judiciary shall rely, when interpreting this Constitution, on the publicly known meaning of the words contained in the Constitution at the time such words were adopted.

THE SECOND BILL OF RIGHTS 2. [29. ONE CATEGORY OF CITIZEN, LIBERTY RIGHTS, EXERCISE PRESUMED VALID.]

1. All persons born or naturalized in the United States and subject to the jurisdiction thereof are citizens of the United States. Section 1 of Amendment XIV is repealed.

1

2. The freedoms, privileges, and immunities—together, the liberty rights—held by citizens at the adoption of this Constitution are retained by the people, are not surrendered to government, and shall not be abridged by the United States. Citizens are endowed with inalienable power to exercise their liberty rights under the Rule of Law. Neither Congress, nor the Executive, nor the Judiciary shall have power to create or grant liberty rights.

3. Liberty rights include, but are not limited to, the rights to life, liberty, and pursuit of happiness; to property in one's own labor and industry; to preserve and secure personal health and safety; to keep and bear arms; to acquire, inherit, purchase, lease, sell, hold, convey, and enjoy real and personal property; to religious liberty; to freedom in matters of conscience; to freedom in making and enforcing lawful contracts of all kinds (including freedom not to contract); to establish a family, to care for and to raise children, and to secure the health, education, and safety thereof; to freedom of press, speech, assemblage, and petition; to pursue any lawful livelihood or avocation; to engage in a profession, trade, business, or calling; and to privacy in one's person, effects, papers, preferences, and affairs.

4. The exercise by a citizen of liberty rights shall be presumed valid by the Judiciary against any law made by Congress and any rule or order made by the Executive that denies or abridges such rights; Provided, that this presumption shall not prevail with respect to laws made pursuant to an enumerated power; and Provided Further, that where Congress relies in part upon the necessary and proper clause of Article 1 Section 8 to make any such law, this presumption may be rebutted upon a showing by the Executive that such law: (i) is plainly necessary in the exercise of an enumerated power; (ii) could not achieve the purpose of an enumerated power by other means not so restrictive of liberty rights, and (iii) is consistent with the Rule of Law.

THE SECOND BILL OF RIGHTS 3. [30. DUE PROCESS UNDER THE RULE OF LAW, EQUAL PROTECTION OF THE LAW.]
Neither Congress nor the Executive, and no State shall deprive any citizen of life, liberty, or property without due process in accord with the Rule of Law; nor deny to any citizen the equal protection of the laws; nor discriminate for or against any citizen on the basis of race, color, national origin, or gender, or on the basis of belief or non-belief in any creed or religion.

THE SECOND BILL OF RIGHTS 4. [31. THE POLICE POWER OF STATES; LIBERTY RIGHTS AND STATE LAW.]

1. The police power is reserved to each of the States under Amendment 10 and includes the power to promote the health, good order, morals, peace, and safety of citizens residing therein through laws of general application that preserve the common exercise of liberty rights.

2. The exercise by a citizen of liberty rights shall be presumed valid against any state law that denies or abridges such rights; Provided, that this presumption may be rebutted upon a showing by the state that such law could not achieve the purpose of the police power by other means not so restrictive of liberty rights.

3. Neither Congress nor the Executive shall make any law, rule, or order requiring a State to exercise the police power in a specific manner as a condition of receiving grants, appropriations, funds, or benefits from, or avoiding penalties imposed by, the federal government. All such conditions shall be held illegal and void.

4. All cases, in law and equity, arising under this amendment shall be heard in the courts of the several States. The Supreme Court may review such cases, with due deference to each State's exercise of the police power.

The Finance and Revenue Amendments (5 and 6)

THE SECOND BILL OF RIGHTS 5. [32. TRANSPARENCY AND ACCOUNTABILITY IN FINANCES; A STABLE CURRENCY.]

1. The fiscal year for the federal government shall begin on April 1 and end on the following March 31. Before October 1, the President shall present to Congress government-wide financial statements in accord with generally accepted government accounting principles for the previous fiscal year with comparisons to the prior two fiscal years, and which shall: include a statement of net assets and a statement of activities; report all of the assets, the condition thereof, current and future liabilities, revenues, expenses, gains and losses of government; distinguish between governmental and business-type activities; and include discussion and analysis. Before October 1, the President shall present to Congress his recommended budget for the next fiscal year, in a format consistent with the government-wide financial statements, with projected revenues, ex-

penses, gains, and losses, changes in assets and the condition thereof, current and future liabilities, along with discussion and analysis.

2. Congress shall by law establish the number of grains of gold nine-tenths fine that shall be the standard unit of value equivalent to the U.S. dollar, which standard shall thereafter be adjusted only through legislation originating in the House of Representatives, and passed by three fifths of both the House of Representatives and the Senate. All forms of money issued or coined by the United States shall be in parity with this standard. Congress shall not delegate the setting or adjustment of this standard to anyone, including the Executive.

THE SECOND BILL OF RIGHTS 6. [33. SUBSTITUTION OF CON-SUMPTION TAX FOR INCOME, ESTATE, GIFT TAXES.]
1. Congress shall have the power to lay and the States to collect on its behalf, a uniform consumption tax on all retail sales of new goods and services to all purchasers, including local, state, and federal government purchasers; Provided, that Congress shall at the same time establish uniform rebates for adults and for children, indexed for inflation and deflation, to shield basic household necessities from such consumption tax, paid monthly to each citizen, legal resident, or the guardian thereof, by the State in which they then reside.

2. Congress shall have no power to levy federal taxes on income, estates, and gifts; no power to lay or collect a Value Added Tax; and no power to levy any excise tax measured by wages. The sixteenth article of amendment to this constitution is repealed.

ALTERNATE 6
THE SECOND BILL OF RIGHTS 6. [33. TAX SIMPLIFIED; MANU-FACTURES AND INFRASTRUCTURE]
1. Congress shall have no power to levy other than a single tax on the income of individuals, and a single tax on the net income of business entities determined in accordance with generally accepted accounting principles under the common law. The highest rate of tax imposed on ordinary income shall not exceed thirty percent and shall not exceed two times the lowest rate so imposed. The rate of tax imposed on income from (i) property held for one year or more, including property so held by or on behalf of individuals for retirement; (ii) the domestic manufacture of durable goods for sale; and (iii) the design, construc-

tion, repair, maintenance and operation of domestic infrastructure facilities (including water supply and treatment, energy supply and generation, road, port, airport, rail, transit, and such other facilities as may be identified by Congress) shall not exceed one-half of the lowest rate of tax imposed on ordinary income.

2. Congress shall establish for individuals: (i) separate personal exemptions from gross income uniformly applicable to each adult and dependent child; (ii) a separate maximum exemption uniformly applicable to each adult deferring from gross income funds actually set aside by the taxpayer during the year for retirement, but not in excess of 20% of gross income; (iii) separate exemptions from gross income uniformly applicable to each adult and dependent child who has contracted for basic health care coverage, as defined by the state in which the taxpayer resides; and (iv) an annual deduction not in excess of 20% of adjusted gross income uniformly applicable to each taxpayer for funds actually contributed to charitable organizations during the year. Exemptions shall be indexed for inflation and deflation. No other adjustment to income or to tax on income shall depend on a taxpayer's level of income, value of assets held, or applicable rate of tax.

3. Congress shall have no power to levy any excise tax on employers measured by wages and no power to levy any tax on the estates of, or on gifts made by, citizens and residents of the United States. Gifts and bequests shall not be income to recipients.

4. Congress shall have no power to lay or collect a Value Added Tax or a Consumption Tax.

The Citizenship and Representation Amendments (7 and 8)
THE SECOND BILL OF RIGHTS 7. [34. NATURALIZATION; RESIDENCE.]

As part of a uniform Rule of Naturalization, Congress shall provide a process in law: (i) for any person not a citizen to make application for residence or for naturalization (that is, citizenship) in the United States, (ii) for clear standards for approval and prompt review of each such application; and (iii) if approved, for an applicant to thereby become subject to the jurisdiction of the United States as a citizen or as a resident.

THE SECOND BILL OF RIGHTS 8. [35. ENUMERATION; DISTRICT BOUNDARIES; WASHINGTON CITY, MD.]

1. No decennial Enumeration shall be other than an actual count of citizens, and shall in no event include estimates. Based upon each Enumeration, every State with more than one district shall establish district boundaries for the House of Representatives that are substantially different from the preceding Enumeration, without regard to race, color, gender, creed, religion, or party affiliation of persons therein. Each district shall comprise an area that is contiguous and not of unusually irregular shape. The quotient obtained from dividing the sum of the outer circumference of each district by the square root of the area of the district shall be as close as reasonably practicable to that obtained for all other districts and as close as reasonably practical to four—that of a square. Boundaries with other States and with navigable waters may be approximated by straight lines. The cognizant United States Court of Appeals shall have original trial jurisdiction in an action by a citizen to enforce this Amendment for a district in which the citizen resides.

2. One year after the effective date of this amendment, the Seat of Government—Washington DC—shall be limited to the land, as Congress shall identify prior to such date by legislation, now comprising the National Mall with its museums and libraries, the Lincoln and Jefferson Memorials, the Houses of Congress and their existing office buildings, the Supreme Court, Lafayette Park and its existing office structures, the White House, and such other immediately adjacent facilities. The rest of the District of Columbia shall return to Maryland as Washington City, and its citizens included in the enumeration for Maryland. Amendment XXIII is repealed.

The Federalism Amendments (9, 10, and 11)

THE SECOND BILL OF RIGHTS 9. [36. THE POWER TO REGULATE COMMERCE AMONG THE STATES.]

Congress' power to regulate Commerce among the several States shall only extend to transportation, trade, or exchange of goods and services in such Commerce. Congress shall have no power to require any citizen, resident, or legal entity to engage in such commerce. Congress shall have no power to require any citizen, resident, or legal entity to participate in or contribute to any retirement, annuity, insurance, medical, disability, or similar plan established, managed, or controlled by the United States.

THE SECOND BILL OF RIGHTS 10. [37. THE JUDICIARY; AP-POINTMENTS; JURISDICTION.]

1. The Judicial power shall be exercised to preserve liberty rights, the Rule of Law, the police power of each of the several States, and the republican form of government. Section 2 of Amendments XIII, XV, XXIV, and XXVI; Sections 1 and 5 of Amendment XIV; and the second paragraph of Amendment XIX are repealed.

2. The President in nominating, and the Senate in advice and consent, shall consider the experience of each judicial nominee in the practice of the common law.

3. In all Cases before the Courts of the United States between Citizens of different States, the prevailing party or parties shall be awarded reasonable attorneys' fees, costs, and expenses.

4. No inferior court of the United States shall have jurisdiction over: (i) any matter involving a uniformed military service, its policies and regulations, its personnel, its code of military justice, or the conduct of such personnel in military service; or (ii) any case or controversy which the President declares in writing involves terrorism with some foreign element. The President need not disclose specifics of such elements in the notice.

5. Citizens accused of terrorism against the United States may be tried for treason in the Courts of the United States in accord with the Rule of Law.

THE SECOND BILL OF RIGHTS 11. [38. RE-CODIFICATION OF STATUTES OF THE UNITED STATES; TRANSITION.]

1. From the effective date of Amendments 28 to 38 (the Second Bill of Rights), the Executive shall not execute or enforce any law, rule, or order, or make any new rule or order inconsistent with the Constitution, as amended. Congress shall promptly modify the statutes of the United States for an orderly transition to conform herewith.

2. Congress may enact legislation that: (i) preserves social security payments and medicare benefits under current law, but free of income tax, for persons who at the date of this amendment are 65 years of age and older; (ii) gives the option to persons then between 45 and 64 years

of age (a) to contribute to social security and medicare under current law and (b) at age 65 to receive such payments and benefits, free of income tax; and (iii) establishes a means test of general application to all persons for reductions, in whole or part, and in amount or time, with respect to one or more of these payments and benefits.

Editor's Note:

The *Constitution of the United States,* including *The Second Bill of Rights,* is set forth in the Appendix.

The New Federalist Papers

Fifty Papers that Present

The Second Bill of Rights

NUMBER 1.
Fouled with Barnacles, the Hull of the
US(S) Constitution Needs a Scrub

One of the most thrilling sights in America today is the *USS Constitution*, the oldest commissioned warship in the U.S. Navy, under sail[1] from its Charlestown yard into Boston harbor on July 4. The *Constitution* has been refitted numerous times. When funds were short, contributions came from ordinary citizens.[2]

President George Washington authorized the construction of six frigates in 1794. One of these, the *USS Constitution* was finished in 1797. Built in Boston from some 2,000 trees, its original cannons were made in Rhode Island. Paul Revere provided copper interior fastenings.

The ship earned its nickname, "Old Ironsides," during a naval battle in the War of 1812, when its wooden hull seemed to be made of iron and enemy cannon balls just bounced off. President George Washington named the ship in honor of the document upon which our republic is based: the Constitution of the United States.

Algae, barnacles, and other sorts of foul organisms have always tried to permanently attach themselves to the sides and to the bottom of the *USS Constitution*. The ship has been repaired in dry dock numerous times. The hull has been cleaned and scraped, repainted, and refinished, with rotted timbers and planks replaced. This kind of maintenance never stops—it is ongoing—because the ship is under constant daily attack from new organisms, algae, and barnacles.

In the 225 years since the Constitutional Convention in 1787, similar organisms, algae, and barnacles—in the form of factions—have attached themselves to the hull of the written U.S. Constitution, tilting our founding

---

1   *http://www.youtube.com/watch?v=69kr5WpYjgA*
2   *http://en.wikipedia.org/wiki/USS_Constitution#Sail_200*

document right and left, up and down, forward and backward. The analogy between the attacks of organisms on the hull of the warship *USS Constitution* and those on our founding document, the U.S. Constitution, is irresistible.

In 2012, the 225th anniversary of the Constitutional Convention, our founding document is in need of a good scrubbing—*not* to change the structure the Founders' established and *not* to force the ship one way or another, but rather to allow our founding "ship," and its central dream of individual freedom in the common exercise of liberty rights—to both endure and sail free again.[3]

Regular maintenance and repairs—a thorough scrubbing in dry dock and the addition of several new navigational aids (as auxiliary precautions)—will be sufficient.[4] A respectful refitting is the simple goal of *The Second Bill of Rights and the New Federalist Papers.*

Valerius

---

3   The *USS Constitution* does not yet need to be careened. Careening a sailing vessel is the practice of beaching it at high tide and then tipping it sideways by pulling the top of the mast. This is usually done in order to expose one side or another of the ship's hull for maintenance and repairs below the water line when the tide goes out.

4   The *Constitution of the United States*, including *The Second Bill of Rights,* is set forth in the Appendix.

NUMBER 2.
A New Birth of Freedom—The Second Bill of Rights

"With malice toward none, with charity for all. . ."
Abraham Lincoln's 2nd Inaugural Address, March 4, 1865

Lincoln ended the Gettysburg Address with a hope consistent with *The Second Bill of Rights.*

> [T]hat this nation under God *shall have a new birth of freedom,* and that government of the people, by the people, for the people shall not perish from the earth.

In Article V of the Constitution,[5] the Founders provided citizens with a direct route to amend the Constitution—a 2/3 vote of both Houses of Congress, followed by ratification by 3/4 of the States. In one election cycle—the people of the United States have the means and the power to elect a Congress that will adjust the Constitution to once again protect citizens against the Founders' perennial concern—*inappropriate administration of the national government.* Ratification in the States would then follow. The Executive[6] and the Judiciary are not involved.

Congress and the Executive have been overrun by what the Founders called factions—and the media now calls special interests. They are numerous, self-perpetuating, and destructive. No longer housed in outside interest groups, factions are embedded in Congress and the Executive branch. Factions have produced: (i) program after program that reach ever further into the choices of free men and women; (ii) ballooning expenditures that are unsustainable, with extraordinary deficits, preposterous national debt;

---

5   Appendix A sets forth the *U.S. Constitution* and its 27 amendments, with *The Second Bill of Rights* inserted to show how the resulting changes would then appear in a revised Constitution.

6   The term "Executive" means the President and the Vice President, the only two people named in Article II of the Constitution. The appointees and officials working for the Executive comprise the "Executive Branch."

and (iii) ever greater interference with the individual's opportunities to explore and pursue his or her own talents, preferences, and choices.

If men were angels, no government would be necessary. If angels were to govern men, neither external nor internal controls on government would be necessary. In framing a government which is to be administered by men over men, *the great difficulty lies in this: you must first enable the government to control the governed; and in the next place oblige it to control itself.*[7]

Government has not been obliged to control itself. As Madison foresaw, a process to amend the Constitution would be necessary to require government to do so.

Obliging Government to Control Itself

The original constitutional framework is healthy, though *factions* have fouled some of the machinery.[8] *The Second Bill of Rights* simply points government back toward familiar middle ground—with individual liberty secure from inappropriate administration by some over others.

Neutral Principles Applicable to All Citizens

Although the Founders recognized each citizen's inalienable individual freedom and liberty in 1789 they failed to agree to treat slaves the same way.[9] The Civil War Amendments were supposed to extend inalienable freedom and liberty to all citizens (particularly former slaves). As described in Num-

---

7   Madison, *The Federalist Papers 51*, at p. 322 (Mentor, 1961). All references are to the 1961 Mentor edition.

8   Substantially all *The Second Bill of Rights* could be enacted by a single Congress, without amending the Constitution. Exceptions are the presumption of liberty applied to States, Am. 4, §2; the return of Washington City to Maryland, Am. 8, §2.

9   Madison notes this fundamental defect in the draft constitution, at *The Federalist Papers 42, supra*, at p. 266. "It were doubtless to be wished that the power of prohibiting the importation of slaves had not been postponed until the year 1808, or rather that it had been suffered to have immediate operation. But it is not difficult to account either for this restriction on the general government, or for the manner in which the whole clause is expressed. It ought to be considered as a great point gained in favor of humanity that a period of twenty years may terminate forever, within these States, a traffic which has so long and so loudly upbraided the barbarism of modern policy; that within that period it will receive a considerable discouragement from the federal government, and may be totally abolished, by a concurrence of the few States which continue the unnatural traffic in the prohibitory example which has been given by so great a majority of the Union. Happy would it be for the unfortunate Africans if any equal prospect lay before them of being redeemed from the oppression of their European brethren!"

ber 11, key elements of these amendments were ineffective for more than eighty years through a series of political and judicial missteps.

The Second Bill of Rights reestablishes neutral application of individual freedom and liberty for all citizens, offering no greater advantage to one citizen or group over any other. Its principles are those of the Founders—neither left nor right as characterized in the press; neither conservative nor socialist—focused instead upon protecting individual freedom in the exercise of liberty rights, with respect for fellow citizens under the common law. *The Second Bill of Rights* is liberal, but in the way the Founders used the word, as an extensive (liberal) acknowledgement of the inalienable power held by the individual to pursue his or her own talents, perspectives, and preferences. *The Second Bill of Rights* is neither anarchist nor purely libertarian. Congress, the Judiciary, the Executive, the States, and the People retain dynamic and substantive roles.

In 1863, at Gettysburg, Abraham Lincoln recalled the nation's founding, and its unique focus:

> Fourscore and seven years ago our fathers brought forth on this continent a new nation, *conceived in liberty and dedicated to the proposition that all men are created equal.* Now we are engaged in a great civil war, *testing whether that nation or any nation so conceived and so dedicated can long endure.*

Broadest Discussion of First Principles in the Context of Federal Elections

We hope to encourage careful consideration of our republic's Founding principles, and the broadest possible exchange of views among Independents, Democrats and Republicans in support of the preservation of individual freedom and liberty from government administered not by angels, but by men and women. The Founders agreed upon this middle ground, based on the common fear of what freedom and liberty would be like in the hands of opposing factions.

We can, and must re-discover that same middle ground. A new birth of freedom, of which Lincoln dreamed, is the gift we hope to give each other through *The Second Bill of Rights.*

Amicus

NUMBER 3.
The Humble Logic of Individual Freedom and Liberty Rights

Most of the human genome was mapped [sequenced] by 2003. Highly trained, specialized scientists and doctors assembled millions upon millions of facts to do it. They confirmed what Washington, Franklin, Adams, Jefferson, and Madison (among others) knew in 1789. Although an overwhelming percentage of our genetic code is the same, each of us is special—unique.

In part, our genetic uniqueness explains why we each have different talents, perspectives, and preferences. Each of us feels a unique satisfaction from learning what these talents are, learning our limitations, pursuing talents we prefer, and excelling at what we love to do.

We admire the *explorers*, those who pursue their individual talents with astonishing results:

- The singers, musicians, dancers, composers, authors, playwrights, and athletes (professional, collegiate, and amateur), whose talents are known and appreciated throughout the world;
- The professional basketball player with a 42 inch vertical jump;
- The medical researchers who bring different talents, training, and skills to the creation of new ways to treat or prevent disease;
- The inventors who develop and bring improved devices and technology to market.

We admire the *competent*, those who choose to acquire a deep understanding of activities that are valuable to other citizens:

- The farmers who feed the nation, and consistently improve productivity in vigorous markets;
- The mechanics who are able to disassemble, repair, and reassemble complex machinery primarily through intuition (a set of skills most of us can only imagine, with envy);

- The craftsmen (electricians, plumbers, carpenters, masons, welders, tin knockers, fabricators, and laborers) who bring the same intuition and skill to construction, repair, and operations of homes, commercial buildings, and infrastructure accessible to the public;
- The crane operator who can position steel columns of great weight within a fraction of an inch many stories above New York City;
- The shopkeepers, grocers, distributors, and wholesalers who seamlessly organize and operate the most complex logistics system in the world (the US economy);
- The medical doctors, nurses, and health professionals who bring different talents, training, and skills to the diagnosis and treatment of disease;
- Manufacturers and managers—in small, medium, and large firms—who produce and bring devices, applications, services, and tools to market.

We admire the *balancers*, those who juggle work with other talents and preferences:

- Those who love the outdoors, whose preferences, beyond employment, lead them to ski, swim, hike, canoe, hunt, sail, fish, ride, golf, fly;
- Those who love the city, and whose preferences lead them to the theatre, the arts, professional sports contests, and the amenities of city life;
- Those who love to travel, whose preferences lead them to visit the country and the world;
- Those immersed in the written word—so many books, so little time;
- Those balancing one (or two) careers with the responsibilities of marriage, children, and raising a family.

We admire the *flexible*, those who re-direct their lives along different talents and preferences, by choice or because chance or fate requires it:

- The professional basketball player who no longer has a 42 inch vertical jump, and moves on to become a successful coach, a Senator, or a businessman/woman;
- The professional boxer who retires to run a successful business, or who becomes a world-wide ambassador of good will;

16

- The parent who re-enters the workforce after the children are grown;
- The craftsmen, surgeons, and mechanics that change their work as their vision ages.

The gift Americans received from the Founders—Washington, Franklin, Adams, Jefferson, and Madison (among others)—was not a set of facts. It wasn't a genomic map. It was much deeper, more enduring, and more important than all the scientific facts known before or after 1789.

The Founders established the constitutional premise that citizens possess inalienable liberty rights that guarantee individual freedom in the pursuit of their own talents, views, preferences, capabilities and tastes. The national government was not to arbitrarily interfere!

Americans consume this gift every day, free to be *explorers, competent, balancers,* and *flexible* throughout their lives. Time and courage are regularly required to appreciate and pursue our talents and preferences. And, because preferences sometimes don't sufficiently match talents, the pursuit can be bumpy. (My preference to sing like Nat King Cole never matched my talent. My preference to understand and play basketball like Bill Russell fell similarly short.) Health and age interfere. (My ability to run every day has deteriorated with my knees.) The responsibilities of work and family also interfere, forcing each of us to be *explorers, competent, balancers,* and *flexible.*

In 1789, the Founders were not yet armed with the innumerable scientific, engineering, and medical facts of modern textbooks. They could not anticipate that their American descendants would learn to build or fly airplanes, or travel to the moon. Yet, among the Founders were some of the most notable scientists and philosophers of the age. Their gift— *the vision of individual freedom through liberty rights*—enabled scientific, engineering, and medical advances to occur in the United States. Millions of American *explorers, balancers,* the *competent,* and the *flexible* transformed the world by developing and deploying modern science and engineering—physics, biology, medicine, computing, aeronautics, railroads, roads, bridges, airports, water supply, and waste water treatment. Millions have been employed in fields and jobs that free individuals created. They transformed the quality and duration of life. They raised the standard of living for countless millions. All of this was inextricably tied to the exercise of liberty rights—the individual freedom to pursue one's own talents, views, preferences, capabilities, and tastes.[10]

The Founders' humble solution was to flip the status quo on its head: to create a constitutional presumption in favor of individual freedom in the pursuit of preferences over arbitrary government power. Individual freedom would be secured by a republic with a national government of limited powers. The states retained the general police power. Citizens retained their liberty rights. The limited power of the national government was further divided among three equal branches—legislative power vested in, and exclusively exercised by, an elected Congress; executive power to faithfully execute the laws vested in the President; and judicial power vested in an appointed Supreme Court. This separation of national power would provide still further structural checks and balances to restrain a privileged few, clothed with the authority of the national government, from interfering with individual freedom and liberty.

James Madison put it this way, in 1787, when explaining why federal power was to be both limited and divided among three branches, with the police power confirmed to the states, and liberty rights retained by the people:

> It may be a reflection on human nature that such devices should be necessary to control the abuses of government. But what is government itself but the greatest of all reflections on human nature? If men were angels, no government would be necessary. If angels were to govern men, neither external nor internal controls on government would be necessary. In framing a government which is to be administered by men over men, the great difficulty lies in this: you must first enable the government to control the governed; and in the next place oblige it to control itself. A dependence on the people is no doubt, the primary control on the government; but experience has taught mankind the necessity of *auxiliary precautions*.[11]

---

10   The Founders were aware of the ongoing struggle to prevent arbitrary state power from interfering with individual freedom, from Magna Carta (1215) and the Petition of Right (1628) to the Declaration of Independence (1776). The Founders themselves were the victims of petty colonial officials who issued Writs of Assistance for warrantless searches of homes, private papers, ships, and goods.
11   Madison, *The Federalist Papers 51*, at p. 322.

Each living American is still special—unique, 225 years after the Constitution was written. A new group of even better trained, even more specialized scientists is assembling millions upon millions of additional new facts in the exploration of the genetic code that uniquely defines us. Will the next advances tell us how our genetic code determines individual talents, perspectives, and preferences? Our physical, emotional, and medical strengths and weaknesses? I may be skeptical, but if science leads us down this path, the Founders' wisdom in protecting individuals from the arbitrary coercion of government will seem even more visionary. As science reveals more about each of us, future Americans may discover that the protections and the privacy our liberty rights provide are even more essential than the Founders imagined.

To me, it seems more likely that different groups of *explorers, balancers,* the *competent,* and the *flexible* will find still more questions with every newly discovered fact. Principles of individual freedom and liberty rights buried deep in the United States Constitution will be ever more vital, more sacred. *The Liberty Rights Amendments* (in particular, Amendments 2 and 3) strengthen the Founder's humble logic by formally establishing a constitutional presumption in favor of individual freedom as the means of controlling the most recent abuses of government.

Each of us *is* special—unique. Yet, the Constitution unites us in the freedom and in the liberty to separately pursue the preferences, perspectives, and talents that flow so naturally from these differences.

Amicus

NUMBER 4.
Our Defense against Factions:
Individual Freedom and Liberty

James Madison, a principal author of the Constitution and *The Federalist Papers*, feared for individual freedom and liberty under *any* government administered by men over men. Madison concluded that both external and internal controls were required. His reasons ring true today.

"Men" are *not* Angels—The Danger of Self-Interest by Government Officials

If men were angels, no government would be necessary. If angels were to govern men, neither *external nor internal controls* on government would be necessary. [12]

Madison saw a great difficulty for *any* government administered by some men over other men.

In framing a government which is to be administered by men over men, *the great difficulty lies in this:* you must first enable the government to control the governed; *and in the next place oblige it to control itself.*[13]

The Founders placed external controls in the Constitution to oblige government to control itself—a limited national government with eighteen (18) enumerated powers; the general police power over everyday life left to the States; and individual freedom and liberty retained by citizens. The Founders also placed internal controls in the Constitution. The national power was divided among three equal branches—legislative, executive, and judicial. This separation of powers established durable checks and balances to restrain officials, clothed with the authority of

---

12   Madison, *The Federalist Papers 51*, at p. 322.
13   *Ibid.*

the national government, from interfering with the individual freedom of ordinary citizens.

> A dependence on the people is no doubt[14] the primary control on the government; but *experience* has taught mankind the necessity of *auxiliary precautions.*

Experience taught the Founders to expect a government of men, not angels. These *external* and *internal* controls were the *auxiliary precautions* Madison believed necessary to curb the inherent abuses of *any* government by men over men.

Factions are *not* Angels—The Danger that Factions Would Misuse the Coercive Power of Government to Interfere with Individual Freedom and Liberty Rights

Madison devoted much of Federalist No. 10 to describing the Constitution's tendency to break and control the violence of faction. The Founders were aware in 1789 of the dangers we still face from faction, more than two hundred years later.

> By a faction I understand a number of citizens *whether amounting to a majority or minority of the whole* who are united and actuated by some common impulse of passion, or of interest, *adverse to the rights of other citizens,* or to the permanent and aggregate interests of the community.[15]

Madison did not believe the causes of faction could be removed. To do so "by destroying the liberty which is essential to its existence" would be a "remedy [ ] worse than the disease." To do so by "giving to every citizen the same opinions, the same passions, and the same interests" would be "as impracticable as the first would be unwise."[16]

---

14   Madison is referring to federal elections every two years, for all of the House and for one-third of the Senate.

15   *The Federalist Papers 10, supra,* pp. 77-84, is quoted extensively throughout this Number 4.

16   *Ibid.*

Two centuries of experience confirm Madison's view. The causes of faction exist because each of us has different views, preferences, opinions, and tastes.

> The latent causes of faction are . . . sown in the nature of man
> . . . A zeal for different opinions concerning religion, . . government, and many other points, . . an attachment to different leaders ambitiously contending for pre-eminence and power; . . have, in turn, divided mankind into parties, inflamed them with mutual animosity, and rendered them much more disposed to vex and oppress each other than to co-operate for their common good.
>
> . . .
>
> But the most common and durable source of factions has been the various and unequal distribution of property. Those who hold and those who are without property have ever formed distinct interests in society. Those who are creditors, and those who are debtors . . . A landed interest, a manufacturing interest, a mercantile interest, a moneyed interest, with many lesser interests, grow up of necessity in civilized nations, and divide them into different classes, actuated by different sentiments and views.

The Founders knew that those elected to office by factions face an inherent conflict of interest. Madison put it this way:

> No man is allowed to be a judge in his own cause, because his interest would certainly bias his judgment, and, not improbably, corrupt his integrity. With equal, nay with great reason, a body of men are unfit to be both judges and parties at the same time; yet what are many of the most important acts of legislation but so many judicial determinations[?] And what are the different classes of legislators but advocates and parties to the causes which they determine?
>
> It is in vain to say that enlightened statesmen will be able to adjust these clashing interests and render them all subservient to the public good. Enlightened statesmen will not always be at the

22

helm. Nor, in many cases, can such an adjustment be made at all[.]

Stripped to its essentials—the Founders worried that part of any electorate (a faction), inflamed by leaders ambitiously contending for pre-eminence and power, would attempt to restrict the freedom and liberty of some citizens to reward others. The Founders understood that *the deeper the national government reached into the everyday affairs of citizens—spurred forward by the passion of factions—the greater the danger that the coercive power of government would, in effect, be captured by factions* to promote the interests and preferences of some citizens while interfering with those of other citizens.

Madison wrote *The Federalist Papers 10* before Democrats, Whigs, or Republicans existed—before logrolling and lobbying were added to our vocabulary. Since 1789, factions have organized into political parties, trade associations, foundations, and other NGOs. Washington DC teems with factions. All intend to push [influence] members of Congress, the President, and petty officials. All seek to promote, shape, or interfere with legislation, regulations, orders, or discretionary decisions. All seek to capture the coercive power of government to promote the interests of some citizens over those of others.

The danger factions present to individual freedom and liberty is *not* partisan: Democrat or Republican. Despite passionate claims by leaders ambitiously contending for pre-eminence and power, this danger is not reduced by substituting one faction for another: left for right, Democrat for Republican, liberal for conservative.

The danger is precisely as Madison stated: factions (minority or majority), inflamed by passion and self-interest, will attempt to use the coercive power of government to promote the interests and preferences of some citizens while interfering with those of others.

What to do? THIS IS NOT A NEW QUESTION. MADISON ADDRESSED IT.

Madison concluded that the *causes* of faction can never be removed, and that in framing the Constitution, relief had to be found by controlling their *effects*. The structure of the republic allows the majority to defeat a minority faction by regular elections. A minority "might clog the administration, or convulse the society, but it would be unable to execute and mask its violence under the forms of the Constitution."[17]

Madison also feared that a majority faction might sacrifice both the public good and the rights of other citizens to further its own passions or interests. In these circumstances, protecting individual rights was one of Madison's *great objects* in writing the Constitution.

> To secure the public good and private rights against the danger of such a [majority] faction, and at the same time to preserve the spirit and form of popular government, is then the *great object* to which our inquiries are directed.

The *auxiliary precautions* Madison placed in the Constitution—i.e. *internal* and *external controls*—were to reduce this *great object* to a manageable one. Government administered by men over men was not to be perverted by the passions and self-interest of faction. Madison's solution was: (a) to establish a national government with limited, enumerated powers; and (b) to confirm the police power (i.e., management of everyday affairs) to the States, where the mischief of faction could be separately and better managed by multiple state and local legislatures.

Madison concludes *The Federalist Papers 10* this way:

> The influence of factious leaders may kindle a flame within their particular States but will be unable to spread a general conflagration through the other States. A religious sect may degenerate into a political faction in a part of the [nation]; but the variety of sects dispersed over the entire face of it must secure the national councils against any danger from that source. A rage for paper money, for an abolition of debts, for an equal division of property, or for any other improper or wicked project, will be less apt to pervade the whole body of the Union[.] . . In the extent and proper structure of the Union, therefore, we behold a republican remedy for the diseases most incident to republican government. [. .]

---

17   *Ibid.*

The first four amendments in *The Second Bill of Rights* (the *Liberty Rights Amendments*)[18] preserve Madison's humble solution by strengthening the auxiliary precautions and controls that protect all citizens from the perennial problem of *faction* (special interests).

Amicus

---

18   The *Constitution of the United States,* including *The Second Bill of Rights,* is set forth in the Appendix.

NUMBER 5.
A Choice the Founders Avoided: Which Faction Will Best Regulate Us?

The framers and ratifiers of our Constitution assumed that men are not angels, but they did not expect us to be devils. A republican government still requires a certain degree of virtue—willingness to recognize a common good that is more than a calculation of individual or group goods. At the very least, republican government requires that we use public power only for genuinely public purposes, not to advance private interests. As Madison put it in Federalist 55:

> As there is a degree of depravity in mankind which requires a certain degree of circumspection and distrust, so there are other qualities in human nature which justify a certain portion of esteem and confidence. Republican government presupposes the existence of these qualities in a higher degree than any other form.

The Second Bill of Rights summons the virtue of the American people, assuming that they can recognize the problems which beset us and can take the necessary steps and make the necessary sacrifices to rectify them. Above all, we ask this generation to look out for the future—for our children and their children—to promote the welfare of future generations rather than to exploit them as conveniently un-enfranchised citizens upon whom we can defer debts and burdens.[19]

Fortunately, the Constitution's amendment process makes this possible.

The Constitution is not foolproof. The problem of faction, "sown in the nature of man," will always manifest itself in new ways. As long as

---

19   The auxiliary precautions and controls that Madison placed in the Constitution to protect citizens from arbitrary government power have, in general, served us well, and have certainly prevented us from experiencing the extreme suffering caused by tyrannical regimes all over the world since 1789. And, these precautions still provide more durable protection for individual freedom and liberty than the troubled democracies of Europe.

we are human, we must struggle with the question of the legitimacy of power and guard against its perversion to selfish ends. As Lincoln put it, there is an "eternal struggle" between the principles of right and wrong. These principles have always "stood face to face, one of them asserting the divine right of kings, the same principle that says you work, you toil, you earn bread, and I will eat it. It is the same old serpent."[20]

The framers of the Constitution did not expect to solve the problem of faction, but did aspire to help control its effects. Yet twentieth-century political scientists came to embrace the unlimited contentions of factions as something inherently positive. From the advent of the New Deal, we have heard that a system of "interest group liberalism," in which government provides an arena in which factions are free to contend, is adequate. And, perversely, they have attributed this system to Madison. But Madison, who defined factions as groups opposed to the permanent and aggregate interests of the community, would never throw up his hands and attempt to make a virtue of this vice.

The Second Bill of Rights reinforces our ability to contend against the force of faction. Section 2 of Amendment 2 begins with a restatement of the principles of the Declaration of Independence: that our rights derive from Nature and Nature's God. Our rights do not come from government; we institute government to protect our preexisting rights.

Section 2 of Amendment 2 brings into the Constitution an expansive definition of our civil rights—as that term was understood in the classical liberal tradition of the Founders. It uses the language of two essential articulations of civil rights—the 1823 opinion by Bushrod Washington in *Corfield v. Coryell,* 6 Fed. Cases 546 (1823), and the *1866 Civil Rights Act,* the foundation of the Fourteenth Amendment. Section 2 of Amendment 2 declares that our liberty rights (civil and economic rights) include the following:

> the rights to life, liberty, and pursuit of happiness; to property in one's own labor and industry; to preserve and secure personal health and safety; to keep and bear arms; to acquire, inherit, purchase, lease, sell, hold, convey, and enjoy real and personal property; to religious liberty; to freedom in matters of conscience; to

---

20   See, Number 21, at footnote 5, below.

freedom in making and enforcing lawful contracts of all kinds (including freedom not to contract); to establish a family, to care for and to raise children, and to secure the health, education, and safety thereof; to freedom of press, speech, assemblage, and petition; to pursue any lawful livelihood or avocation; to engage in a profession, trade, business, or calling; and to privacy in one's person, effects, papers, preferences, and affairs.

Section 2 overcomes the Court's narrow interpretation of §1 of the Fourteenth Amendment, that was supposed to extend the privileges and immunities held by white citizens to all.[21] It is ironic that the original Constitution, which contained many more detailed provisions about the structure of the government than it did broad declarations of rights, received much more intense scrutiny and debate about structure than the Fourteenth Amendment did about liberty rights. The listing of liberty rights in Section 3 of Amendment 2 cures this deficiency.

Section 4 of Amendment 2 preserves the doctrine of implied or *necessary and proper* powers by establishing a presumption of validity in the exercise by a citizen of liberty rights.[22] Section 4 permits this presumption of liberty to be "rebutted upon a showing... that such law is plainly necessary in the exercise of an enumerated power." Section 4 adopts the language that Chief Justice John Marshall used when he vindicated Madison's view of the Tenth Amendment.

> Let the end be legitimate, let it be within the scope of the constitution, and all means which are appropriate, which are plainly adapted to that end, which are not prohibited, but consist with the letter and spirit of the constitution, are constitutional.[23]

The presumption for liberty rights addresses another aspect of the problem factions have posed since the first *Federalist Papers*. Madison and the Founders were particularly concerned about the problem of majority

---

21   The first section of the Fourteenth Amendment received very little debate in Congress, and even less in the state legislatures that ratified it. See, Numbers 11 and 12, below.

22   It avoids the overly restrictive language of the Articles of Confederation and the original, anti-federalist draft of the Tenth Amendment. Those provisions limited the Congress to only those powers expressly granted.

23   *McCulloch v. Maryland*, 17 U.S. 579, at p. 421 (U.S. S.Ct., 1819).

tyranny. Madison noted in Federalist No. 10 that "If a faction consists of less than a majority, relief is supplied by the republican principle, which enables the majority to defeat its sinister views by regular vote."

By limiting the power of the national government to a list, and confirming that the police power was distributed to each of the States, Madison confirmed that he understood the peculiar advantage of small numbers in democratic systems. The political scientist Mancur Olson described this in his 1965 book, *The Logic of Collective Action.* When great benefits are concentrated among a small number of beneficiaries, and costs are spread among a large number of contributors, beneficiaries will expend a great deal of time and money to retain their benefits, while contributors will not think it worth their time and money to organize against it.[24] As the national government has taken more power in the progressive era, factions have become increasingly successful at exploiting this advantage when lobbying Congress and the Executive. Small numbers of beneficiaries work hard to impose tiny contributions from all of us: through the tax code, permits, licenses, and all sorts of federal approvals. Minority factions have become more dangerous to individual liberty than even Madison supposed, because Madison's vision of distributed power has been substantially eroded by expanding national power.

The *Liberty Rights Amendments* also restore the holistic view of rights as described by John Locke, a view that the Founders embraced.[25] John Locke wrote the following:

> Though the earth and all inferior creatures are common to all men, yet every man has a property in his own person. This nobody has any right to but himself. The labor of his body, and the work of his hands, are properly his.[26]

---

24   For example, if a tariff on imported sugar increases the profits of a handful of domestic sugar-growers by millions of dollars, and raises the price of sugar in the domestic market by a few cents per pound, the small minority of sugar-growers has a great advantage over the large majority of sugar-consumers.

25   The Founders often used the term "property" and "right" interchangeably. They did not refer to only tangible goods as "property."

26   When Locke wanted to talk about material possessions—land, chattels, jewelry, cash—he used the term "estates." Locke also devised the famous "labor theory of value" by which one came to possess something by mixing one's own labor with it.

James Madison had a similar view. In a 1792 essay he wrote that the term property:

> embraces everything to which a man may attach a value and have a right; and which leaves to everyone else the like advantage…. A man has a property in his opinions and the free communication of them. He has a property of peculiar value in his religious opinions, and in the profession and practice dictated by them. He has a property very dear to him in the safety and liberty of his person. He has an equal property in the free use of his faculties and free choice of objects on which to employ them. In a word, as a man is said to have a right to his property, he may be equally said to have a property in his rights.

The Liberty Rights Amendments thus restore not only the Founders' presumption of liberty but also a more appropriate understanding of rights.

Prosperus

NUMBER 6.
Our Defense against Arrogance:
Individual Freedom and Liberty

As noted in Number 2 and Number 3, the Founders were concerned whether individual freedom and liberty rights could be preserved under *any government which was to be administered by men over men.* They knew that men weren't angels. Clothed with the coercive power of government, they feared that men would act in their own self-interest, or in the interest of factions. *Auxiliary precautions, external controls,* and *internal controls* were placed in the Constitution to protect the individual freedom and the liberty rights of all citizens from the self-interest of officials and factions in the administration of government.

Madison dismissed the notion that enlightened statesmen could adjust the clashing interests of factions and the self-interest of officials. Madison knew that some interests of factions could not be adjusted. This latter point, italicized below, is remarkable for its humility.

> It is in vain to say that enlightened statesmen will be able to adjust these clashing interests and render them all subservient to the public good. Enlightened statesmen will not always be at the helm. *Nor, in many cases, can such an adjustment be made at all.*[27]

Madison knew there was a different, insurmountable barrier facing any government that presumed itself capable of understanding and deciding among the clashing interests of its citizens. No person has the mental capacity to fully understand and judge among the competing preferences, capabilities, and tastes of millions of Americans. F. A. Hayek, winner of the Nobel Prize in Economics, describes this impossibility:

> [I]t would be impossible for any mind to comprehend the infinite variety of different needs of different people which compete

---

27   Madison, *The Federalist Papers 10*, at p. 84.

for the available resources and to attach a definite weight to each ... Whether his interests center round his own physical needs, or whether he takes a warm interest in the welfare of every human being he knows, the ends about which he can be concerned will always be only an infinitesimal fraction of the needs of all men.[28]

The Founders had sufficient humility to know: (i) that they, too, were not angels; (ii) that no collection of Presidents, Senators and Representatives could ever be aware of more than a tiny fraction of the preferences, capabilities, and tastes of all Americans; (iii) that no Congress could ever possess the information and, thus, the capacity, to pick and choose which combinations of these preferences, capabilities, and tastes would or would not produce common good, welfare, or happiness for [all, now 300+ million] Americans.

The Founders implemented a humble solution. They put the national government out of the business of managing everyday affairs of citizens. Organizing everyday interactions among citizens—the police power—including the basic law of contracts, torts, and the criminal law, was left to the States and the people. The Founders placed structural precautions and controls upon the national government to protect each individual's choices from interference by the national government, except in those limited, enumerated areas authorized to Congress. The Constitution's federal system (i) precluded detailed central planning of the minutiae of commerce as an inevitable interference with both liberty rights and individual freedom, and (ii) left the police power to the several States, where local differences and preferences would be best observed and managed by locally elected legislatures.

One can only marvel at the preposterous notion that any Congress, any President, and any of their appointees have the mental capacity to appreciate, consider, *and* efficiently and effectively prioritize and choose among the individual preferences, capabilities, and tastes of 300+ million people as they move through a $14-trillion-dollar annual economy. This absurdity would be no different if every federal official had full-time advice from the world's ten thousand smartest experts in all fields.

---

28   F. A. Hayek, *The Road to Serfdom*, Text and Documents, The Definitive Edition, Edited by Bruce Caldwell, 2007, The University of Chicago Press, at p. 102. Hayek later described those who claim to have the capacity to comprehend this infinite variety of needs as burdened with a fatal conceit. (All references are to this edition.)

No human mind can grasp—let alone communicate to another human mind—the complexity of 300 million different sets of preferences, capabilities, and tastes; likewise, none can judge the relative weights that should be given to each. This type of arrogance was noted in 1776 by Adam Smith. Smith's views were known to, and shared by the Founders. Only arrogant, presumptuous men would find themselves fit to exercise such power.

> The statesmen who should attempt to direct private people in what manner they ought to employ their capitals [editor's note: efforts], would not only load himself with a most unnecessary attention, but assume an authority which could safely be trusted to no council and senate whatever, and which would nowhere be so dangerous as in the hands of a man who had folly and presumption enough to fancy himself fit to exercise it.[29]

Little has changed since 1789. There is still no guarantee that "enlightened statesmen" will be elected to Congress, the Senate, or the Presidency, or be appointed to fill the Executive branch. Indeed, whether *any* public person is enlightened *anywhere* in the United States is regularly debated in the press, on the Internet and on television. Members of Congress, the Senate, or the Executive branch are met with vitriol every day in our 24/7 media cycle. Views enlightened to some are impractical, silly, vicious, or worse to others. Indeed, if elected officials were disqualified based on the scurrilous things said by opposing factions, the House, the Senate, and the Presidency would lie vacant.

Madison foresaw our current situation, in which ambitious and arrogant leaders would contend for pre-eminence and power through factions. Factions would seek to capture the coercive power of any government administered by men over men. They attempt to use that power to interfere with other citizen's freedom and liberty rights. It was happening when the Founders created the nation, has happened since, is happening now, and will happen again.

> The latent causes of faction are . . sown in the nature of man .
> . . [A]n attachment to different leaders ambitiously contending for pre-

---

29   *Inquiry Into the Nature and Causes of the Wealth of Nations,* Book IV, Ch. II, p. 456, ¶10. Adam Smith called this arrogant, presumptuous person "the man of system."

eminence and power . . . [h]ave, in turn, divided mankind into parties, inflamed them with mutual animosity, and rendered them much more disposed to vex and oppress each other than to co-operate for their common good.[30]

In a nation of 300 million unique people, it is *not* surprising that citizens disagree about whether particular ideas, views, and preferences are enlightened. It *is* surprising, however, that the American people have been diverted from its humble (yet effective) defense against the arrogance and self-interest of factions—individual freedom and liberty rights. Madison's great object—placing precautions and controls in the Constitution to protect individual freedom and liberty from a government administered by men over men—needs constant renewal and support.

Tolerance, respect, and humility are deeply embedded in the Constitutional concepts of individual freedom and liberty rights: (i) tolerance and respect for another's preferences, capabilities, and tastes that differ from our own; (ii) humility with respect to the limitations of the human mind and the impossibility that any individual or group has the capacity to refashion our complex, unpredictable world into an order imposed by man. Tolerance, respect, and humility are concepts that have gone missing from today's public discourse.

As Madison feared, leaders of factions still ambitiously contend for pre-eminence and power, and arrogantly assert they can refashion the world—an appealing, but fatal conceit. Indeed, much of the twentieth century was marred by the fatal conceit of a handful of leaders who possessed sufficient folly and presumption (arrogance) to assert they could refashion the world—Lenin, Stalin, Hitler, Mussolini, Mao, Pol Pot.[31]

The Founders knew that clashing interests of factions could not be resolved by compromise when factions sought to interfere with bedrock principles of individual freedom and liberty. The passions, ambition, arrogance, and self-interest of factions and their leaders were to be broken on the protective walls of the auxiliary precautions and controls that

---

30   Madison, *The Federalist Papers 10,* at p. 79.
31   Even in America, the arrogance of leaders during each World War led to the internment of large numbers of our fellow U.S. citizens—men and women of German, Italian, and Japanese descent.

the Founders wrote into the Constitution to protect individual freedom and liberty.

Ben Franklin's exchange with a Philadelphia woman at the close of the 1787 Convention illustrates the Founders' concern.

> "Well, Doctor, what have we got—a Republic or a Monarchy?"
> "A Republic, if you can keep it."[32]

The Liberty Rights Amendments (1—4) scrub the constitutional bottom, allow a manageable mid-course correction, and strengthen the auxiliary precautions and the external and internal controls that Madison, Washington, Franklin, Adams, and the other Founders placed in the Constitution obliging government to control itself.

Amicus

---

32   *Notes of Dr. James McHenry*, published in The American Historical Review, vol. 11, 1906, at p. 618.

NUMBER 7.
Pursuit of Individual Preferences and Talents Is Not Selfish

One of my favorite pictures is a shot of Boston Celtic William F. (Bill) Russell, with his 11 NBA Championship rings in the palm of his two hands—smiling. Russell was my childhood sports hero. I doubt there will ever be another person who assembles and brings the same combination of intellect, hard work, character, desire, and talent to the game of basketball. Russell has more rings than fingers—eleven championships in thirteen years as an NBA player—to go along with two consecutive NCAA championships, and a gold medal at the 1956 Summer Olympics. He may be the most accomplished winner in the history of modern sports.

Would any American conclude that it was selfish of Bill Russell to develop and apply his intellect, character, and desire, along with very hard work over many years in the pursuit of his preferences and his talents? Was it really necessary to win all of those titles? All those rings? Wouldn't it have served a greater good for Russell and his teammates not to be so selfish? Was Russell selfish? While any NBA player might wish Russell well for trying, each would work hard to deny Russell and his teammates every title.

The vast majority of Americans[33] might conclude that bouncing an orange ball and throwing it at an orange rim is not worth years of effort. But, Americans are free to value all such activities—from poetry to physics—differently.

As his books describe, Russell faced innumerable challenges and choices along the path to fourteen championships—both personal and professional—from easy to hard, *very hard*—from fair to unfair, *very unfair*. Yet, Bill Russell's relentless pursuit of his preferences, values, and talent (in the circumstances presented to him) is remarkable, extraordinary, and widely admired.

---

33 Many Americans have not yet acknowledged the cosmic importance of basketball.

Surely, the choices Bill Russell made with respect to his basketball career had corresponding effects and consequences (positive, neutral, and negative) in other aspects of his life. In this respect, Bill Russell is little different from most Americans—forced to choose among many different paths with inevitably different results in family, friends, and acquaintances, and in the nature of relationships. And, just like so many other Americans, the road each of us travels cannot effectively be compared with any of the numerous roads we chose *not* to travel.

Did Bill Russell's unique combination of intellect, hard work, character, and talent lead him to decisions and choices that his friends and family might not have made? Surely, yes. In this respect, Bill Russell is little different from most Americans—forced to balance not only among his own competing desires, needs, and preferences, but also those closest to him.

Other than securing his individual freedom and liberty rights under the constitution, could the 535 members of the U.S. House and Senate have achieved for Bill Russell what he achieved for himself? Could any Congress first understand and then fashion legislation that would have been of timely help to Bill Russell as he made each of the millions of decisions that led him to fourteen different championships, several books, an interesting career, and an interesting life?

The Founders would have said *no*! Russell's path is the very essence of individual freedom, though, at times, it was unnecessarily hard and stupidly unfair. F. A. Hayek would also say *no*! No 535 humans have ever had sufficient capacity to even conceptualize such results.

> [It] is impossible for any man to survey more than a limited field, to be aware of the urgency of more than a limited number of needs. Whether his interests center round his own physical needs, or whether he takes a warm interest in the welfare of every human being he knows, the ends about which he can be concerned will always be only an infinitesimal fraction of the needs of all men.[34]

And no—all those rings don't mean William F. Russell was a selfish man. Instead, they confirm that an individual armed with freedom can successfully follow his own values and preferences rather than someone

---

34   F. A. Hayek, *The Road to Serfdom, supra,* at p. 102.

else's, not only with success, but with great personal satisfaction and dignity, even in the face of difficult and unfair obstacles.

> [I]ndividualism . . . does not assume, as is often asserted, that man is egoistic or selfish or ought to be. It merely starts from the indisputable fact that the limits of our powers of imagination make it impossible to include in our scale of values more than a sector of the needs of the whole society, and that, since, strictly speaking, scales of value can exist only in individual minds, nothing but partial scales of values exist . . . From this the individualist concludes that individuals should be allowed, within defined limits, to follow their own values and preferences rather than somebody else's; that within these spheres the individual's system of ends should be supreme and not subject to any dictation by others.[35]

The Liberty Rights Amendments (1 to 4) are intended to confirm that each of us must be allowed, within the defined limits of the Rule of Law, to follow our own values and preferences rather than somebody else's, and that within our own sphere of individual liberty, our own values and preferences are supreme, not subject to dictation by others.

I have heard Bill Russell speak and read each of his books. My impression is that Russell would be fully supportive of any young citizen with different talents, intellect, and character pursuing his or her own course. Russell's admiration of and respect for the professional singing career of his high school track teammate—Johnny Mathis—is but one example. Russell's advice to young people—athletes or not—black or white—male or female— would seem to be the same: make and learn from your own choices, pursue your own talents in your own way, and develop your own intellect and character. It is the exercise of this freedom across our lives that has value, produces satisfaction, and builds integrity, *not* the specific path taken. Such choices are not selfish. Rather, they are the basic elements of individual freedom and liberty. Understanding and pursuing each of our individual talents, capacities, and intellect is never selfish in a society structured around individual freedom and liberty and governed by the Rule of Law.

Amicus

NUMBER 8.
A Mandatory Reboot for Liberty Rights

Thirty-one (31) of *The New Federalist Papers* relate to the first four Amendments of *The Second Bill of Rights*. These amendments are a package, operating together to secure individual freedom and liberty in the United States. This introduction to the group—the *Liberty Rights Amendments*—is appropriate, before giving individual attention to each of the four amendments.

The *Liberty Rights Amendments* 1—4 focus on the rights, privileges, and immunities of individuals—the building blocks for a nation founded on equal exercise of these rights by all citizens.

Establishing durable protections for individual citizens from the arbitrary power of government was the overarching concern of most Americans when the Declaration of Independence was signed and published on July 4, 1776. The thirteen colonies went to war over individual freedom and liberty. Before the Constitution was ratified in 1789, each of the thirteen States enacted constitutions that protected each citizen's liberty rights from the arbitrary power of States.[36] The first Bill of Rights assured the States and the people that the new national government would be similarly curbed from interfering with liberty rights.[37] The Founders and the States successfully reduced the most important concept ever devised by mankind—*individual freedom under law*—into each of the written state and federal constitutions.

The Founders got this most important concept right! But, *individual freedom under law* did not yet apply to slaves,[38] only to free persons. The error was in application, not in content.

---

36   Massachusetts had adopted its constitution in 1780. Its listing of "the natural, essential, and unalienable rights" of citizens is exhaustive. See Number 16, below.
37   See, Numbers 14, 15, and 16, below.
38   Several States had already banned slavery. Some Founders expected that slavery would end by itself or be limited to States in which it already existed. Although the original U.S. Constitution does not refer to slavery, Article I, Section 2 provided that

This error produced the very things Madison most feared: unequal administration of government by free men (who weren't angels) over those who were not free; a Civil War among the States; and unending opportunities for factions to divide men into parties and to inflame them with animosity. The error caused incalculable suffering, and continues to generate misunderstanding, fear, and suspicion among groups of American citizens. Factions (special interests) of all sorts have exploited these fertile opportunities to contend for pre-eminence and power, and to encourage citizens to vex and oppress each other rather than cooperate. While the Civil War Amendments might have offered a path to equal application of individual freedom and liberty rights, the actual path was twisted and turned by the decision of the Supreme Court in *The Slaughterhouse Cases*, subsequent enactment of Jim Crow laws, and piecemeal intervention by the U.S. Supreme Court.[39]

Numbers 1 through 31 of *The New Federalist Papers* describe some of the historical events that led us down a path the Founders never intended—a path they tried hard to avoid. Instead of relying on the written constitutional protections of individual freedom and liberty, we have increasingly looked to government and to officials to protect individual freedom and liberty on our behalf. For more than a century, American citizens have hoped that elected and appointed officials would be disinterested, all-knowing angels, capable of using expansive legislative and regulatory power wisely. Our experience over the last century is like "a group of people [agreeing] to take a journey together without agreeing where they want to go . . . [T]he result [is] they . . [all] . . make a journey which most of them do not want at all."[40] While debating the journey, the original premise is forgotten—individual freedom and liberty in making the trip.

All of the limitations inherent in such an approach were identified by the Founders.[41] Pitting fifty state legislatures and Congress against one another, fifty state regulators and federal regulators against one another, with fifty state court systems and the federal court system on top of it all, has produced the very confusion and complexity Madison tried so hard

---

only "three-fifths of all other Persons" counted in the census that determined seats in the House of Representatives.

39   See, Numbers 11, 12, 17, 20, and 21, below. The destructive influence of factions is highlighted throughout *The New Federalist Papers*.

40   F. A. Hayek, *The Road to Serfdom, supra*, at pp. 103-104.

41   These limitations are pointed out throughout *The New Federalist Papers*.

to prevent. Madison knew that such confusion and complexity could only lead to arbitrary administration of the power of government, *unequal* right to individual freedom and liberty, and, in the end, infringement of individual freedom and liberty.

The Founders focused on the protection of liberty rights from the coercive power of government. In an environment of government v. government, regulator v. regulator, with federal and state judges on top of the confusion, the Founders' focus on liberty rights is simply lost.

Can the equilibrium for which the Founders fought—balancing the enumerated federal powers, the police power of States, and common exercise of liberty rights—be restored?

The approach offered in the *Liberty Rights Amendments* is the one Bill Gates created early in the development of MS DOS. If a PC is frozen, or has been taken over by a hacker, all MS DOS computers (PCs) allow the user to hit three keys together—CTRL + ALT + DEL—forcing the computer to move to screen that allows the user to Reboot (and to restore the default settings).

The *Liberty Rights Amendments* are equivalent to CTRL + ALT + DEL—a mandatory Reboot back to 1789 to restore the default settings for liberty rights. The amendments work together, in the steps described below.

AMENDMENT 2 OF THE SECOND BILL OF RIGHTS

1. The first sentence of Section 2 of Amendment 2 moves the clock back to 1789 to define liberty rights, and confirms that the freedoms, privileges, and immunities—together, the liberty rights—held by citizens at the adoption of this Constitution are retained by the people, are not surrendered to government, and shall not be abridged by the United States. The second sentence of Section 2, Amendment 2 brings this definition of liberty rights forward to today, and applies it to all citizens.

2. Section 3 of Amendment 2 includes a non-exhaustive list of liberty rights, using the formulation written by Bushrod Washington (George Washington's nephew) in 1823.[42] The list is an expansive one, but consistent with the preference of the Founders for individual freedom. The

---

42   See Number 5, above, and Number 18, below.

list is consistent with the Founders' views of the Enlightenment—citizens did not support government intrusion into the preferences, talents, and perspectives of fellow citizens.

3. Section 4 of Amendment 2 establishes a new "auxiliary precaution"[43] to protect liberty rights, a presumption that the exercise by a citizen of liberty rights is valid against any law made by Congress and any rule or order made by the Executive that denies or abridges such rights. The presumption does not apply when Congress is exercising one of its enumerated powers.[44]

AMENDMENT 3 OF THE SECOND BILL OF RIGHTS

4. Amendment 3 solidifies existing protections previously set forth in Section 1 of the Fourteenth Amendment with respect to due process and equal protection of the laws. Amendment 3 expands these protections to ban discrimination. Most importantly, Amendment 3 extends these protections to apply to both Congress and the Executive, in addition to confirming these same protections with respect to States.[45]

AMENDMENT 4 OF THE SECOND BILL OF RIGHTS

5. Section 1 of Amendment 4 confirms that the police power is reserved to each of the States and includes the power to promote the health, good order, morals, peace, and safety of citizens through laws of general application that preserve the common exercise of liberty rights. Section 2 of Amendment 4 adds an "auxiliary precaution" at the state level confirming that the exercise by a citizen of liberty rights is presumed valid against any law made by the State that denies or abridges such rights.

6. Section 3 of Amendment 4 prohibits the national government from bullying states in the exercise of their police power. Federal laws, rules, and orders requiring a State to exercise its police power in a specific

---

43   Madison used the term frequently when describing how federal power was controlled in the Constitution. See, Number 3, above.

44   See, Number 18, below.

45   With the addition of this separate, stand alone Amendment 3, strengthening the protections of due process, equal protection of the laws, and banning discrimination, Section 1 of the Fourteenth Amendment is repealed. See, Section 1 of Amendment 2 of *The Second Bill of Rights*. The *Constitution of the United States*, including *The Second Bill of Rights*, is set forth in the Appendix.

manner as a condition of receiving benefits from the federal government are invalidated.[46]

AMENDMENT 1 OF THE SECOND BILL OF RIGHTS

7. Amendments 2, 3, and 4 are tied together by Amendment 1, which defines the Rule of Law in the United States to include the constitutional structure, and the continued development of the common law by an independent judiciary.[47]

The Founders got the most important concept right—*individual freedom under law*! Amendments 1—4 provide for a Reboot that is long overdue.

Amicus

---

46   See, Number 30, below.
47   See, Number 9, below.

NUMBER 9.
Government under The Rule of Law in the United States

The first four amendments in *The Second Bill of Rights* are the *Liberty Rights Amendments.* The *Liberty Rights Amendments* re-affirm to all citizens that the freedoms, privileges, and immunities—that is, *the liberty rights*—held by citizens when the American Revolution was won are retained by the people and are not surrendered, all under the Rule of Law. Section 1 of the first amendment defines the Rule of Law in the United States:

> 1. The Rule of Law in the United States shall forever be comprised of: allocated powers among the people, the states, and the national government under this Constitution; broad liberty rights retained by the people; the police power retained by each State to preserve the common exercise of liberty rights; limited, enumerated legislative powers vested in and exercisable only by an elected Congress; separation of national powers among Congress, the Executive, and the Judiciary; and development of the common law consistent therewith by an independent state and federal judiciary.

The U.S. Constitution was different from other constitutions when adopted—indeed unique—and has remained so since 1789. Why?

THE UNITED STATES CONSTITUTION WAS ESTABLISHED BY THE PEOPLE AND CANNOT BE ALTERED BY THE GOVERNMENT.

Madison confirms this most important of differences—the Constitution was the paramount law of the land, established by the people, *and unalterable by the government serving them.*

> *The important distinction so well understood in America between a Constitution established by the people and unalterable by the government* [on the one hand], *and a law established by* [another] *government and alterable by* [that] *government, seems to have been little understood and less observed in any other country. Wherever the*

44

supreme power of legislation has resided, has been supposed to reside also a full power to change the form of the government. *Even in Great Britain, where the principles of political and civil liberty have been most discussed, and where we hear most of the rights of the Constitution, it is maintained that the authority of the Parliament is transcendent and uncontrollable* as well with regard to the Constitution as the ordinary object of legislative provision.[48]

In our constitutional republic, the agents of the people—Representatives, Senators, the President—are merely the temporary occupants of the seats of government, without authority to alter the Constitution by legislation or regulation.

A constitution is, in fact, and must be regarded by the judges as, a fundamental law. . . . If there should happen to be an irreconcilable variance between the two, that which has the superior obligation and validity ought, of course, to be preferred; or, in other words, *the Constitution ought to be preferred to the statute, the intention of the people to the intention of their agents. .*

They teach us that the prior act of a superior [the people] ought to be preferred to the subsequent act of an inferior and subordinate authority [their agents]; and that accordingly, whenever a particular statute contravenes the Constitution, it will be the duty of the judicial tribunals to adhere to the latter and disregard the former.[49]

The Founders clearly intended to construct competing tensions among the three co-equal branches of the government. These tensions were viewed favorably as the means to provide equilibrium within the republic, and to prevent the usurpation of power by the legislative or the executive branches.

The Founders were well aware that the Judiciary would be called upon to protect the Constitution from encroachment by the other branches and to protect the liberty rights of citizens.

If, then, the courts of justice are to be considered as the *bulwarks of a limited Constitution against legislative encroachments*, this

---

48   Madison, *The Federalist Papers 53*, at p. 331.
49   Hamilton, *The Federalist Papers 78*, at pp. 467-68.

consideration will afford a strong argument for the permanent tenure of judicial offices, since nothing will contribute so much as this to that independent spirit in the judges which must be essential to the faithful performance of so arduous a duty.

This independence of the judges is equally requisite to guard the Constitution and the rights of individuals from the effects of those ill humors which the arts of designing men, or the influence of particular [circumstances], sometimes disseminate among the people themselves, and which, though they speedily give [way] to better information, and more deliberate reflection, have a tendency, in the meantime, to [lead to] dangerous innovations in the government, and serious oppression of the minor party in the community.[50]

The Founders well understood that they were establishing a constitutional republic with a hierarchy of constitutional, federal, and state law, all of which was balanced by the common law decisions of an independent judiciary. All of this was different from any other country.

A Fresh Start for Liberty Rights under the Rule of Law

The experience of 225 years with the American Constitution has taught us that factions have been periodically successful in stressing the original framework. Although their influence waxes and wanes, we seem to be in another period of highly contentious competition among factions for manipulation of government administered by some men over others.

In 1873, the Supreme Court's decision in *Slaughterhouse* unwisely jettisoned judicial protection of the privileges and immunities to which individuals are entitled from government. Factions were quick to take advantage of this surprising decision, which indicated that state interference with economic, political, and civil rights (privileges and immunities) would be overlooked by the federal judiciary. One result was a steady decline in the effectiveness of individual economic rights. Other results include 140 years of controversy relating to voting, race, gender, and privacy—arising from the divisive interplay of factions with numerous Congresses, Presidents, States, and courts in the vacuum the *Slaughterhouse* decision created.

---

50   *Ibid*, at p. 469.

A fresh start is not only possible (with a thorough scrub of algae and barnacles from the Constitution) but required to meet the most recent challenge. Once again, factions:

> have, in turn, divided mankind into parties, inflamed them with mutual animosity, and rendered them much more disposed to vex and oppress each other than to co-operate for their common good.[51]

The Founders' basic concept for a constitutional republic is still sound: allocated powers among the people, the states, and the national government; broad liberty rights retained by the people; limited, enumerated powers granted by the people to the national government; separation of these powers among Congress, the Executive, and the Judiciary; and development of the common law consistent therewith by an independent state and federal judiciary.

Little has changed since 1787. Still, men are not angels. Government administered by men over other men still faces the unbridled self-interest of factions, their passions, and their leaders. *The Second Bill of Rights* allows the people of the nation to pause, to carefully consider the consequences of allowing factions to continue to vex and oppress each other, to put the flames of mutual animosity aside, and to cooperate for their common good.

The Founders still point the way toward (i) a rediscovery of common interests, (ii) a lowering of divisive rhetoric, (iii) re-affirmation of individual freedom and liberty rights, and (iv) a shift to more stable middle ground. On that middle ground, the constitutional lines separating individual liberty from federal power and from the police power of States will again be visible across our society. Clarity (of these constitutional lines) is *all* an independent federal and state judiciary needs to fulfill the role the Founders intended—impenetrable bulwark for individual freedom and liberty rights.[52]

Valerius

---

51   The danger of which Madison was so concerned in *The Federalist Papers 10*. See, Number 3, above.
52   The first section of Amendment 10, *The Second Bill of Rights*, confirms that "[t]he Judicial power shall be exercised to preserve liberty rights, the Rule of Law, and the republican form of government." See Number 47, below, for a further discussion of Amendment 10.

NUMBER 10.
For the Purpose of Common Defense and General Welfare

Amendment 1, Section 2 of the *Liberty Rights Amendments* reads as follows:

> 2. The Preamble to this Constitution is a statement of general purpose, and not a grant of powers to the government. The language in Article I, Section 8 "to pay the Debts and provide for the common Defence and general Welfare of the United States" is a limitation on the power of Congress to lay and collect taxes, duties, imposts, and excises, not an independent grant of power in addition to those otherwise set forth in Section 8. The Judiciary shall rely, when interpreting this Constitution, on the publicly known meaning of the words contained in the Constitution at the time such words were adopted.

Section 2 restores the "precautions" Madison placed in the Constitution to ensure that the new national government would not simply run over the police power reserved to the several States or the liberty rights retained by citizens.

First, the Founders included a Preamble to the Constitution that clearly set forth the overall purpose of the people in forming a union of the several States:[53]

> We the People of the United States, in Order to form a more perfect Union, establish Justice, insure domestic Tranquility, provide for the common defence, promote the general Welfare,

---

53 First-year law students learn that a "Preamble" is not an operative part of a legal document—it is prefatory only. They also learn common law rules of interpretation, including that when interpreting any legal document, you should rely on the publicly known meaning of words at the time those words were adopted. These parts of Section 2 simply state what was obvious to the Founders, but is conveniently forgotten by some of today's federal officials.

and secure the Blessings of Liberty to ourselves and our Posterity, do ordain and establish this Constitution for the United States of America.

Second, the Founders limited congressional power over taxation in Article I, Section 8, ¶1:

> The Congress shall have Power To lay and collect Taxes, Duties, Imposts and Excises, *to pay the Debts and provide for the common Defence and general Welfare* of the United States. . . ;

The words in italics were included to *limit* congressional power to lay and collect taxes to the general purposes listed. *This was never intended to be an independent grant of power for Congress to enact whatever it wished* in the name of "the common defence and general welfare."

Is the Founders' intent a guess? No!

This exact issue was discussed in *The Federalist Papers 41*, while the Constitution was being ratified (and before New York and Virginia did so). These very words were addressed by James Madison. Rarely in *The Federalist Papers* does Madison show a higher level of impatience than with absurd interpretations by opponents of the Constitution who were attempting to stop ratification in New York State. "An absurdity" was the term he used to describe the opponents' contention that these words would give Congress unlimited power to enact whatever legislation Congress thought to be for the general welfare. Here are detailed excerpts from Madison's discussion:

> Some who have not denied the necessity of the power of taxation have grounded a very fierce attack against the Constitution, on the language in which [the taxing power] is defined. It has been urged and echoed that the power "*to lay and collect taxes, duties, imposts, and excises, to pay the debts, and provide for the common defense and general welfare of the United States,*" amounts to an unlimited commission to exercise every power which may be alleged to be necessary for the common defense or general welfare. No stronger proof could be given of the distress under which these writers labor [search] for objections, than their stooping to such a misconstruction.

Had no other enumeration or definition of the powers of the Congress been found in the Constitution than the general expression just cited, the authors of the objection might have had some color [basis] for it; though it would have been difficult to find a reason for so awkward a form of describing an authority to legislate in all possible cases. A power to destroy the freedom of the press, the trial by jury, or even to regulate the course of descents [inheritance], or the form of conveyances [sales] must be very singularly expressed by the terms "to raise money for the general welfare."[54]

But what color [basis] can the objection have, when a specification of the objects alluded to by these general terms immediately follows and is not even separated by a longer pause than a semicolon? If the different parts of the same [document] ought to be [read] as to give meaning to every part . . ., shall one part of the same sentence be excluded altogether from a share in the meaning; and shall the more doubtful and indefinite terms be [given full effect], and the clear and precise expression be denied any signification whatsoever? For what purpose could the enumeration of particular powers be inserted, if these and all others were meant to be included in the preceding general power? Nothing is more natural nor common than first to use a general phrase, and then to explain and qualify it by a recital of particulars. But the idea of an enumeration of particulars which neither explain nor qualify the general meaning, and can have no other effect than to confound and mislead, is an absurdity . . . .

. . . .

How difficult it is for error to escape its own condemnation.[55]

(Editor: Emphasis in the original, explanatory words in [brackets].)

Two years later, in 1791, then Secretary of State Thomas Jefferson expressed the same view in a letter to President Washington as part of his

---

54   Madison is saying that only a tortured construction of these words can lead to the conclusion that Congress has power to legislate to raise money for whatever Congress decides is "the general welfare."

55   Madison, *The Federalist Papers 41*, at pp. 264-64.

opinion that the Constitution did not give Congress the power to establish a National Bank.[56]

> [Congress] are not *to do anything they please* to provide for the general welfare, but only to lay taxes for that purpose. To consider the latter phrase not as describing the purpose of the first, but as giving a distinct and independent power to do any act they please which might be for the good of the Union, would render all the preceding and subsequent enumerations of power completely useless. It would reduce the whole instrument to a single phrase, that of instituting a Congress with power to do whatever would be for the good of the United States; and, as they would be the sole judges of the good or evil, it would be also a power to do whatever evil they please... Certainly no such universal power was meant to be given them. It was intended to lace them up straitly within the enumerated powers and those without which, as means, these powers could not be carried into effect.[57]

(Editor: Emphasis in the original, explanatory words in [brackets].)

In 1817, eight years after his two terms as President were concluded, Jefferson again confirmed his views in a letter to his former Secretary of the Treasury, Albert Gallatin:

> Our tenet ever was . . that Congress had *not* unlimited powers to provide for the general welfare, but were restrained to those specifically enumerated, and that, as it was never meant that they should provide for that welfare but by the exercise of the enumerated powers, so it could not have been meant they should raise money for purposes which the enumeration did not place under their action; consequently, that the specification of powers is a limitation of the purposes for which they may raise money.[58]

---

56   Alexander Hamilton, the Secretary of the Treasury had given a separate opinion to President Washington that the "necessary and proper" clause (discussed in more detailed in Number 18, below) authorized the government to establish a national bank.
57   The Writings of Thomas Jefferson, Memorial Edition (Lipscomb and Bergh, editors) 20 Vols., Washington DC, 1903-04, at Vol. 3 p. 148 (ME 3:148).
58   *Ibid*, Letter to Albert Gallatin, 1817, at Vol. 15 p. 133 (ME 15:133).

Jefferson hoped the courts would never accept what Madison had called an absurd construction of the words "for the general welfare"—what the New Deal Court did anyway in the 1930s:

> I hope our courts will never countenance [accept] the sweeping pretensions which have been set up under the words 'general defence and public welfare.' These words only express the motives which induced the [Constitutional] Convention to give to the ordinary legislature [Congress] certain specified powers which they enumerate, and which they thought might be trusted to [Congress], and not to give them the unspecified [powers] also; or why any specification? [The Convention] could not be so awkward in language as to mean, as we say, 'all and some.' *And should this construction prevail, all limits to the federal government are done away.*[59]

The Founders would not have imagined Section 2 to be necessary. Yet, when a Speaker of the House of Representatives states that Congress can enact what it pleases for the general welfare of the nation, *experience teaches* that the precautions placed by Madison need to be strengthened.

Valerius

---

59   *Ibid*, Letter to Spencer Roane, 1815, at Vol. 14 p. 350 (ME 14:350).

NUMBER 11.
The Privileges and Immunities of American Citizens

Since 1789, the Constitution has ensured that the rights of citizens could not be infringed upon when visiting or transacting business in another State:

> The Citizens of each State shall be entitled to all Privileges and Immunities of Citizens in the several States.[60]

On April 9, 1866, the Civil War was over and the so-called "Radical" Republicans were in charge of Congress. Relying on the Privileges and Immunities Clause, Congress enacted the *Civil Rights Act of 1866*, over the veto of Democrat President Andrew Johnson. Section 1 confirmed that former slaves born in the United States were citizens of the United States with the same economic rights [listed in the Act] "as [are] enjoyed by white citizens."

Section 1 declared:

> That all persons born in the United States and not subject to any foreign power, excluding Indians not taxed, are hereby declared to be citizens of the United States; and such citizens, of every race and color, without regard to any previous condition of slavery or involuntary servitude, except as a punishment for crime whereof the party shall have been duly convicted, shall have *the same right, in every State and Territory in the United States, to make and enforce contracts, to sue, be parties, and give evidence, to inherit, purchase, lease, sell, hold, and convey real and personal property, and to full and equal benefit of all laws and proceedings for the security of person and property, as is enjoyed by white citizens, and shall be subject to like punishment, pains, and penalties, and to none other,* any law, statute, ordinance, regulation, or custom, to the contrary notwithstanding.

---

60   The privileges and immunities clause is set forth at Article IV, Section 2, in the first paragraph.

Three practical questions put the Act's constitutionality in doubt:

- *Could the Privileges and Immunities clause now support a result after the Civil War that it did not support before the War?* Prior to the Civil War, in states allowing slavery, slaves were "property", *not* citizens. Prior to the War, slaves could not make and enforce contracts, could not sue, inherit, purchase, lease, sell, or hold property. Before 1866, the "privileges and immunities" clause protected citizens, *not* "property"—that is, *not* slaves.

- *Although Congress could enforce the Civil Rights Act in federal territories, did the Constitution authorize Congress to dictate to States as to their police power?* The police power—that is, the state law and the common law governing relationships among citizens within the States—had been assigned by Amendment 10 to the States. Before the Civil War, it was the States, not the federal government, that controlled who could make and enforce contracts, sue, inherit, purchase, lease, sell, hold property.

- *Would the Civil Rights Act of 1866 be upheld by the Supreme Court?* The Supreme Court's 1833 decision in *Barron v. Baltimore*, 32 U.S. 243 (1833), ruled that the Bill of Rights limited federal powers, *not* those of the states. "In the years leading up to the Civil War . . . local officials routinely suppressed abolitionist speech and the freedom of the abolitionist press. They denied abolitionists and free blacks the equal protection of the laws from mob violence and terrorism. After the war, the black codes and other measures violated the right of blacks and Republicans to keep and bear arms to protect themselves from mobs and other violence, as well as the natural rights of blacks to hold property and enter into contracts. Under the Constitution [as construed in *Barron v. Baltimore*], did Congress or federal courts have power to provide relief from [state] violations of [liberty] rights."[61]

---

61 *Restoring the Lost Constitution*, The Presumption of Liberty, by Randy E. Barnett, Princeton University Press, 2004, ISBN-13: 978-0-691-12376-9, at p. 192. For a more complete treatment of all of these issues, see, *Constitutional Law, Cases in Context*, Randy E. Barnett, 2008, ISBN 978-0-7355-6344-5, Wolters Kluwer Law & Business, Aspen Publishers.

Unsure of the Supreme Court, Congress was also concerned that a future Congress might repeal the Act (with a different composition after the southern States were readmitted). The Republicans decided to directly protect the liberty rights of citizens from states through a new *Fourteenth Amendment*, debated in 1866. Borrowing language from the privileges *and* immunities clause, the amendment expressly protected the privileges *or* immunities of citizens—including former slaves—from abuse by their own state, just as the original privileges *and* immunities clause protected citizens from abuse when traveling in other states. New York Congressman John Bingham made this clear in debating the amendment on February 29, 1866:

> Is it not essential to the unity of the people that the citizens of each State shall be entitled to all the privileges and immunities of citizens of the several states?

Despite some controversy, Congress declared the Amendment to be ratified in July 1868. The Radical Republicans in Congress now believed that all "citizens," including freed slaves, were entitled to the same privileges *or* immunities held by citizens prior to the constitution.[62]

> All persons born or naturalized in the United States and subject to the jurisdiction thereof, *are citizens of the United States and of the State wherein they reside.* No State shall make or enforce any law which shall abridge *the privileges or immunities of citizens of the United States.*

Five years later, these same two sentences were turned on their heads in a 5-4 Supreme Court decision that *instead* declared that the amendment had established two separate (U.S. and state) classes of citizenship. *The Slaughterhouse Cases*, 83 U.S. 36 (1873) arose out of a Louisiana statute that awarded an exclusive 25-year franchise to provide all slaughterhouse services in the City of New Orleans. More than one thousand butchers were required to relocate from their own premises to a single slaughterhouse managed by a private entity selected by the state. Could Louisiana interfere with the place of business chosen by over a thousand butchers—some former slaves? Wasn't an individual's choice to set up

---

62   See, for example, the *1780 Massachusetts Constitution*, adopted well before the U.S. Constitution.

a butcher shop a privilege protected by the Fourteenth Amendment? A number of butchers thought so, and sued. The majority opinion read these two sentences in a way no member of Congress had expected.

> *It is quite clear, then,* that there is a citizenship of the United States, and a citizenship of a State, which are distinct from each other, and which depend upon different characteristics or circumstances in the individual. *The Slaughterhouse Cases, at 74.*

THIS WASN'T "CLEAR" AT ALL.

The Court concluded that Louisiana wasn't interfering with the privileges *or* immunities of citizens of the United States. Using its police power, Louisiana could interfere with privileges of persons in their other citizenship status—as citizens of Louisiana. *Wow!*

The dissenting opinions by Justices Field (p. 83), Bradley (p. 111), and Swayne (p. 124) excoriated the majority opinion and correctly predicted what was to follow over the next 140 years. State legislatures were now free to interfere with the liberty rights of *state* citizens because the rights of state citizens were different from those protected by the Constitution for *U.S. citizens.* State and local governments soon separated much more than butchers—rail passengers, hotel guests, and school children—by race, not only erecting Jim Crow, but leading to discrimination by states against other disfavored groups—including the Irish and the Chinese.

The decision "interpreted" the Amendment's most important sentence out of the Constitution:

> No state shall make or enforce any law which shall abridge the privileges or immunities of citizens of the United States.

Slaughterhouse authorized states to ignore the privileges and immunities held by citizens at the time of the Constitution, and to avoid applying these privileges to all citizens after the Civil War.

A series of regrettable Supreme Court decisions followed, delaying equal right to the privileges and immunities of all citizens for more than 140 years. Among the worst: *United States v. Cruikshank*, 92 U.S. 542 (1875), *The Civil Rights Cases*, 109 U.S. 3 (1883), and *Plessy v. Ferguson*,

163 U.S. 537 (1896). In 1954, the decision in *Brown v Board of Education* overturned *Plessy*, but it did not overturn this aspect of *Slaughterhouse*. Hindered by its own decision in *Slaughterhouse* from relying on the privileges *or* immunities clause to directly ban separate but equal publicly funded schools as an interference with the privileges *or* immunities of black citizens, the Court has instead tortured the *due process* and the *equal protection* clauses in the Fourteenth Amendment to judicially incorporate selective provisions of the Bill of Rights into the Fourteenth Amendment, *a process that looks awfully like judges are legislating from the bench.* The contortions continue today. Worse still, due process and equal protection concepts focus primarily on procedural rights. These concepts are a poor substitute for protecting the substantive privileges and immunities of American citizens.

The *Liberty Rights Amendments* (1—4) in *The Second Bill of Rights* sweep this aspect of *Slaughterhouse* away, reinstate a single category of citizenship, and confirm that the freedoms, privileges, and immunities held by citizens at the time of the Founding now apply to everyone.

Valerius

NUMBER 12.
A Single Category of Citizenship—American

In Number 11, we described how a central pillar of the Civil War Amendments—the first sentence of the Fourteenth Amendment—was construed in *The Slaughterhouse Cases* to conclude that each citizen wore two citizenship hats simultaneously—one subject to the police power of his state of residence and a second hat subject to the requirements of the federal constitution. After *Slaughterhouse,* a state could exercise its police power to interfere with the privileges and immunities of a citizen wearing his *state citizen hat* but couldn't interfere with the privileges and immunities of the very same citizen when he put on his *federal citizenship hat.*[63] *Only lawyers can construct such a muddle! Incomprehensible nonsense!*

America's experience with this two-category-of-citizenship construction over the 140 years since *Slaughterhouse* has been exceptionally poor. The Supreme Court has struggled ever since to construct a substitute legal home for the privileges and immunities of citizens of the United States, a home that the 1873 Supreme Court discarded from the Fourteenth Amendment. During much of this period, the Court, Congress, and the Executive have wrangled, argued, and fussed with each other, with the media, and with individual citizens over how to repair the damage—particularly in areas relating to racial discrimination and gender equality.

Consider the one hundred year period between the Supreme Court decisions in *Slaughterhouse* and in *Roe v. Wade.* The Black Codes and Jim Crow were erected in numerous states and then destroyed piecemeal through years of litigation across the courtrooms of the entire country; *Plessy v. Ferguson* (allowing states to establish "separate but equal" racial separation) was decided, then overturned in *Brown v. Board of Education*

---

63   The silliest aspect of the *Slaughterhouse* majority opinion may be that the "privileges or immunities of citizens of the United States" was a legal dead end. The term is not defined in the Constitution, and the Bill of Rights is not such a list. Madison and Hamilton promised a Bill of Rights during the ratification process that would restrain the federal government, not the States. See, Number 11 and Number 14.

(mandating an end to racial separation in public schools, again through years of litigation in courtrooms across the country, and sometimes, with the assistance of federal troops); and both *Griswold v. Connecticut* (recognizing a right to privacy) and *Roe v. Wade* (establishing a judicial line between a woman's right to choose an abortion and a state's right to protect the unborn) were decided.

Factions of all sorts found fertile ground throughout this period to advance their own interests and to obstruct the interests of their fellow citizens—just the kind of dangerous opportunity Madison feared and described in *The Federalist Papers 10*. Ambitious leaders took advantage of both real and perceived injustice and unfairness to contend for pre-eminence and power, divide mankind into parties, inflame them with mutual animosity, and render them much more disposed to vex and oppress each other than to co-operate for their common good.[64]

The Court's decision in *Slaughterhouse* created a vacuum filled by the very factions the Founders feared, inflaming mutual animosity, and assigning millions of American citizens into the inexorable tug-of-wars upon which factions thrive. This vacuum has provided authors and commentators, ministers and preachers, newspapers, radio, TV, and thousands of elected officials with endless opportunities to tear at the Founders' basic structure: a citizenry in possession of inalienable rights, privileges, immunities, and freedoms.

The impact of *Slaughterhouse* and its progeny does not end at civil rights. Equally damaging has been subsequent interference with the other pillar of individual freedom—economic rights (or economic liberty). *Slaughterhouse* allowed direct interference in the economic liberty of classes of citizens by a State, an outcome the privileges *or* immunities clause in the Fourteenth Amendment was expressly intended to prevent. And in the subsequent struggle to re-establish the most basic civil rights for black citizens—where each citizen may sit, ride, drink, and learn—the swipe that *Slaughterhouse* took at the economic liberty of citizens of every race and gender has received little attention.[65]

---

64   A few leaders did just the opposite—The Rev. Dr. Martin Luther King, Jr. is at the top of this list.

65   The clause is still there, though the decision in *Slaughterhouse* instructed lower courts to ignore it. This aspect of the decision has never been overturned. The Court could have said in 1873, and it could say now, that this aspect of *Slaughterhouse* was

Trapped in a two-year election cycle in which appealing to one's base and staying away from controversy is a political necessity, a string of Congresses, Presidents, and Supreme Courts have been unable to fundamentally address and fix the problems created by the decision in *Slaughterhouse*. It is easier for incumbent politicians to continue to wrangle, argue, and fuss at the head of competing factions than address these issues.

The *Liberty Rights Amendments* [1—4] in *The Second Bill of Rights* sweep this aspect of *Slaughterhouse* away, reinstate a single category of citizenship, and restore the freedoms, privileges, and immunities held by all citizens at the time of the Founding of the Republic.

Section 1 of Amendment XIV is replaced in its entirety, establishing a single category of citizenship without substantially altering the constitutional structure or diminishing the protections of due process and equal protection under the Rule of Law.

The first sentence of Amendment XIV, Section 1 now reads as follows:

> 1. All persons born or naturalized in the United States and subject to the jurisdiction thereof, are citizens of the United States *and of the State wherein they reside.*

Section 1 of Amendment 2 to *The Second Bill of Rights* amends this first sentence by deleting the italicized words:

> 1. All persons born or naturalized in the United States and subject to the jurisdiction thereof are citizens of the United States. Section 1 of Amendment XIV is repealed.

With this change, every citizen is an American, in whatever state he or she resides. Sections 2 and 3 of Amendment 2 explicitly define the freedoms, privileges, and immunities held by citizens at the adoption of the Constitution as liberty rights that are retained by citizens. And, upon adoption of *The Second Bill of Rights*, there is a single category of citizenship—American.

Valerius

---

incorrectly decided, and that henceforth, no state may interfere with the privileges and immunities of any citizen, as those privileges and immunities were defined in 1789.

NUMBER 13.
The Exhaustive List in Our Constitution

List-making is a problem that plagues all of us every day. It is hard to make a list that is complete—of friends, of books to read . . . and of liberty rights. Most lists I've made—groceries, errands, or repairs—are incomplete. My bucket list today is different from that of last year, next year, and a decade in either direction. Subjective lists are even more difficult—best movies or songs. If my kids made lists of my ten best and worst traits, each list would be quite different—2 or 3 items on the best list, and an incomplete sampling whittled down to 10 on the worst list.

We learn the hard way that list-making causes misunderstandings, if we're lucky, and controversy at other times. Is the list you made an exhaustive one or one with examples? Reasons to call the doctor—exhaustive or example? Reasons for a child to call you at work—exhaustive or example? Our lists are bad, not just because we're human and make mistakes, but because lists require judgment and the words we use mean different things to different people.

It should not surprise us that list-making plagued the Founders, too. The exhaustive and the example lists they included in the Constitution are still at the heart of two key issues facing Americans today. The Founders made several lists: a list of things States can't do in Article 1, Section 10; a list of things Congress can't do in Article 1, Section 9; and a list of cases that can be heard by the federal judiciary in Article 3, Section 2.

But, by far, two other lists have been most important. Over 225 years— each of these two lists has generated substantial misunderstandings— among judges, elected officials, and the leaders of factions, *ambitiously contending for pre-eminence and power.* Both lists are now out of whack—so far out that the original purpose of each list has been turned 180 degrees around.

The *first* is the list of the eighteen (18) enumerated powers granted by the people of the United States to Congress in Article I Section 8. The *second*, discussed in greater detail in Number 14, is the list of exclusions from federal power in the first Bill of Rights.

The Founders understood the advantages and disadvantages that the inclusion of lists would pose to the American Republic. These issues were discussed in *The Federalist Papers* and in various "broadsides" [newspapers] published throughout the country during the debates over ratification. As with every list any of us might make today, the Founders tried to strike an appropriate balance between the powers granted to the new government, the powers reserved to the States, and the rights reserved to the People who had created the States and were about to create a new nation.

The First List—An Exhaustive List of Enumerated Powers.

The *first* list—the eighteen (18) enumerated powers in Article I, Section 8—was intended to limit the power of Congress, and, because the President can only execute the laws approved by Congress, the entire national government. The eighteen powers were these (numbers added):

The Congress shall have Power [1] To lay and collect Taxes, Duties, Imposts and Excises, to pay the Debts and provide for the common Defence and general Welfare of the United States; but all Duties, Imposts and Excises shall be uniform throughout the United States;

[2] To borrow money on the credit of the United States;

[3] To regulate Commerce with foreign Nations, and among the several States, and with the Indian Tribes;

[4] To establish an uniform Rule of Naturalization, and uniform Laws on the subject of Bankruptcies throughout the United States;

[5] To coin Money, regulate the Value thereof, and of foreign Coin, and fix the Standard of Weights and Measures;

[6] To provide for the Punishment of counterfeiting the Securities and current Coin of the United States;

[7] To establish Post Offices and Post Roads;

[8] To promote the Progress of Science and useful Arts, by securing for limited Times to Authors and Inventors the exclusive Right to their respective Writings and Discoveries;

[9] To constitute Tribunals inferior to the supreme Court;

[10] To define and punish Piracies and Felonies committed on the high Seas, and Offenses against the Law of Nations;

[11] To declare War, grant Letters of Marque and Reprisal, and make Rules concerning Captures on Land and Water;

[12] To raise and support Armies, but no Appropriation of Money to that Use shall be for a longer Term than two Years;

[13] To provide and maintain a Navy;

[14] To make Rules for the Government and Regulation of the land and naval Forces;

[15] To provide for calling forth the Militia to execute the Laws of the Union, suppress Insurrections and repel Invasions;

[16] To provide for organizing, arming, and disciplining the Militia, and for governing such Part of them as may be employed in the Service of the United States, reserving to the States respectively, the Appointment of the Officers, and the Authority of training the Militia according to the discipline prescribed by Congress;

[17] To exercise exclusive Legislation in all Cases whatsoever, over such District (not exceeding ten Miles square) as may, by Cession of particular States, and the acceptance of Congress, become the Seat of the Government of the United States, and to exercise like Authority over all Places purchased by the Consent of the Legislature of the State in which the Same shall be, for the Erection of Forts, Magazines, Arsenals, dock-Yards, and other needful Buildings; And

[18] To make all Laws which shall be *necessary and proper* for carrying into Execution the foregoing Powers, and all other Powers vested by this Constitution in the Government of the United States, or in any Department or Officer thereof.

The eighteenth (18th) power is the so-called *necessary and proper* clause, or the sweeping clause as it was known at the time of the Founding. Congress has the authority to do what is necessary and proper to exercise the other seventeen enumerated powers. Madison described these powers in *The Federalist Papers 45*.

The powers delegated by the proposed Constitution to the federal government are *few and defined*. Those which are to remain in the State governments are numerous and indefinite. The former will be exercised principally on external objects, as war, peace, negotiation, and foreign; with which last the power of taxation will, for the most part, be connected. The powers reserved to the several States will extend to all the objects which, in the ordinary course of affairs, concern the lives, liberties, and properties of the people, and the internal order, improvement, and prosperity of the State.[66]

In *The Federalist Papers 33*, Hamilton defended the *necessary and proper* clause as limited by its terms to the execution of *the foregoing powers*.[67] He argued that the clause could be relied on only when Congress was exercising one of the other seventeen (17) powers.

The last clause of [Article 1, Section 8] authorizes the national legislature "to make all laws which shall be *necessary* and *proper* for carrying into execution *the powers* by that Constitution vested in the government of the United States, or in any department or officer thereof"; and the second clause of the sixth article [the supremacy clause] declares that "the Constitution and the laws of the United States made *in pursuance thereof* and the treaties made by their authority shall be the *supreme law* of the land, anything in the constitution or laws of any State to the contrary notwithstanding."

These two clauses have been the source of much virulent invective and petulant declamation against the proposed Constitution. They have been held up to the people in all the exaggerated colors of misrepresentation as the pernicious engines by which their local governments were to be destroyed and their liberties exterminated; as the hideous monster whose devouring jaws would spare neither sex nor age, nor high nor low, nor sa-

---

66   Madison, *The Federalist Papers 45*, at p. 292.
67   Hamilton, *The Federalist Papers 33*, at pp. 201-203. Two hundred and twenty-five years later, the fears of those who opposed the sweeping clause are realized. Since 1933, an ever expanding federal government believes that necessary and proper is a separate grant of power, limited only by what Congress believes is necessary and proper. If the language is interpreted this way, there no need for items 1 through 17. Madison believed such an expansive interpretation of the necessary and proper clause to be an absurdity. Jefferson used an eighteenth century nursery rhyme, "The House that Jack Built," to ridicule this interpretation. See Number 10, above, and Number 19, below.

cred nor profane; and yet, strange as it may appear, after all this clamor, to those who may not have happened to contemplate them in the same light, it may be affirmed with perfect confidence that the constitutional operation of the intended government would be precisely the same if these clauses were entirely obliterated or if they were repeated in every article. . . Why then was it introduced? The answer is . . . for greater caution.

The *Liberty Rights Amendments* (1—4) restore the Founders' original settings by moving back toward an exhaustive list of Congress' powers (with principled flexibility), and an example list of liberty rights (with a presumption that the exercise of liberty rights is valid). At the Founding, these two lists were opposite sides of the same coin, always in equilibrium, inextricably related, and maintaining the balance between the liberty rights of a free people and the faithful exercise of limited powers delegated by the people to the national government.

Amicus

NUMBER 14.
Our Constitution's List of Examples—The First Bill of Rights

As noted in Number 13, two of the lists in the Constitution have generated substantial discussion and debate among judges, officials, and factions. The *first* was described in Number 13. The *second* is the list of exclusions from federal powers in the Bill of Rights.

From May 25, 1787 to September 17, 1787, George Washington served as President of the Constitutional Convention that prepared, debated, and transmitted the draft Constitution to the Continental Congress. During ratification, the absence of a Bill of Rights was argued to be a reason not to ratify the entire document. Ratification of the constitution hung in the balance.

Opponents—Don't Ratify Without a Bill of Rights.

Opponents claimed that the inclusion of other lists created an ambiguity. Were the powers of the federal government in fact limited to the 18 enumerated powers in Article I, Section 8?

> *But rulers have the same propensities as other men; they are as likely to use the power with which they are vested, for private purposes, and to the injury and oppression of those over whom they are placed, as individuals in a state of nature are to injure and oppress one another.* It is therefore as proper that bounds should be set to their authority, as that government should have at first been instituted to restrain private injuries.

This principle, which seems so evidently founded in the reason and nature of things, is confirmed by universal experience. *Those who have governed, have been found in all ages ever active to enlarge their powers and abridge the public liberty. This has induced the people in all countries, where any sense of freedom remained, to fix barriers against the encroachment of their rulers.* The country from which we have derived our origin, is an eminent example of this. Their *magna charta* and bill of rights have long been the boats, as well as the security of that nation. I need say no more, I presume, to an American, than that this principle is a fundamental one . . .

. . .

We find they have, in the ninth section of the first article declared, that the writ of habeas corpus shall not be suspended, unless in cases of rebellion, that no bill of attainder, or ex post facto law, shall be passed, that no title of nobility shall be granted by the United States, etc. *If everything which is not given is reserved, what propriety is there in these exceptions?* Does this Constitution anywhere grant the power of suspending the habeas corpus, to make ex post facto laws, pass bills of attainder, or grant titles of nobility? It certainly does not in express terms. The only answer that can be given is that these are implied in the general powers granted. With equal truth it may be said, that all the powers which the bills of rights guard against the abuse of, are contained or implied in the general ones granted by the this Constitution.[68]

Other opponents made still another list argument: the absence of a Bill of Rights (itself a list).

[M]en of the greatest purity of intention may be made instruments of despotism in the hands of the *artful and designing.* . . .

From this investigation into the organization of this government, it appears that it is devoid of all responsibility or accountability to the great body of the people, and that so far from being a regular balanced government, it would be in practice a *permanent* ARISTOCRACY.

The framers of it, actuated by the true spirit of such a government, which ever abominates and suppresses all free enquiry and discussion have made no provision for the liberty of the press, that *grand palladium of freedom*, and *scourge of tyrants*, but observed a total silence on that head. . . . [69]

---

68   Barnett, *Constitutional Law: Cases in Context, supra,* at pp. 32 and 34, quoting Brutus II, the *New York Journal,* November 1, 1787.
69   *Constitutional Law, Cases in Context,* Barnett, *supra,* at pp. 27-28, quoting Centinel I, Oct. 5, 1787.

Proponents—Ratify Without A Bill of Rights.

Hamilton made several arguments why New Yorkers should ratify without a Bill of Rights. Hamilton's first argument contrasted the origin of previous bill(s) of rights with the source of power under the American Constitution. Concessions from a king to his subjects, Hamilton argued, were entirely different from the consent of THE PEOPLE OF THE UNITED STATES.

> [B]ills of rights are . . . stipulations between kings and their subjects, abridgements of [royal] prerogative in favor of [a subject's] privilege, reservations of [a subject's] rights not surrendered to the prince. . . . Here, [in the U.S. Constitution] the people surrender nothing; and as they retain everything they have no need of particular reservations. "WE, THE PEOPLE OF THE UNITED STATES, to secure the blessings of liberty to ourselves and our posterity, do ordain and establish this Constitution for the United States of America." Here is a better recognition of popular rights than volumes of [bills of rights.][70]

Hamilton's second and third arguments were both prophetic and direct.

> [B]ills of rights . . are not only unnecessary in the proposed Constitution but would even be dangerous. They would contain various exceptions to powers which are not granted; and, on this very account, would afford a colorable pretext to claim more than were granted. *For why declare that things shall not be done which there is no power to do?*

> The truth is . . . that *the Constitution is* itself, in every rational sense, and to every useful purpose, *a BILL OF RIGHTS.*[71]

James Wilson argued to the Pennsylvania ratification convention on October 28, 1787, and December 4, 1787, that it was impossible to make a complete list of rights in a Bill of Rights.

> October 28, 1787: *[I]n a government consisting of enumerated powers, such as is proposed for the United States, a bill of rights would not only be unnecessary, but. . . highly imprudent.* In all societies, there

---

70   Hamilton, *The Federalist Papers 84*, at p. 513.
71   *Ibid*, at pp. 513-15.

are many powers and rights which cannot be particularly enumerated. A bill of rights annexed to a constitution is an enumeration of the powers reserved. *If we attempt an enumeration, everything that is not enumerated is presumed to be given.*

December 4, 1787:

All the political writers . . . have treated [written] on this subject; *but in no[t] one of those books, nor in the aggregate of them all, can you find a complete enumeration of rights appertaining to the people as men and as citizens.*

There are two kinds of government—that where general power is intended to be given to the legislature and that where the powers are particularly enumerated. In the last case, the implied result is that nothing more is intended to be given than what is so enumerated . . . *But in a government like the proposed one, there can be no necessity for a bill of rights, for on my principle, the people never part with their power. Enumerate all the rights of men! [No one] in the late Convention would have attempted such a thing.*

James Iridell made the same point to the North Carolina ratification convention on July 29, 1788.

It would be the greatest absurdity for any man to pretend that, when a legislature is formed for a particular purpose, it can have any authority [other than] what is expressly given to it. . . . [F]or example, if I had three tracts of land, one in Orange, another in Caswell, and another in Chatham, and I gave a power of attorney to a man to sell the two tracts in Orange and Caswell, and he should attempt to sell my land in Chatham, would any man of common sense suppose he had authority to do so? In like manner, I say, the future Congress can have no right to exercise any power but what is contained in that paper. . . . *Let anyone make what collection or enumeration of rights he please, I will immediately mention twenty or thirty more rights not contained in it.*[72]

---

72   Quotations from Wilson and Iridell, *Constitutional Law, Cases in Context*, Barnett, *supra*, at pp. 30-31.

Eighty years later, James F. Wilson[73] made the same argument for the 1866 Civil Rights Act:

> Before our Constitution was formed, the great fundamental rights which I have mentioned, belonged to every person who became a member of our great national family. *No one surrendered a jot or tittle of these rights by consenting to the formation of the Government.*[74]

Most historians agree that without the Federalists' public promise to add a Bill of Rights, the required nine states would not have ratified. Number 15 describes how that promise was kept.

Amicus

---

73 Co-author of the Thirteenth Amendment and Chairman of the House Judiciary Committee.

74 *Restoring the Lost Constitution*, Randy E. Barnett, *supra*, at p. 64.

NUMBER 15.
The Judiciary: Impenetrable Bulwark for Individual Liberty?

On June 8, 1789, James Madison, then a member of the first Congress, and one of the principal drafters of the Constitution, gave a speech supporting the addition of a Bill of Rights as the first twelve (12) amendments. The Constitution had been in effect since June 21, 1788, when nine States had ratified it. Virginia and New York ratified shortly thereafter. When Madison spoke, there were still only eleven States in the union. North Carolina and Rhode Island joined later.

Madison understood Hamilton's argument that any Bill of Rights could not include an exhaustive list of rights protecting citizens from the general government. Madison also understood the political reality that Pennsylvania and New York had ratified after a public promise to add a Bill of Rights to the Constitution after the government formed. Of the twelve draft amendments Madison submitted, following debate and revision, ten were adopted by Congress and ratified by the States, pursuant to the amendment process of Article V. Amendments I (1) through X (10), are commonly known as the Bill of Rights.

Amendment 1
Congress shall make no law respecting an establishment of religion, or prohibiting the free exercise thereof; or abridging the freedom of speech, or of the press; or the right of the people peaceably to assemble, and to petition the Government for a redress of grievances.

Amendment 2
A well regulated Militia, being necessary to the security of a free State, the right of the people to keep and bear Arms, shall not be infringed.

Amendment 3
No Soldier shall, in time of peace be quartered in any house, without the consent of the Owner, nor in time of war, but in a manner to be prescribed by law.

Amendment 4
The right of the people to be secure in their persons, houses, papers, and effects, against unreasonable searches and seizures, shall not be violated, and no Warrants shall issue, but upon probable cause, supported by Oath or affirmation, and particularly describing the place to be searched, and the persons or things to be seized.

Amendment 5
No person shall be held to answer for a capital, or otherwise infamous crime, unless on a presentment or indictment of a Grand Jury, except in cases arising in the land or naval forces, or in the Militia, when in actual service in time of War or public danger; nor shall any person be subject for the same offense to be twice put in jeopardy of life or limb; nor shall be compelled in any criminal case to be a witness against himself, nor be deprived of life, liberty, or property, without due process of law; nor shall private property be taken for public use, without just compensation.

Amendment 6
In all criminal prosecutions, the accused shall enjoy the right to a speedy and public trial, by an impartial jury of the State and district wherein the crime shall have been committed, which district shall have been previously ascertained by law, and to be informed of the nature and cause of the accusation; to be confronted with the witnesses against him; to have compulsory process for obtaining witnesses in his favor, and to have the Assistance of Counsel for his defence.

Amendment 7
In Suits at common law, where the value in controversy shall exceed twenty dollars, the right of trial by jury shall be preserved, and no fact tried by a jury, shall be otherwise re-examined in any Court of the United States, than according to the rules of the common law.

Amendment 8
Excessive bail shall not be required, nor excessive fines imposed, nor cruel and unusual punishments inflicted.

Amendment 9
The enumeration in the Constitution, of certain rights, shall not be construed to deny or disparage others retained by the people.

Amendment 10
The powers not delegated to the United States by the Constitution, nor prohibited by it to the States, are reserved to the States respectively, or to the people.

Madison struggled with how to leave *open* the list of rights in the Bill of Rights. As noted in Number 14, several had argued that an exhaustive list was impossible. James Iridell quipped the following:

> *Let anyone make what collection or enumeration of rights he please, I will immediately mention twenty or thirty more rights not contained in it.*[75]

Madison believed his draft of what became Amendment 9 to the Bill of Rights provided a solution, *leaving the door open to every one of the rights Iridell might name.*

> [B]y enumerating particular exceptions to the grant of power, it would disparage those rights which were not placed in that enumeration, and it might follow by implication, that those rights which were not singled out, were intended to be assigned into the hands of the general government, and were consequently insecure. *This is one of the most plausible arguments I have ever heard urged against the admission of a bill of rights into this system; but, I conceive, that may be guarded against.* I have attempted it, as gentlemen may see by turning to the last clause of the 4th resolution.

Madison's draft of what later became Amendment 9 to the Bill of Rights confirmed that the Bill of Rights was *not* an exhaustive list:

---

75   *Constitutional Law, Cases in Context,* Barnett, Aspen Publishers, 2008, at pp. 30-31.

The exceptions here or elsewhere in the constitution, made in favor of particular rights, shall not be so construed as to diminish the just importance of other rights retained by the people; or as to enlarge the powers delegated by the constitution; but either as actual limitations of such powers, or as inserted merely for greater caution.

In final form, Amendment 9 in the Bill of Rights (Amendment IX to the Constitution) said the same in fewer words.

Amendment 9. The enumeration in the Constitution of certain rights shall not be construed to deny or disparage others retained by the people.

In his June 8 speech to Congress, Madison argued that the addition of a Bill of Rights would have a "salutary effect against the abuse of power." Madison expected the Judiciary to serve as guardian of these rights against federal government intrusion—an impenetrable bulwark [in favor of the individual].

If [liberty rights] are incorporated into the constitution, *independent tribunals of justice will consider themselves in a peculiar manner the guardians of those rights; they will be an impenetrable bulwark against every assumption of power in the legislative or executive,* they will be naturally led to resist every encroachment upon rights expressly stipulated for in the constitution by the declaration of rights.

Since the *Slaughterhouse* decision in 1873, discussed in Numbers 11 and 12, the Judiciary has *infrequently* served the people as an impenetrable bulwark for individual liberty against encroachment by either the national government or state governments. Much of the confusion today over the role of the Judiciary as guardians of individual liberty comes not from federal judges, but from federal legislative and regulatory encroachment against (i) the police power of the States and (ii) the economic and political liberty rights of citizens. Lost in the confusion has been the judicial protection the Civil Rights Act of 1866 tried to guarantee for all Americans.

The fears of Brutus II and Centinel I, cited in Number 14, are too close to reality in 2012.

Those who have governed have been found in all ages ever active to enlarge their powers and abridge the public liberty. This has induced the people in all countries, where any sense of freedom remained, to fix barriers against the encroachment of their rulers.[76]

[M]en of the greatest purity of intention may be made instruments of despotism in the hands of the *artful and designing . . .* From this investigation into the organization of this government, it appears that it is devoid of all responsibility or accountability to the great body of the people, and that so far from being a regular balanced government, it would be in practice a *permanent* ARISTOCRACY.[77]

The *Liberty Rights Amendments* (1—4) take direct aim at these concerns, in a measured, principled way. The Founders intended the *necessary and proper* clause and a non-exclusive listing of individual liberty rights to be two sides of the same coin. The *Liberty Rights Amendments* restore this concept.

These mutually reinforcing protections—the operation of the government and full realization of liberty rights—are managed as the Founders intended in the *Liberty Rights Amendments*.[78] On the one hand, the flexibility required in the *necessary and proper* clause is given a filter in Amendment 2, Section 4, through a presumption of validity in the exercise of liberty rights, entirely rebutted when Congress is executing one of its enumerated powers, and rebuttable when Congress is relying, in whole or in part, on the *necessary and proper* clause. This logic is applied to the states in Amendment 4, Section 2, with respect to the police power. On the other hand, Madison's intent that any listing of individual rights be and remain a list of examples is re-affirmed expressly in Amendment 2, Sections 2 and 3.

Amicus

---

76   Barnett, *Constitutional Law: Cases in Context, supra,* at pp. 32 and 34, quoting Brutus II, the *New York Journal,* November 1, 1787.

77   Barnett, *Constitutional Law: Cases in Context, supra,* at pp. 27-28, quoting Centinel I, *Independent Gazetteer,* October 5, 1787.

78   The *Constitution of the United States,* including *The Second Bill of Rights,* is set forth in the Appendix.

NUMBER 16.
Where Did Madison Find the Ideas He Set Forth in the First Bill of Rights?

When James Madison proposed the addition of the Bill of Rights, he offered twelve draft amendments on the floor of the House. Ten were approved by 2/3 of both Houses of Congress and by 3/4 of the States to become the (first) Bill of Rights. Where did these ideas come from? Did Madison have any inkling that they would be acceptable to his colleagues in the House? In the Senate? In 3/4 of the States?

Was he just lucky? No!

These ideas were close at hand. The thirteen colonies had formed the Continental Congress, had declared themselves to be independent states, and had successfully fought the War of Independence. Most had already established written constitutions as States between 1775 and 1783, well before the Constitutional Convention met in 1787. These constitutions contained written protections for liberty rights, restraints on the power of legislatures and officials, and an independent judiciary. Madison did not have to look far for the content of the Bill of Rights. His draft was little more than a short summary of rights already enshrined in the various constitutions of the several States. But this time, the list would protect citizens from the new national government. The constitutions of Massachusetts and Virginia confirm that Madison's list of restrictions on the new government was just what he said it was on June 8, 1789—a list of examples—and not an exhaustive list. Recall his draft of Amendment 9 from Number 15.

> The exceptions here or elsewhere in the constitution, made in favor of particular rights, shall not be so construed as to diminish the just importance of other rights retained by the people; or as to enlarge the powers delegated by the constitution; but either as actual limitations of such powers, or as inserted merely for greater caution.

The 1780 Massachusetts Constitution

The 1780 Massachusetts Constitution also confirmed that rights do not come from government. A few of these rights appear below. They are entirely familiar. This was no coincidence.

PREAMBLE . . .
We, therefore, the people of Massachusetts, acknowledging, with grateful hearts, the goodness of the great Legislator of the universe, in affording us, in the course of His providence, an opportunity, deliberately and peaceably, without fraud, violence, or surprise, of entering into an original, explicit, and solemn compact with each other, and of forming a new constitution of civil government for ourselves and posterity; and devoutly imploring His direction in so interesting a design, do agree upon, ordain, and establish the following declaration of rights and frame of government as the constitution of the Commonwealth of Massachusetts.

PART THE FIRST
A Declaration of the Rights of the Inhabitants of the Commonwealth of Massachusetts.

Article I. *All men are born free and equal, and have certain natural, essential, and unalienable rights; among which may be reckoned the right of enjoying and defending their lives and liberties; that of acquiring, possessing, and protecting property;* in fine, that of seeking and obtaining their safety and happiness.

. . .

Art. IV. *The people of this commonwealth have the sole and exclusive right of governing themselves as a free, sovereign, and independent State, and do, and forever hereafter shall, exercise and enjoy every power, jurisdiction, and right which is not, or may not hereafter be, by them expressly delegated to the United States of America in Congress assembled.*

. . .

Art. XII. No subject shall be held to answer for any crimes or offence until the same is fully and plainly, substantially and formally, described to him; or be compelled to accuse, or *furnish evidence against himself*; and every subject shall have a right to produce all proofs that may be favorable to him; *to meet the witnesses against him face to face,* and to be fully heard in his defence by himself, or his *counsel* at his election.

And *no subject shall be arrested, imprisoned, despoiled, or deprived of his property, immunities, or privileges, put out of the protection of the law, exiled or deprived of his life, liberty, or estate, but by the judgment of his peers, or the law of the land.*

. . .

Art. XIV. Every subject has a right to be *secure from all unreasonable searches and seizures of his person, his houses, his papers, and all his possessions.* All warrants, therefore, are contrary to this right, if the cause or foundation of them be not previously supported by oath or affirmation, and if the order in the warrant to a civil officer, to make search in suspected places, or to arrest one or more suspected persons, or to seize their property, be not accompanied with a special designation of the persons or objects of search, arrest, or seizure; and no warrant ought to be issued but in cases, and with the formalities, prescribed by the laws.

Art. XV. In all controversies concerning property, and in all suits between two or more persons, except in cases in which it has heretofore been otherways used and practised, the parties have a *right to a trial by jury*; and this method of procedure shall be held sacred . . .

Art. XVI. The *liberty of the press* is essential to the security of freedom in a State; it ought not, therefore, to be restrained in this commonwealth.

Art. XVII. The people have a *right to keep and to bear arms* for the common defence. And as, in time of peace, armies are dangerous to liberty, they ought not to be maintained without the consent of the legislature; and the military power shall always be held in an exact subordination to the civil authority and be governed by it.

. . .

Art. XXIV. Laws made to punish for actions done before the existence of such laws, and which have not been declared crimes by preceding laws, are unjust, oppressive, and inconsistent with the fundamental principles of a free government.[79]

. . . .

Art. XXVI. *No magistrate or court of law shall demand excessive bail or sureties, impose excessive fines, or inflict cruel or unusual punishments.*

. . . .

Art. XXVII. In time of peace, no soldier ought to be quartered in any house without the consent of the owner; and in time of war, such quarters ought not be made but by the civil magistrate, in a manner ordained by the legislature.

. . . .

Art. XXIX. It is essential to the preservation of the rights of every individual, his life, liberty, property, and character, that there be an impartial interpretation of the laws, and administration of justice. *It is the right of every citizen to be tried by judges as free, impartial, and independent as the lot of humanity will admit.* It is, therefore, not only the best policy, but for the security of the rights of the people, and of every citizen, that the judges of the supreme judicial court should hold their offices as long as they behave themselves well, and that they should have honorable salaries ascertained and established by standing laws.

Art. XXX. In the government of this commonwealth, *the legislative department shall never exercise the executive and judicial powers,* or either of them; *the executive shall never exercise the legislative and judicial powers,* or either of them; *the judicial shall never exercise the legislative and executive powers,* or either of them; *to the end it may be a government of laws, and not of men.*

---

79   Art. XXIV prohibits "bills of attainder"—laws that turn an act legally done in the past into a crime.

The 1776 Virginia Declaration of Rights

Similarly, the *Virginia Declaration of Rights* had already established, for citizens of Virginia, the rights later listed in Madison's draft of the Bill of Rights. The full text of the Virginia Declaration of Rights confirms that virtually nothing contained in the Bill of Rights was new. Section I, for example, confirms that citizens are free to use whatever *means* [trade] to acquire property in the pursuit of happiness and safety.

> SECTION I. That all men are by nature equally free and independent and have certain inherent rights, of which, when they enter into a state of society, they cannot, by any compact, deprive or divest their posterity; *namely, the enjoyment of life and liberty, with the means of acquiring and possessing property, and pursuing and obtaining happiness and safety.*

Madison did not intend to establish new ground. Madison drafted the Bill of Rights to confirm to opponents of the new constitution that the rights already embedded in the State constitutions were safe from interference by the new federal government. The Bill of Rights fulfilled the promise Madison made before ratification—to restrain the federal government.[80]

Amicus

---

80 See, the discussion of the decision in *Barron v. Baltimore* (1833) in Number 11 above. The Bill of Rights did not restrain the States. The States were already restrained by their own constitutions. The Bill of Rights restrained the new national government.

NUMBER 17.
The Liberty Rights of Americans

As noted in Numbers 9, 10, 11, and 12, the first four amendments in *The Second Bill of Rights* are called the *Liberty Rights Amendments* because they re-affirm to all Americans the freedoms, privileges, and immunities—together, *the liberty rights*—held by citizens of the United States at the close of the Revolution and prior to the adoption of the Constitution. Liberty rights are retained by the people, are not surrendered to the government, and are exercisable under the Rule of Law.

The *Liberty Rights Amendments* achieve this result by revising Section 1 of Amendment XIV, the second of the Civil War amendments. The protections regarding due process and equal protection in Section 1 of Amendment XIV are kept, but are moved and expanded. Section 1 of Amendment XIV is revised in its entirety.[81]

Four separate substitutions are provided in Amendments 2, 3, and 4 of *The Second Bill of Rights* to more effectively secure liberty, due process, and equal protection, and to deter discrimination.

First, *liberty rights* are broadly defined in Section 2 of Amendment 2 to describe these freedoms, privileges, and immunities in one place, and to reinstate them in full. Americans are endowed by citizenship, not by government, with power to exercise these rights. Liberty rights are not created or granted by the national government. These rights pre-date it.

---

81   As noted in Number 11, the first sentence of Amendment XIV, Section 1, is revised to establish a single category of citizenship—American. The second sentence is deleted—first phrase, second phrase, and third phrase. This is the old language—now deleted. "No State shall make or enforce any law which shall abridge the privileges or immunities of citizens of the United States; nor shall any State deprive any person of life, liberty, or property, without due process of law; nor deny to any person within its jurisdiction the equal protection of the laws."

2. The freedoms, privileges, and immunities—together, the liberty rights—held by citizens at the adoption of this Constitution are retained by the people, are not surrendered to government, and shall not be abridged by the United States. Citizens are endowed with inalienable power to exercise their liberty rights under the Rule of Law. Neither Congress, nor the Executive, nor the Judiciary shall have power to create or grant liberty rights.

Second, a list of examples of liberty rights, identified as such and *not* as an exhaustive list, is included in Section 3 of Amendment 2 [adapted from *Corfield v. Coryell*, 6 Fed. Cases 546 (1823) and from the 1780 Massachusetts Constitution]. Economic liberty rights that were (i) protected at the Founding, (ii) confirmed in the Civil Rights Act of 1866, and (iii) undone by the decision in the *Slaughterhouse Cases* are also listed and restored.

3. Liberty rights include, but are not limited to, the rights to life, liberty, and pursuit of happiness; to property in one's own labor and industry; to preserve and secure personal health and safety; to keep and bear arms; to acquire, inherit, purchase, lease, sell, hold, convey, and enjoy real and personal property; to religious liberty; to freedom in matters of conscience; to freedom in making and enforcing lawful contracts of all kinds (including freedom not to contract); to establish a family, to care for and to raise children, and to secure the health, education, and safety thereof; to freedom of press, speech, assemblage, and petition; to pursue any lawful livelihood or avocation; to engage in a profession, trade, business, or calling; and to privacy in one's person, effects, papers, preferences, and affairs.

Third, Amendments 2 and 4 establish rebuttable presumptions in favor of the citizen when the exercise of a liberty right is in conflict with the power of the national government or with the police power of one of the several States. The rebuttable presumptions provide a workable mechanism to balance the protection of liberty rights, on the one hand, with the exercise of (i) the limited, enumerated powers of the national government, and (ii) the police powers of the several States, on the other.

Amendment 2, Section 4. The exercise by a citizen of liberty rights shall be presumed valid by the Judiciary against any law made by

Congress and any rule or order made by the Executive that denies or abridges such rights; Provided, that this presumption shall not prevail with respect to laws made pursuant to an enumerated power; and Provided Further, that where Congress relies in part upon the necessary and proper clause of Article 1 Section 8 to make any such law, this presumption may be rebutted upon a showing by the Executive that such law: (i) is plainly necessary in the exercise of an enumerated power; (ii) could not achieve the purpose of an enumerated power by other means not so restrictive of liberty rights, and (iii) is consistent with the Rule of Law.

Amendment 4, Section 2. The exercise by a citizen of liberty rights shall be presumed valid against any state law that denies or abridges such rights; Provided, that this presumption may be rebutted upon a showing by the state that such law could not achieve the purpose of the police power by other means not so restrictive of liberty rights.

Fourth, the protections of due process and equal protection under the Rule of Law (as defined in Amendment 1) are made applicable to *both* the federal government and the States.

Amendment 3. Neither Congress nor the Executive, and no State shall deprive any citizen of life, liberty, or property without due process in accord with the Rule of Law; nor deny to any citizen the equal protection of the laws; nor discriminate for or against any citizen on the basis of race, color, national origin, or gender, or on the basis of belief or non-belief in any creed or religion.

The wording of Amendment 3 closely tracks the second and third phrases from the Fourteenth Amendment, and adds a requirement barring discrimination for or against any citizen on the basis of race, color, national origin, or gender, or on the basis of belief or non-belief in any creed or religion. There will naturally be differences among the several States in how the police power is exercised. The *Liberty Rights Amendments* (1—4) will fully protect citizens from *both* state and federal infringement of their constitutional liberty rights.

Valerius

NUMBER 18.
The American Filtration System:
the Presumption for Liberty Rights

Filters are an integral part of human life. Our blood vessels are filters—allowing nutrients through the filter's walls into other parts of the body. Our lungs are filters—allowing oxygen to pass into the bloodstream and both nitrogen and carbon dioxide to pass out. Our skin is a filter—keeping harmful substances from getting in, but letting perspiration out. Our intestines and kidneys serve different functions, but are complex filters—the basic stuff of human life. Our body's filters are extraordinary sieves that can keep substances smaller than one (1) micron in their proper place—i.e. inside or outside the filter wall.

Imitating the elegance of human filters has been a goal of mankind for centuries, from the earliest production of metal. Millions of Americans have been engaged, and are engaged now, in the business of filtration—the straining, sifting, or separation of one substance from another. Americans are heavily involved in filtration systems, inspired by the creativity, the innovation, and the entrepreneurial nature of a free people. A simple window screen allows air through, but keeps flies out. High-tech fabrics—such as Gore-Tex®—allow a select amount of air through while keeping liquids (water) out. A stone-crushing plant uses various sizes of sieves to separate 2 inch stone from 1 inch stone, from ½ inch stone, from stone dust.

A search for filters on the Web confirms the technological diversity of American companies in this business. It would be difficult to identify any segment of everyday American life that does not rely on some type of filters—those that exist in nature and those created by mankind.[82]

---

82 Filtering is an important element in the manufacture of adhesives, ceramics, colors, lubricants, paint, oil, resins, rubber, ethanol, biofuels, food, chocolate, candy, juice, alcohol, wine, baking products, processed corn, edible oils, processed fruits and vegetables, machining fluids, spray nozzles, catalysts, deionized water, kerosene, amines,

Filters Embedded in the Constitution

The framework established by the Founders can easily be viewed as a collection of filters—sieves—strainers—specifically designed to separate the enumerated powers of the federal government (the eighteen powers listed in Article 1, Section 8) from the retained liberty rights of citizens and from the retained police power of the States.

One of these constitutional filters—the last of these eighteen (18) powers—the *necessary and proper* clause—or the *sweeping clause*—is encrusted with the barnacles of faction, and needs to be scrubbed. The presumption of validity in favor of a citizen's exercise of liberty rights set forth in Amendment 2, against federal intrusion, and in Amendment 4, against state intrusion, reestablish the vision of the Founders—separation of the enumerated powers of the national government, the police power of the States, and the liberty rights of citizens, each from the others, by an appropriately sized sieve.

The Founders did *not* want an overreaching national government without limits, interfering with impunity into the private lives of citizens, *nor* did they want a collection of sovereign States with so much power that the national government could not function in its limited, assigned role. And the Founders did *not* want individual freedom and liberty rights to be corrupted into *license*—that is, individual freedom without corresponding responsibility—as this would infringe upon the freedom of other citizens.

The *sweeping clause*[83] reads as follows:

> To make all Laws which shall be necessary and proper for carrying into Execution the foregoing Powers, and all other Powers vested by this Constitution in the Government of the United States, or in any Department or Officer thereof.

In *McCulloch v. Maryland*, 17 U.S. 316 (1819), the Supreme Court decided the first major case construing the necessary and proper clause.

---

paper, vitamins, mechanical seals. And filtration is an important element in a number of processes, including acid removal, CO2 injection, seawater injection, water injection, water treatment, water filtration, waste water filtration, air filtration, scrubbing exhaust air of all types.

83   Article I, Section 8, paragraph 18.

John Marshall's opinion describes both sides of the "filter" role that the "sweeping clause" was intended to fill:

> Let the end be legitimate, let it be within the scope of the constitution, and all means which are appropriate, which are plainly adapted to that end, which are not prohibited, but consist with the letter and spirit of the constitution, are constitutional.

> . . .

> Should Congress, in the execution of its powers, adopt measures which are prohibited by the constitution; or should Congress, under the pretext of executing its powers, pass laws for the accomplishment of objects not entrusted to the government; it would become the painful duty of this tribunal, should a case requiring such a decision come before it, to say that such an act was not the law of the land.

The *necessary and proper* clause simply does *not* grant a stand-alone power to Congress. The words limit the clause to laws "for carrying into Execution the foregoing Powers"[84] and the other powers vested in the national government. The words confirm that the *sweeping clause* does not give Congress the authority to do whatever it thinks is necessary and proper.

If that were so, the clause would be a filter that filters nothing. If that were so, why did the Founders: (i) enumerate seventeen powers elsewhere in Section 8; (ii) ban the Congress from other actions in Article I, Section 9; and (iii) add a Bill of Rights. [85]

If the Founders intended that the *sweeping clause* give Congress authority to do whatever it thinks is necessary and proper, Article I, Section 8 would have only one paragraph:

> Congress shall have power to enact whatever legislation it decides is necessary and proper.

---

84   The "foregoing powers" are the 17 powers listed before, in the same sentence as the "sweeping clause."
85   Madison called such a construction "an absurdity" and Jefferson used an eighteenth century nursery rhyme to ridicule it. See, Number 10 above, and Number 19, below.

The *sweeping clause*—the Founders' filter—is wrongly perceived by many current elected and appointed officials. It is *not* a sand sieve with holes big enough to let boulders through; a mosquito screen with holes so big that mosquitoes fly through; or a colander to wash fruit with holes so large that apples fall through.

Voluminous federal laws (which few, if any, elected officials have read before passage, and which no human could ever retain at once)[86] are claimed to pass the sieve of the *necessary and proper* clause, a result clearly against the express words of the Constitution, against explanations of the clause by Hamilton and Madison in *The Federalist Papers*,[87] and against the decision in *McCulloch v. Maryland*.[88]

The presumption of validity in a citizen's exercise of liberty rights is simply the original filter the Founders intended. The presumption restores the balance between the power of governments (federal and state) and the liberty rights of citizens.

> Amendment 2, Section 4.
> The exercise by a citizen of liberty rights shall be presumed valid by the Judiciary against any law made by Congress and any rule or order made by the Executive that denies or abridges such rights; Provided, that this presumption shall not prevail with respect to laws made pursuant to an enumerated power; and Provided Further, that where Congress relies in part upon the necessary and proper clause of Article 1 Section 8 to make any such law, this presumption may be rebutted upon a showing by the Executive that such law: (i) is plainly necessary in the exercise of an enumerated power; (ii) could not achieve the purpose of an enumerated power by other means not so restrictive of liberty rights, and (iii) is consistent with the Rule of Law.

---

86   The Patient Protection and Affordable Care Act, enacted in January 2010; 2.5MB in PDF format, 900+ pages; or Dodd-Frank Wall Street Reform and Consumer Protection Act, 3.5MB in PDF format, 2,300+ pages.

87   Hamilton's and Madison's explanations are found in *The Federalist Papers 33* and *44*, respectively.

88   See Number 5, above.

Amendment 4, Section 2.

The exercise by a citizen of liberty rights shall be presumed valid against any state law that denies or abridges such rights; Provided, that this presumption may be rebutted upon a showing by the state that such law could not achieve the purpose of the police power by other means not so restrictive of liberty rights.

Valerius

NUMBER 19.
Federal Examples of the Presumption in Action

The inescapable problem in any human society is the balance of individual freedom and public power. But, as Supreme Court Justice George Sutherland said a century ago, "freedom of contract is, nevertheless, the general rule and restraint the exception." It has always been a difficult problem for legislators, judges, and citizens to determine this balance.

As John Marshall said of the problem of determining the boundary between federal and state power, "The question respecting the extent of the powers actually granted, is perpetually arising, and will probably continue to arise, so long as our system shall exist." [89] It is equally difficult to define the boundary between public power and private rights.

No constitution can provide a foolproof answer to every political dispute that might arise in the future. Abraham Lincoln observed that "no organic law can ever be framed with a provision specifically applicable to every question which may occur in practical administration. No foresight can anticipate nor any document of reasonable length contain express provisions for all possible questions." [90] We do not want to give our Constitution, as Marshall put it, the prolixity of a legal code. [91]

The new *Liberty Rights Amendments* (1—4) make the presumption of liberty much clearer. Specific examples show how it will shift the burden of proof from the individual to the government.

Should a farmer be allowed to grow wheat on his own farm, for seed, and to feed his family and livestock? In 1942, an Ohio farmer, Roscoe Filburn, was fined $117 for cultivating eleven acres more than the Department of Agriculture permitted him under the Agricultural Adjustment Act of 1938.

---

89 *McCulloch v. Maryland*, 17 U.S. 316, 405 (1819).
90 First Inaugural Address, March 4, 1861.
91 *McCulloch v. Maryland*, 17 U.S. 316, 407 (1819).

Congress claimed that it was exercising its power to "regulate commerce among the states" via this scheme to limit agricultural production. Limiting production would raise the prices and income of farmers, Congress reckoned, giving them more power to purchase industrial goods. Roscoe Filburn was obliged to limit his wheat production whether he wanted to participate in the scheme or not. And he was fined even though his *excess* wheat never crossed a state line—indeed, never left his farm.

The Court upheld the conviction, accepting the claim that, however miniscule, Filburn's 239 bushels of wheat would affect the national price of wheat. Justice Jackson said the following:

> It supplies a need of the man who grew it which would otherwise be reflected by purchases in the open market. Home-grown wheat thus competes with wheat in commerce.

How did we get to the point where a bureaucracy could undertake such a scheme of central planning—exactly what Hamilton assured the people that the new government would not be empowered to attempt? Hamilton wrote the following in *The Federalist Papers 17*:

> The administration of private justice between the citizens of the same State, the supervision of agriculture and of other concerns of a similar nature, all those things, in short, which are proper to be provided for by local legislation, can never be desirable cares of a general jurisdiction.[92]

In addition to being a significant expansion in constitutional limits to federal power, the Agricultural Adjustment Act of 1938 was a policy disaster. In 1933, Government began paying farmers to reduce wheat production. By 1935, the U.S. was importing foreign wheat.[93]

Thomas Jefferson used the eighteenth century nursery rhyme—*The House That Jack Built*—to ridicule the claim that Congress could use cause and effect logic to control every activity in the nation.[94]

---

92 Hamilton, *The Federalist Papers 17*, at p. 118
93 Neither legislatures nor bureaucracies have ever been effective central planners. See, Numbers 20-26, below.
94 Letter from Thomas Jefferson to Edward Livingston (Apr. 30, 1800), *The Papers of Thomas Jefferson* 31:547 (B. Oberg ed. 2004), cited in *U.S. v. Comstock*, 551 F.3d 274.

Congress [is] authorized to defend the nation. Ships are necessary for defense; copper is necessary for ships; mines necessary for copper; a company necessary to work mines; and who can doubt this reasoning who has ever played at 'This is the House that Jack built?' Under such a process of filiation of necessities the sweeping clause makes clean work.

What was an *absurdity* to Madison and a ridiculous rhyme to Jefferson was relied on for the result in *Wickard*. The concept was much like the butterfly effect in chaos theory—Congress might regulate a butterfly flapping its wings in Brazil if it concludes that it might ultimately cause a hurricane in Texas.

The power to regulate commerce among the states has been converted, by a series of Congresses, administrations, and the Court, into a confusing, duplicative federal version of the police power reserved to the States. The *Liberty Rights Amendments*, and in particular, Amendment 2, Section 4, and Amendment 4, will reverse this.

It all began innocently enough. A century ago, Congress began to regulate the interstate traffic in things that were widely regarded as harmful or immoral—adulterated food products, patent medicines, narcotics, even lottery tickets (when every state prohibited gambling). In the Victorian era, public disapproval of these practices made most observers loosen their constitutional standards. Congress took a major step forward in 1910 when it prohibited the transportation of women across state lines for "prostitution or debauchery, or for any other immoral purpose."

The Supreme Court went along, although Chief Justice Fuller warned in his dissent in the lottery case, "In countries whose fundamental law is flexible it may be that the homely maxim 'to ease the shoe where it pinches' may be applied, but under the Constitution of the United States it cannot be availed of to justify action by Congress or by the courts."

Congress relied on its powers to control the mail and to tax as ways to regulate similar perceived evils. The Court temporarily blocked this path when Congress tried to prohibit the interstate shipment of goods made using child labor, reasoning that Congress could only interdict things that were harmful in themselves. The absence of a clear distinction from

91

different results reached in cases involving gambling, narcotics, and adulterated food put the Court in an embarrassing position.

Many of the remaining limitations on congressional power over commerce were swept away by a change in outlook by the Supreme Court during the New Deal. In 1937, after President Franklin D. Roosevelt threatened to *pack* the Court, it accepted the National Labor Relations (Wagner) Act that required employers to bargain exclusively with the organization chosen by a majority of its employees. Strikes had an adverse effect on interstate commerce, the Court reasoned, and employer resistance to unions caused strikes. Such attenuated cause-and-effect reasoning has continued to lead to a perception by federal officials that Congress can regulate anything because, ultimately, everything might affect commerce.

As the dissenters observed, the logic of the Wagner Act would extend congressional power into almost every field of human industry.[95] A chain of indirect and progressively remote events would eventually present such questions as the following:

> May a mill owner be prohibited from closing his factory or discontinuing his business because so to do would stop the flow of products to and from his plant in interstate commerce? May employees in a factory be restrained from quitting work in a body because this will close the factory and thereby stop the flow of commerce? May arson of a factory be made a federal offense whenever this would interfere with such flow? If the business cannot continue with the existing wage scale, may Congress command a reduction?

Almost anything from birth to death may in some fashion affect commerce.

For almost six decades, with the Court silent in its role as bulwark for the protection of liberty rights, Congress has continued to regulate everything under the sun. When the Court upheld the Fair Labor Standards Act of 1938, which set maximum hours and minimum wages and prohibited most child labor, it dismissed its earlier qualifications as "a departure from the principles which have prevailed in the interpretation of commerce" before and since.

---

95   *N.L.R.B v. Friedman-Harry Marks Clothing, Co.*, 301 U.S. 58, 97-98 (1937).

Congress is now in the habit of assuming that it can justify anything as a regulation of interstate commerce. In the 1990s it made it a federal crime to possess a firearm within a thousand feet of a school and made *domestic violence* a federal offense. The Supreme Court struck down these acts as too remotely related to commerce to be rational. It said, "Indeed, we can think of no better example of the police power, which the Founders denied the National Government and reposed in the states, than the suppression of violent crime and vindication of its victims."[96]

But these decisions were hardly a restoration of the original intent of the Founders. The Court was only able to trim some of the more extravagant growth of federal duplication of the state police power. Most of the twentieth-century experiments by progressives in central planning—especially those regulating the economy—remained safe. "Although I might be willing to return to the original understanding," Justice Clarence Thomas wrote, "I recognize that many believe that it is too late in the day to undertake a fundamental reexamination of the past sixty years. Considerations of stare decisis[97] and reliance interests may convince us that we cannot wipe the slate clean."

The Court may not be willing to wipe the slate clean, but the people can.[98] The original Constitution was the work of "We the People," and it provided means by which the people could change it. For decades now, Congress and the Courts have taken it upon themselves to change what the Constitution means, not through the front door of the amendment process but through the back door. It remains within the people's power to restore the original Constitution's presumption of liberty through the front door—by amendment.

Prosperus

---

96 *U.S. v. Morrison*, 529 U.S. 598, 618 (2000).

97 Editor: This means "sticking with judicial precedent."

98 The *Constitution of the United States*, including *The Second Bill of Rights*, is set forth in the Appendix. There are no changes to the text of the original Constitution or the first Bill of Rights (Amendments 1 to 10). Portions of the language in Amendments 13, 14, 15, 16, 19, 23, 24, and 26 are deleted, and shown as strikethrough text—~~as shown here~~. The Second Bill of Rights is inserted as Amendments 28 to 38 to the Constitution of the United States of America.

NUMBER 20.
The Presumption for Liberty against the Power of States

Seventy-five years ago, when the Supreme Court was resisting the expansion of government regulation during the New Deal, President Roosevelt complained that the Court had created a "'no-man's land' where no government—state or federal—can function." The Court had held that neither federal nor state government could establish a minimum wage for women.

As long-forgotten Nebraska Senator Edward Burke told F.D.R.'s Assistant Attorney General (and future Supreme Court Justice) Robert Jackson,

> Do you not recognize that there is a vast power that does not lie in either the federal government or any state government, but has been reserved so far by the people themselves, and they have not yet been willing to turn over to any government, no matter how beneficial its purpose may be?[99]

The basic assumption of twentieth-century progressives and liberals was that every human activity—at least those of an economic variety—must be *regulatable* by government at some level. But the Founders' Constitution was based on the opposite presumption—liberty of individual action and limits on government power—were assumed. Thus, the Ninth Amendment in the original Bill of Rights declares the following: "[t]he enumeration in the Constitution, of certain rights, shall not be construed to deny or disparage others retained by the people."

Indeed, Hamilton and Madison were so insistent that the Constitution was a grant of certain, specified powers to the national government that Hamilton believed it would be dangerous to introduce a list of guaranteed rights. To make a list of "exceptions to powers which are not

---

99 *Reorganization of the Federal Judiciary,* Hearings before the Committee on the Judiciary, U.S. Senate, 75th Cong., First Session (Washington: GPO, 1937), p. 57.

granted," Hamilton warned, might "afford a colorable pretext to claim more than were granted."

Restoring this principle of federalism—that powers not delegated to the federal government belong to the States or the people—is important, but we do not want to replace an overreaching national government with a system of grassroots tyranny. The founding generation faced a similar situation. When they overthrew the King and Parliament, who had claimed the power to rule the colonists without their consent in all cases whatsoever, they soon found that the thirteen state legislatures had adopted similar pretentions to sovereign power. As Thomas Jefferson noted in 1782, "One hundred and seventy-three despots [the number of seats in the Virginia legislature] would surely be as oppressive as one."[100]

The Constitution was meant to strengthen the United States in a dangerous world of sovereign states and to prevent the American states from discriminating against one another in the domestic market. But it also aimed to improve republican government within the states. When preparing for the Constitutional Convention, James Madison reviewed many of the problems of state government in an essay titled *The Vices of the Political System of the United States.* In addition to the threats that bad state governments posed to the Union and to the other states, Madison noted that existing laws displayed multiplicity, mutablility, and injustice. Madison was principally concerned with paper money laws and other schemes by which debtors evaded their obligations to creditors. He noted "how easily are base and selfish measures, masked by pretexts of public good and apparent expediency." Madison identified a fundamental problem facing all republican governments—the difficulty of discerning genuinely sound public measures from those based on self intent, but eloquently hidden by assertions of public good."

In the nineteenth century, such acts were known as *class legislation*—intended for the good *not* of the public, but of particular interest groups, or what Madison called *factions.* The original Constitution contained several provisions meant to limit *class legislation.* These are principally found in Article I, Section 10, which imposed exceptions to the reserved powers of the states.

---

100 Madison, *The Federalist Papers 48,* at p. 311.

Many of these restrictions are similar to those in the Articles of Confederation, prohibiting states from engaging in their own foreign policies, or discriminating against other states. But the most important ones tried to prevent local majorities from violating the property rights of minorities. Thus, the states could not make anything but gold and silver coin a tender in payment of debts.

Above all, the original Constitution, before the Bill of Rights, barred States from passing any law impairing the obligation of contracts. The contract clause became the most important constitutional provision preventing state legislatures from violating private rights. In 1810, Chief Justice John Marshall called the contract clause "a bill of rights for the people of each state."

In the nineteenth century, the constitutional provision that gave Congress the power to *regulate commerce among the states* then principally protected the rights of individual citizens against state power. The federal courts prevented states from regulating commerce in ways that discriminated against out-of-state residents, and prevented state legislatures from insulating local business from foreign competition.

The Fourteenth Amendment should have removed any doubt about the states' power to violate the fundamental rights of American citizens. After defining U. S. citizenship in the first sentence, the second sentence of Section 1 declared the following:

> No state shall make or enforce any law which shall abridge the privileges or immunities of citizens of the United States; nor shall any State deprive any person of life, liberty, or property, without due process of law; nor deny to any person within its jurisdiction the equal protection of the laws.

This amendment should have protected the former slaves, and all citizens, against arbitrary *class legislation*. When the Supreme Court first interpreted the amendment in 1873, it decided that the language had virtually no effect on States, upholding an act of the Louisiana legislature (possibly the result of bribery) establishing a monopoly in the slaughtering business in New Orleans. The dissenting justices noted that "equality of right, with exemption from all disparaging and partial enactments, in the lawful pursuits of life, throughout the whole country, is the distin-

guishing privilege of citizens of the United States . . . This is the fundamental idea upon which our institutions rest, and, unless adhered to in
the legislation of the country, our government will be a republic only in
name."[101] They argued that "grants of exclusive privilege... are opposed
to the whole theory of free government, and it requires no aid from any
bill of rights to render them void." Justice Bradley added that "the right
of any citizen to follow whatever lawful employment he chooses to adopt
(submitting himself to all lawful regulations) is one of his most valuable
rights, and one which the legislature of a state cannot invade, whether
restrained by its own constitution or not."

"Even if the Constitution were silent," they went on, "the fundamental
privileges and immunities of citizens, as such, would be no less real and
no less inviolable than they now are." It was not necessary to say in words
that the citizens should have and exercise all the privileges of buying,
selling, and enjoying property; the privilege of engaging in any lawful
employment for a livelihood. To compel butchers to "slaughter their
cattle in another person's slaughterhouse and pay him a toll therefore .
. . is onerous, unreasonable, arbitrary and unjust."

Over the following six decades, the Court occasionally used the Fourteenth Amendment to protect individual rights against state legislation,
but without the clear mandate of the privilege or immunities clause that
it had eviscerated in *Slaughterhouse*. Despite the reputation of an era of
"laissez-faire jurisprudence" before the New Deal, the Court usually accepted the flimsiest pretexts as legitimate exercises of the state police
power. One example is *Plessy v. Ferguson*, in which it accepted Louisiana's
argument that it needed to segregate the races to prevent race riots.

In the 1930s, the Court gave up the effort altogether, permitting all sorts
of state price-fixing laws and regulations limiting entry into certain businesses. States such as New York set a minimum price at which grocers
could sell milk to raise the income of dairy farmers. A Rochester grocer, Leo Nebbia,[102] was fined for selling milk at less than nine cents per
quart. A Jersey City tailor, Jacob Maged, went to jail for pressing a pair
of pants for thirty-five cents, because the New Jersey dry-cleaning code
established forty cents as the minimum price.

---

101 *The Slaughterhouse Cases*, 83 U.S. 36 (1873). See Number 11, *supra*.
102 See Number 23, below.

Since the New Deal, the Court has taken it upon itself to protect some rights—personal rights—but not others—primarily economic rights.

The *Liberty Rights Amendments*, in particular, the definition of *liberty rights* in Section 3 of Amendment 2[103] and the presumption of validity in Section 2 of Amendment 4,[104] restore the Founders' presumption in favor of individual liberty over the regulatory power of the state.

Prosperus

---

103 Section 3 provides reads this way: "3. Liberty rights include, but are not limited to, the rights to life, liberty, and pursuit of happiness; to property in one's own labor and industry; to preserve and secure personal health and safety; to keep and bear arms; to acquire, inherit, purchase, lease, sell, hold, convey, and enjoy real and personal property; to religious liberty; to freedom in matters of conscience; to freedom in making and enforcing lawful contracts of all kinds (including freedom not to contract); to establish a family, to care for and to raise children, and to secure the health, education, and safety thereof; to freedom of press, speech, assemblage, and petition; to pursue any lawful livelihood or avocation; to engage in a profession, trade, business, or calling; and to privacy in one's person, effects, papers, preferences, and affairs."

104 Section 2 reads this way: "2. The exercise by a citizen of liberty rights shall be presumed valid against any state law that denies or abridges such rights; PROVIDED, that this presumption may be rebutted upon a showing by the state that such law could not achieve the purpose of the police power by other means not so restrictive of liberty rights."

NUMBER 21.
[Your] Pursuit of [Your] Happiness—
The Fruit of Your Own Work

Amendment 2 in *The Second Bill of Rights* restores the privileges and immunities of citizens to constitutional status. Section 3 is an example list of these rights, six of which confirm that we are free to pursue our own happiness through our own labor and industry.

> 3. Liberty rights include, but are not limited to, the rights to *life, liberty, and pursuit of happiness; to property in one's own labor and industry; . . . to acquire, inherit, purchase, lease, sell, hold, convey, and enjoy real and personal property; . . . to freedom in making and enforcing lawful contracts of all kinds (including freedom not to contract); . . . to pursue any lawful livelihood or avocation; to engage in a profession, trade, business, or calling; . . . .*

These six liberty rights restore economic rights to the same level of constitutional protection as civil rights such as freedom of speech, freedom of conscience, and freedom from unreasonable searches and seizures. Civil and economic rights are joined together as "liberty rights." All liberty rights are self-operating and do not originate with government, and permission is not required in their exercise.

For five hundred years before the Founding, the *right of Englishmen* to earn a living from their own efforts was acknowledged. Sir Edward Coke confirmed the right at common law of "any man to use any trade . . . to maintain himself and his family" from Magna Carta (1215).[105]

In the year of the Declaration of Independence—1776—each person's right to the fruits of his own labor was confirmed, on each side of the Atlantic: by the Scottish economist Adam Smith and by the Common-

---

105 *Allen v. Tooley*, 80 Eng. Rep. 1055 (K.B. 1614).

wealth of Virginia in its Declaration of Rights. To Smith, the concept was sacred and inviolable:[106]

> The property which every man has in his own labour, as it is the original foundation of all other property, so it is the most sacred and inviolable. The patrimony of a poor man lies in the strength and dexterity of his hands; and *to hinder him from employing this strength and dexterity in what manner he thinks proper, without injury to his neighbor, is a plain violation of this most sacred property.* [emphasis added]

The *Virginia Declaration of Rights*[107] confirmed that citizens are free to use any *means* [follow any trade] to acquire property in the pursuit of happiness and safety.

> SECTION I. That all men are by nature equally free and independent and have certain inherent rights, of which, when they enter into a state of society, they cannot, by any compact, deprive or divest their posterity; *namely, the enjoyment of life and liberty, with the means of acquiring and possessing property, and pursuing and obtaining happiness and safety.*

Slavery interfered directly with the liberty right to earn a living.[108]

> Born a slave, Frederick Douglass recalled how he escaped the home of his master Hugh Auld, reaching New York on the Underground Railroad in 1838. Walking the streets of Rochester, looking for a job, Douglass came across a house where a pile of coal had just been delivered. He had an idea that he might make some money, and he knocked at the door, offering to move the coal inside for the woman who answered. "I was not long in accomplishing the job," he wrote, "when the dear lady put into my hand two silver half dollars. To understand the emotion which swelled my heart as I clasped this money, realizing that I had no master who could take it from me—that it was mine—that my hands were my own, and could earn more of the precious

---

106 Adam Smith, *The Wealth of Nations*, Book I, Ch. 10, Part 2, p. 92. (1776), Classic House Books (2009).
107 George Mason, a friend of George Washington, was the principal author.
108 *The Right to Earn a Living*: Economic Freedom and the Law, Timothy Sandefur, The Cato Institute, 2010, Chapter 1, note 7.

coin—one must have been in some sense himself a slave . . . I was not only a freeman but a free-working man, and no Master Hugh stood ready at the end of the week to seize my hard earnings.

In 1858, as a candidate for Senate, Lincoln described slavery this way:

[T]he same old serpent that says you work and I eat, you toil and I will enjoy the fruits.[109]

Charles Sumner, Radical Republican Massachusetts Senator of the Civil War, said of it:[110]

[The] ever present motive power of slavery was simply to compel the labor of fellow-men without wages, by "excluding them from that property in their own earnings, which the law of nature allows, and civilization secures. . . . It is robbery and petty larceny under the garb of law," which presumed "that for his own good," the slave "must work for his master, and not for himself."

It would have been of little use to Frederick Douglass to earn two silver half dollars, with no contract right to payment at common law in exchange for his labor. The right to contract is inherent in a trade. And, the right to convert cash into a house, or a car, or savings—is inherent in the right to work and to receive the fruits of one's own labor. As described in Number 11, above, the Civil Rights Act of 1866 confirmed that former slaves now possessed the right to earn and acquire property from their own labor. Section 1 of that Act provided the following:

That . . . citizens, of every race and color, . . . shall have *the same right, in every State and Territory in the United States, to make and enforce contracts, to sue, be parties, and give evidence, to inherit, purchase, lease, sell, hold, and convey real and personal property, and to full and equal benefit of all laws and proceedings for the security of person and property, as is enjoyed by white citizens, and shall be subject to like punishment,*

---

109 Quoted at Chapter 1, note 9, *Right to Earn a Living*: Economic Freedom and the Law, Abraham Lincoln, Speech at Chicago, Il. (July 10 1858) in The Collected Works of Abraham Lincoln, ed. Roy P. Basler (Camden, NJ: Rutgers University Press, 1953), Vol. 2, p. 500.
110 *Ibid*, note 8, Chapter 1.

pains, and penalties, and to none other, any law, statute, ordinance, regulation, or custom, to the contrary notwithstanding.

The disputed Louisiana law in *The Slaughterhouse Cases* granted an exclusive, twenty-five year franchise to one company to slaughter and sell meat over an area of 1,154 square miles. The majority opinion ran over the right of hundreds of existing butchers to continue their trade. Three Justices joined the *dissenting* opinion of Justice Field, and recognized the damage inflicted by the majority on the right of each citizen to property in [the benefits from] one's own labor:

> The abolition of slavery and involuntary servitude was intended to make every one born in this country a freeman, and as such *to give to him the right to pursue the ordinary avocations of life without other restraint than such as affects all others, and to enjoy equally with them the fruits of his labor.* A prohibition to him to pursue certain callings, open to others of the same age, condition, and sex, or to reside in places where others are permitted to live, would so far deprive him of the rights of a freeman, and would place him, as respects others, in a condition of servitude. A person allowed to pursue only one trade or calling, and only in one locality of the country, would not be, in the strict sense of the term, in a condition of slavery, but probably none would deny that he would be in a condition of servitude. He certainly would not possess the liberties nor enjoy the privileges of a freeman. The compulsion which would force him to labor even for his own benefit only in one direction, or in one place, would be almost as oppressive and nearly as great an invasion of his liberty as the compulsion which would force him to labor for the benefit or pleasure of another, and would equally constitute an element of servitude.

> This equality of right . . . in the lawful pursuits of life, throughout the whole country, is the distinguishing privilege of citizens of the United States. To them, everywhere, all pursuits, all professions, all avocations are open without other restrictions than such as are imposed equally upon all others of the same age, sex, and condition. . . . This is the fundamental idea upon which our institutions rest, and unless adhered to in the legislation of the country our government will be a republic only in name. The fourteenth amendment, in my judgment, makes it essential

to the validity of the legislation of every State that this equality of right should be respected. How widely this equality has been departed from, how entirely rejected and trampled upon by the act of Louisiana, I have already shown. And it is to me a matter of profound regret that its validity is recognized by a majority of this court, for by it the right of free labor, one of the most sacred and imprescriptible rights of man, is violated.[111]

The ability to move up the economic ladder—"economic mobility"—has been a key element of success for millions of Americans over 225 years. The decision in *Slaughterhouse* substantially undercut the economic privileges and immunities previously held by citizens and protected by courts. The *Liberty Rights Amendments* correct this aspect of *Slaughterhouse* by restoring economic rights alongside civil rights, in the combined protected status of *liberty rights*.

Valerius

---

111 *Slaughterhouse*, pp. 90-91 and 109-111.

NUMBER 22.
The Ice Case—The Dynamic Nature of Freedom in America

In any government administered by some citizens over others, officials are naturally unaware of what might come from the imagination and creativity of their fellow citizens. As noted in Number 8, the human mind is incapable of holding all such knowledge at one time, and it is certainly incapable of evaluating what it cannot hold. Hayek uses the term "needs"—but it is also true of contributions.[112] As noted in Number 25, below, officials with power over other men come to believe there are centrally planned solutions to the "problems they perceive." Two fatally flawed assumptions contaminate such a belief: first, that man has the capacity to control societal outcomes; and second, that the problems to be solved through planning are static—that is, unchanging. Neither is true.

In today's America, Madison's fears are real once again—a government of wider scope than the Founders imagined has been captured by self-interested factions. The possible contributions of citizens outside government are unknown, not considered, or ignored.[113] In their zeal for central planning of all of American society, factions bring experts to Congress and the Executive to promote self-interested solutions to a set of static problems that in fact are dynamic. Static problems are no longer common in our society.[114]

---

112 [I]t would be impossible for any mind to comprehend the infinite variety of different needs of different people which compete for the available resources and to attach a definite weight to each. F. A. Hayek, *The Road to Serfdom, supra,* at p. 102.

113 Paraphrasing Hayek, individualism merely starts from the indisputable fact that the limits of our imagination make it impossible to understand more than a fraction of the needs or the potential contributions of the whole society. From this, the individualist concludes that individuals should be allowed, within the limits of the Rule of Law, to follow their own talents and preferences rather than somebody else's; and that within these limits, the individual should not be subject to dictation by others.

114 "[Collectivist systems] all differ from liberalism and individualism in wanting to organize the whole of society and all its resources for this unitary end and in refusing to recognize autonomous spheres in which the ends of the individuals are supreme." F.

Liberty rights provide a humble defense to individual Americans against the natural arrogance of fellow men placed in positions of power within a government administered over other men. Madison dismissed the notion that "enlightened statesmen" could adjust the "clashing interests" of factions and the self-interest of officials. Madison knew that some interests of factions could not be "adjusted" and, instead, had to be broken to preserve individual freedom. Adam Smith knew in 1776 that any person who believes he or she has the mental capacity to fully understand and judge among the competing preferences, capabilities, and tastes of citizens is a fool. Hayek put this same thought positively—as an inherent limitation of the human mind. Hayek believed that such arrogance is dangerous, especially in collectivist governments—from Nazis and Soviets to European socialists.

The decision of the Supreme Court in *New State Ice Co. v. Liebmann*, 285 U.S. 262 (1932) illustrates how the Judiciary treated the arrogance of officials before FDR's appointments changed the outcomes in 1934. Liebmann started a business in Oklahoma City to manufacture, sell, and distribute ice. He was sued by the New State Ice Company because he had not obtained a permit from the Corporation Commission of Oklahoma, a board established by the legislature. The board was only to issue such a permit after a hearing in which Liebmann showed that there was a need for additional suppliers in the community and that current supply was insufficient. Failure to comply with the board's decision was a misdemeanor punishable by fine. The board's members included persons already in the local ice business. Thus, the legislature—motivated by self-interested factions in the ice business—was micro-managing who could make ice and where.

In a 6-2 decision, the Court relied on the Fourteenth Amendment to invalidate this interference with the economic liberty of citizens. The liberty right to engage in ordinary vocations was one of the privileges and immunities protected by Article IV Section 2, as citizens engaged in commerce from state to state. The Fourteenth Amendment extended this concept to protect every citizen's right to pursue a lawful occupation in each state.

Here we are dealing with an ordinary business . . . . It is a business as essentially private in its nature as the business of the grocer,

A. Hayek, *The Road to Serfdom, supra,* at p. 100.

the dairyman, the butcher, the baker, the shoemaker, or the tailor, each of whom performs a service which, to a greater or less extent, the community is dependent upon and is interested in having maintained; but which bears no such relation to the public as to warrant its inclusion in the category of businesses charged with a public use. It may be quite true that in Oklahoma ice is, not only an article of prime necessity, but indispensable; but certainly not more so than food or clothing or the shelter of a home. . . . .

The Court understood the fleeting nature of the state's interference. And, its ineffectiveness. Refrigeration and electrical service allowed anyone to make ice.[115] Common sense informed the Court that state interference stifled innovation. Common sense and the Fourteenth Amendment were aligned—as the drafters of the amendment intended.

Plainly, a regulation which has the effect of denying or unreasonably curtailing the common right to engage in a lawful private business . . . cannot be upheld consistent with the Fourteenth Amendment. Under that amendment, nothing is more clearly settled than that it is beyond the power of a state, 'under the guise of protecting the public, arbitrarily (to) interfere with private business or prohibit lawful occupations or impose unreasonable and unnecessary restrictions upon them.' . . .

The majority was unimpressed with the assertion by Justice Brandeis, leader of the progressive wing of the Court, that States could experiment

---

115 It has been said that the manufacture of ice requires an expensive plant beyond the means of the average citizen, and that, since the use of ice is indispensable, patronage of the producer by the consumer is unavoidable. . . . But, for the moment conceding the materiality of the statement, it is not now true, whatever may have been the fact in the past. We know, since it is common knowledge, that today, to say nothing of other means, wherever electricity or gas is available (and one or the other is available in practically every part of the country), any one for a comparatively moderate outlay may have set up in his kitchen an appliance by means of which he may manufacture ice for himself. Under such circumstances it hardly will do to say that people generally are at the mercy of the manufacturer, seller, and distributer of ice for ordinary needs. Moreover, the practical tendency of the restriction . . . is to shut out new enterprises, and thus create and foster monopoly in the hands of existing establishments, against, rather than in aid of, the interest of the consuming public.

with such interference.[116] The majority plainly understood that the Constitution placed some matters *beyond experimentation.*

The *New State Ice Co.* case is a metaphor for precisely what the Founders most feared in the establishment of any government administered by men over men.[117] Men are not angels, and can be divided into parties [factions], inflamed with mutual animosity by leaders ambitiously contending for pre-eminence and power; and rendered much more disposed to vex and oppress each other than to co-operate for their common good.

While factions of ice suppliers in Oklahoma were busy organizing themselves to capture the legislature to enact legislation to: (i) oppress new competitors, (ii) maintain captive customers, and (iii) force higher prices; free citizens outside of government were busy (unknowingly) making the entire plan irrelevant. Edison had perfected electric power distribution. Large meat packers were implementing ammonia based refrigeration, following on experiments by Benjamin Franklin in 1756 at Cambridge University in England. With the invention of chlorofluorocarbon (CFC) at the beginning of the twentieth century—household refrigeration was a reality.[118]

This pattern is repeated throughout American history. While factions lobbied Congress and state legislatures on the eastern seaboard for exclusive monopolies to establish canals and roads across the Appalachians from 1789 to 1830,[118] Watt, Fulton, and others were perfecting the steam engine and introducing the riverboat and the train. The scheming of factions to get Congress or a state legislature to prefer one applicant, or one mode of transportation, or one route over another—was entirely disrupted and destroyed. Destroyed *not* by the wisdom of government administrators (who wasted many millions of taxpayer dollars in pursuit of unworkable and even silly schemes), *but* by the ingenuity of citizens disconnected from government.[119]

---

116 It . . . would be strange and unwarranted doctrine to hold that [States] may do so by enactments which transcend the limitations imposed upon them by the Federal Constitution. . . *The opportunity to apply one's labor and skill in an ordinary occupation with proper regard for all reasonable regulations is no less entitled to protection.*
117 See, Number 4 and *The Federalist Papers 10, supra.*
118 Canals in South Carolina, Virginia, Maryland, Pennsylvania, and New York; the National Road
119 The most famous is the Pennsylvania Main Line—a state canal over the Appala-

While factions were busy lobbying Congress to establish the Pony Express, Samuel Morse was finishing the telegraph, changing everything. And, while Western Union deployed the telegraph across the nation, Alexander Graham Bell was perfecting the telephone, changing everything again. On and on, to the cell phone, the satellite phone, the smart phone, the mobile computer, and GPS. Transportation followed the same pattern, from steam boats, to trains, cars, planes, tele-commuting, and movement of information by email. Free individuals—such as Henry Ford (mass producing autos), Andrew Carnegie (producing steel sufficiently strong to cross major rivers), John Roebling (producing wire to build suspension bridges), Thomas Edison (inventing innumerable conveniences); and Bill Gates (creating MS DOS)—contributed what administrators in government could not even imagine—*substitute solutions, not* to the problems government administrators imagined, but to actual difficulties citizens confront in their daily life. These contributors created not only markets, but vocations and millions of jobs. Throughout, factions are busy lobbying Congress, legislatures, and administrators at all levels to advance one tiny agenda over another tiny agenda, all on the assumption of a static world that does not exist. More often than we would like to admit, Congress, legislatures, and administrators are captured by factions whose aim is to oppress their fellow citizens rather than to cooperate in the exercise of individual liberty under the Rule of Law—all as Madison feared.

The majority in *New State Ice Co.* came to the constitutional conclusion that the Founders envisioned in 1789. Men aren't angels, nor are they capable of understanding how a society as complex as the United States works. Nor can they hold this complexity in their minds for the purpose of planning detailed outcomes. The Founders were sufficiently experienced—not only through education, but through practical and commercial knowledge—to be humble regarding the capacity of any government administered by some men over other men.

The Founders placed internal and external controls in the Constitution to prevent Congress, the states, and factions from oppressing the social, economic, and political rights of individual citizens, and they established auxiliary precautions to ensure these rights. The *Liberty Rights*

---

chian Mountains. Canal boats were dragged by mule on a road at high points, where there was no water. It failed. You can't make this stuff up!

Amendments (1—4) re-establish all these rights as *liberty rights*, exercisable under the Rule of Law.

In Number 23, we consider what happened to these rights when Madison's bulwark for individual liberty—the Judiciary—looked away, beginning in 1934.

Amicus

NUMBER 23.
Rational Outcomes with Economic Liberty—
Not Any Rationale to Interfere

Justice Brandeis had his way two years later, in *Nebbia v. New York*, 291 U.S. 502 (1934), a 5-4 decision that established nearly unlimited Supreme Court deference to state legislation infringing on economic liberty rights. *Nebbia* arose when the New York state legislature concluded that the price of milk in New York had to be *raised* because of the *decreased buying power of consumers in the depression.*[120] A New York law established a Milk Board to set prices for selling milk. It was a crime to sell except at this price—not higher, not lower. The Milk Board fixed nine cents as the price to be charged *by a store* for a quart of milk. Nebbia owned a grocery store in Rochester, sold two quarts and a five-cent loaf of bread for eighteen cents; and was convicted for violating the board's order. A 5-4 majority upheld the law, ruling as follows:

> If the laws passed . . . have a *reasonable relation to a proper legislative purpose,* . . . the requirements of *due process* are satisfied . . .

The so-called *rational basis* test was born. Under *Nebbia,* if a court can imagine a rational basis for a state's infringement of individual economic or social rights, the statute prevails over all three of the protections in the Fourteenth Amendment: privileges or immunities, due process, and equal protection.

> In areas of social and economic policy, *a statutory classification . . . must be upheld* against equal protection challenge *if there is any reasonably conceivable state of facts that could provide a rational basis for the classification.*[121]

---

120 *People v. Nebbia*, 262 N.Y. 259, 186 N.E. 694. These were the facts presented to the Court.
121 *FCC v. Beach Communications, Inc.*, 508 U.S. 307, at 315 (1993).

Combining the decisions in *Slaughterhouse* and *Nebbia*, the Court threw three (3) strikes at the economic liberty rights of individual citizens. Strike one came in *Slaughterhouse*, when the Fourteenth Amendment's privileges or immunities clause was judicially stripped out of the amendment through the creation of two categories of citizenship. Strikes two and three came in *Nebbia*, when the rational basis test was applied to diminish the other two Fourteenth Amendment safeguards to individual economic rights—due process and equal protection.

The dissent of Justice McReynolds predicted the path legislatures have since taken.[122]

> *This is not regulation, but management, control, dictation—it amounts to the deprivation of the fundamental right which one has to conduct his own affairs honestly and along customary lines.* The argument advanced here would support general prescription of prices for farm products, groceries, shoes, clothing, all the necessities of modern civilization, as well as labor, when some Legislature finds and declares such action advisable and for the public good.

Justice McReynolds, believing Courts must consider the logic of legislation infringing liberty rights, would have applied the *necessary and proper* test of *McCullough v. Maryland.*

> [T]his Court must have regard to the wisdom of the enactment. At least, we must inquire concerning its purpose and decide whether the means proposed have reasonable relation to something within legislative power—*whether the end is legitimate, and the means appropriate. If a statute to prevent conflagrations should require householders to pour oil on their roofs as a means of curbing the spread of fire when discovered in the neighborhood, we could hardly uphold it.* Here, we find direct interference with guaranteed rights . . . [on the basis that] the purpose was to promote the public welfare by increasing milk prices at the farm. Unless we can affirm that the end proposed is proper and the means adopted have reasonable relation to it, this action is unjustifiable.

---

122 *Nebbia v. New York*, 291 U.S. 502, at 554 through 558 (1934).

Justice McReynolds would not throw away common sense in reviewing legislation.[123]

> Not only does the statute interfere arbitrarily with the rights of the little grocer to conduct his business . . . but it takes away the liberty of 12,000,000 consumers to buy a necessity of life in an open market. . . . *To him with less than 9 cents it says: You cannot procure a quart of milk from the grocer although he is anxious to accept what you can pay and the demands of your household are urgent!* A superabundance; but *no child can purchase from a willing storekeeper below the figure appointed by three men at headquarters!* And this is true although the storekeeper himself may have bought from a willing producer at half that rate and must sell quickly or lose his stock through deterioration. The fanciful scheme is to protect the farmer against undue exactions by prescribing the price at which milk disposed of by him at will may be resold!

The majority, however, claimed the rational basis test precluded asking whether it was legitimate that Nebbia be labeled a criminal if he sold milk at a lower price before it went sour. The Court did not ask whether it was legitimate for New York to simply take Nebbia's investment in good milk—he paid a distributor less than the sales price—if people with no

---

123 The court below has not . . . attempted to indicate how higher charges at stores to impoverished customers when the output is excessive and sale prices by producers are unrestrained, can possibly increase receipts at the farm. The Legislative Committee pointed out as the obvious cause of decreased consumption, notwithstanding low prices, the consumers' reduced buying power. Higher store prices will not enlarge this power; nor will they decrease production. Low prices will bring less cows only after several years. The prime causes of the difficulties will remain. Nothing indicates early decreased output. Demand at low prices being wholly insufficient, the proposed plan is to raise and fix higher minimum prices at stores and thereby aid the producer whose output and prices remain unrestrained! It is not true as stated that 'the State seeks to protect the producer by fixing a minimum price for his milk.' She carefully refrained from doing this; but did undertake to fix the price after the milk had passed to other owners. Assuming that the views and facts reported by the Legislative Committee are correct, it appears to me wholly unreasonable to expect this legislation to accomplish the proposed end—increase of prices at the farm. We deal only with Order No. 5 as did the court below. It is not merely unwise; it is arbitrary and unduly oppressive. Better prices may follow but it is beyond reason to expect them as the consequent of that order. The Legislative Committee reported: 'It is recognized that the dairy industry of the State cannot be placed upon a profitable basis without a decided rise in the general level of commodity prices.'

money failed to buy it before it went sour. The Court simply looked away from the Fourteenth Amendment, from seven hundred years of the common law, and from provisions in state constitutions protecting economic rights to contract and to pursue a vocation under the Rule of Law. The decision took Nebbia's property without due process and without equal protection as compared to distributors, and it interfered with his economic privilege to pursue an ordinary vocation.

Brandeis' dissent in the *New State Ice* case [see Number 22] confirms that he understood these issues in the same way as the Founders.[124] The objections to central planning "are obvious and grave; the remedy might be worse than the disease; the obstacles seemed insuperable; the economic and social sciences were uncharted; the record of success of government in controlling the economy was poor; and the limit of human intelligence was a problem." Madison could easily have written this language. And yet, the *Nebbia* court chose to abandon the protection of individual economic liberty in favor of the rational basis test—converting the Court from Madison's *bulwark for liberty* into FDR's *bulwark of deference* to central planning.

The Brandeis court complicated these issues four years later, when it decided *United States v. Carolene Products*, 304 U.S. 144 (1938). In response to intense lobbying by the dairy industry, attempting to protect its market against competition by cheaper foreign fat, Congress enacted the Filled Milk Act, which made it a crime to transport in interstate commerce filled milk "in imitation or semblance of milk, cream, or skimmed milk." If it looked like milk, cream, or skimmed milk, Congress made it a crime to move it. Carolene Products was indicted for violating[125]

---

124 Whether [the view that many business should be required to obtain permits of necessity] is sound nobody knows. The objections to the proposal are obvious and grave. *The remedy might bring evils worse than the present disease. The obstacles to success seem insuperable. The economic and social sciences are largely uncharted seas.* We have been none too successful in the modest essays in economic control already entered upon. The new proposal involves a vast extension of the area of control. Merely to acquire the knowledge essential as a basis for the exercise of this multitude of judgments would be a formidable task; and each of the thousands of these judgments would call for some measure of prophecy. Even more serious are the obstacles to success inherent in the demands which execution of the project would make upon human intelligence and upon the character of men. Man is weak and his judgment is at best fallible. Yet the advances in the exact sciences and the achievements in invention remind us that the seemingly impossible sometimes happens. . . Brandeis, Dissent, at pp. 309-310.
125 March 4, 1923, c. 262, 42 Stat. 1486, 21 U.S.C. §§ 61 63, 21 U.S.C.A. § 61—63.

the Act by the shipment of Milnut, a compound of condensed skimmed milk and coconut oil that looked like condensed milk. The product was properly labeled. Consumers knew what Milnut was, a cheaper substitute useful in baking and in baby formula.[126]

Carolene Products was engaged in an ordinary business—a variant of skim milk useful in baking and cooking. It deceived no one. It offered a cheaper and better product (with the benefit of modern biology). But, the company ran afoul of self-interested factions, who manipulated Congress into oppressing the product through the criminal law. The trial court had dismissed the indictment, but the Supreme Court, applying its rational basis test, reinstated the indictment.[127]

Most states have now eliminated restrictions on filled milk. The lobbyists were in error.[128]

---

126 "Milnut" was popular with working-class immigrant mothers for use in baby formula.

127 Ironically, every student in law school learns about *Carolene Products*, not because it reached a factually incorrect conclusion, or because it shows the dangers of faction and the misuse of legislative power, but for its footnote number 4, claimed to be "the most famous footnote" in constitutional law. That footnote declared that the Court would impose a higher level of scrutiny upon legislation involving burdens on "discrete and insular minorities" or restrictions on voting rights or free speech. This footnote has led to numerous instances where the court seems to decide on an ad hoc basis whether to apply the low level "rational basis" test or to apply the higher "strict scrutiny" test. Legislation typically passes the low test and fails the high test.

128 Filled milk is skim milk that has been reconstituted with fats, usually vegetable oils, from sources other than dairy cows and only exists as evaporated milk. Like pure evaporated milk, filled milk is generally considered unsuitable for drinking because of its particular flavor, but is equivalent to evaporated milk for baking and cooking purposes. Other filled milk products with substituted fat are used to make ice cream, sour cream, whipping cream, and half-and-half substitutes among other dairy products. *Coconut oil filled milk became a popular cost-saving product sold throughout the United States in the early 20th century. Coconut oil could be cheaply imported, primarily from the Philippines (at the time under American rule), and this product was able to undercut the market for evaporated and condensed milk.* At the time, liquid milk was not widely available or very popular because of the rarity of refrigeration and the problems of transportation and storage. Wikipedia (July, 2011).

Interested readers can learn more about the legislative history of margarine and skim milk from Geoff Miller's articles: "The True Story of Carolene Products," *Supreme Court Review* (1987), 397-428; and "Public Choice at the Dawn of the Special Interest State: The Story of Butter and Margarine," *California Law Review* 77 (1989).

[T]here is no evidence that filled milk, especially as supplemented by vitamins A and D, as it usually is, is less healthy than normal
evaporated milk. There is in fact evidence that the non-saturat-
ed fats in the vegetable oils may be more healthy than the milk
fat in normal milk products.

Brandeis' own fear—expressed in his *New State Ice Co* dissent—has also
been realized.

[W]e must be ever on our guard, lest we erect our prejudices
into legal principles.

Brandeis did just that in *Nebbia* and *Carolene Products*—erecting his own
prejudices into legal principles that allowed the Court to look the other
way [defer] as states infringed the economic privileges and immunities
of citizens. *The rational basis test reflects Brandeis' bias for the notion that there
is no limit to the reach of central planning by government.*

Hayek believed just the opposite—that democracy can only function
where a majority of the society is in agreement on a small range of subjects.[129] To permit the government, as Brandeis did, to extend the reach
of government across all subjects is, in the end, to destroy it. The Founders were 175 years ahead of Hayek. The Constitution established a limited range of subjects upon which a clear majority of the people and
the States did agree. With the rational basis test, the need for majority
agreement is avoided, producing a fertile field for factions to run unrestrained. Eighty years of irrational outcomes from the rational basis is

---

129 "It is the price of democracy that the possibilities of conscious control are restricted to the fields where true agreement exists and that in some fields things must
be left to chance. But in a society which depends on central planning this control cannot be made dependent on a majority's being able to agree; it will often be necessary
that the will of a small minority be imposed upon the people, because this minority
will be the largest group able to agree among themselves on the question at issue.
Democratic government has worked successfully where, and so long as, the functions
of government . . . were restricted to fields where agreement among a majority could
be achieved by free discussion; and *it is the great merit of the liberal creed that it reduced the
range of subjects on which agreement was necessary to one on which it was likely to exist in a society of free men.* It is now often said that democracy will not tolerate "capitalism". If "capitalism" means here a competitive system based on free disposal over private property,
it is far more important to realize that only within this system is democracy possible.
When it becomes dominated by a collectivist creed, democracy will inevitably destroy itself." F. A.
Hayek, *The Road to Serfdom, supra,* at pp. 109-10.

enough. The *Liberty Rights Amendments* (1—4) combine and then secure *both* economic and civil rights.

Amicus

NUMBER 24.
A Right to See? Unnecessary with *The Second Bill of Rights*!

According to the National Eye Institute, 2.3 million American have "low vision." With glasses, vision in their better eye cannot be corrected to 20/40. Another 30 million Americans are near-sighted—correctable to 20/20 with glasses. I am one of the 11.6 million far-sighted Americans— not needing correction until middle age when reading and progressive lenses are required. From 20/20 vision at age 44, my future will include steady decline in eyesight.

During a recent visit to Europe, it was difficult to read in hotels with in- sufficient light. Light bulbs just don't emit enough light. In Germany, I moved lamps to concentrate available light or furniture so I could sit beneath overhead spotlights. In Holland, I turned on every light in my room to comfortably read with my glasses on.

Back home in the United States, the amount of light was back to "nor- mal." Regulations issued by the European Union are nudging hotels across Europe to conserve energy (and reduce lumens) to meet EU en- ergy standards. Was I conserving energy in Germany and Holland? I was engaged in a frustrating attempt to combine sources of inadequate light to be able to read. Conserving energy makes practical sense. Who can argue with that? But, in exchange for the ability to read? To work? And, for millions of Americans who are elderly or ill, reading is an inex- pensive way to experience everything across the world.

A recent Congress authorized the Executive to issue regulations limiting the amount of lumens and the nature of light bulbs manufactured in the United States. Really? Really! Should individuals in a free society be trusted to match their capacity to see with products commonly available in commercial markets? Can the national government interfere with such choices? Is constitutional protection of a "right to see" necessary?

Shouldn't each of us buy what light bulbs, lamps, glasses, and lenses we need, without interference from government?

There is no right to see set forth in the main text of the Constitution, nor in the Bill of Rights. But, we are back to the debate the Founders had as to the wisdom of adding a Bill of Rights in the first place.[130] James Iridell told the North Carolina ratification convention the following:

> Let anyone make what collection or enumeration of rights he please, I will immediately mention twenty or thirty more rights not contained in it.

With Iridell in mind, here is a start of a new list of twenty or thirty rights related to vision:

- The right to move toward adequate light to read;
- The right to purchase a lamp;
- The right to purchase two lamps, and so on;
- The right to purchase a light bulb;
- The right to purchase two light bulbs, and so on;
- The right to purchase glasses with different power, and so on;
- The right to borrow my brother's glasses;
- The right to borrow my brother's lamps . . . [you get the point.]

Benjamin Franklin, a signer of the Declaration of Independence, a delegate to the Constitutional Convention, a member of the Royal Society (London), and one of the world's most famous scientists, was farsighted. Our similarities end there. Unable to focus on near objects without spectacles, he read at night by candle or by lamp, without electric light. Franklin invented bi-focals in the 1750's, a technology that evolved into the progressive lens now worn by millions. Franklin would have applauded Edison's invention of the incandescent light bulb. Franklin and I would likely reach the same conclusion about improving reading light through bulbs, candles, and lamps. And, we would likely agree that the national government of the United States has not been given the power to direct, through legislation, regulation, or court decision, how any citizen may choose to assemble sufficient lumens to read the morning paper or to write a letter.

---

130 See Number 14, *supra.*

For me, one 250 watt bulb is now sufficient with my current eyesight and a good lamp. On a sunny day, near a south-facing window, a low-watt LED bulb is sufficient. And, my eyesight *is much better* than that of the 2.3 million Americans with low vision. For them, more complex equipment, halogen lamps, and vision aids are necessary. Surely, Franklin would conclude that each of the 2.3 million Americans with low vision is at liberty to choose to acquire whatever equipment—including light bulbs—he or she deems necessary to read and write—free from statutory or regulatory interference by the national government.

The European approach to energy conservation begins by accepting the premise that a collective decision by a European government or by the European Commission is within the power of government. The Founders, including Franklin, rejected this premise in the Constitution of the United States. A *limited* national government was established with *enumerated powers*, rather than one with general powers similar to those of the nations in Europe.

The Founder's debate between 1787 and 1791 over these basic issues is still instructive. The national government is still a limited one, with enumerated powers only. It is not a general government that would duplicate, nonsensically, the police powers of the several States. The Constitution gives no power to the national government with respect to managing or dictating the ordinary aspects of everyday American life. There is no power authorizing Congress or Executive officials to substitute their judgment on such matters for the judgment of individual citizens or the judgment of state governments in the appropriate exercise of their police power.

> Amendment 2, Section 4 establishes a presumption of validity against any law made by Congress and any rule or order made by the Executive, when a citizen is exercising liberty rights. The presumption is easily rebutted when Congress is acting pursuant to an enumerated power, and is rebuttable when Congress properly relies, in part, on the *necessary and proper* clause. The amendment places the burden the Founders intended on Congress and the Executive when infringing the liberty rights of citizens.

> The exercise by a citizen of liberty rights shall be presumed valid by the Judiciary against any law made by Congress and any rule or order made by the Executive that denies or abridges such

rights; Provided, that this presumption shall not prevail with respect to laws made pursuant to an enumerated power; and Provided Further, that where Congress relies in part upon the necessary and proper clause of Article 1 Section 8 to make any such law, this presumption may be rebutted upon a showing by the Executive that such law: (i) is plainly necessary in the exercise of an enumerated power; (ii) could not achieve the purpose of an enumerated power by other means not so restrictive of liberty rights, and (iii) is consistent with the Rule of Law.

Amendment 4, Section 2 establishes a similar presumption of validity against any law made by States. The presumption is easily rebuttable, placing an appropriate burden on the States when infringing the liberty rights of citizens.

The exercise by a citizen of liberty rights shall be presumed valid against any state law that denies or abridges such rights; Provided, that this presumption may be rebutted upon a showing by the state that such law could not achieve the purpose of the police power by other means not so restrictive of liberty rights.

There is no enumerated power authorizing Congress or the Executive to interfere with a citizen's right to see or read; nor would it be plainly necessary for Congress to do so in the exercise of an enumerated power.

So, do we need a constitutional right to see? Do we need constitutional protection for any of the rights James Iridell could list? A right to grow a mustache? Wear jeans? Wear a hat? Walk on the other side of the street? Whistle on the way to work?

No!

The presumption in Amendments 2 and 4 of the *Liberty Rights Amendments* restores the filter the Founders intended to protect citizens in the everyday exercise of liberty rights from infringement, except when Congress is exercising one of its enumerated powers or when a State is properly exercising its police power.

Valerius

NUMBER 25.
Tragic Lessons from the 20th Century—Walter Lippmann

The Founders were familiar with various forms of government: the divine right of kings, parliaments, Greek democracies, and at the time the Constitution was being ratified, the French terror. From the start, the Founders' proclaimed that Americans would stand in a different place relative to the coercive power of government. Declaration of Independence (second paragraph).

> WE hold these Truths to be self-evident, *that all Men are created equal, that they are endowed by their Creator with certain unalienable Rights*, that among these are Life, Liberty, and the Pursuit of Happiness—That to secure these Rights, Governments are instituted among Men, *deriving their just Powers form the Consent of the Governed*, that whenever any Form of Government becomes destructive of these Ends, it is the Right of the People to alter or to abolish it, and to institute new Government, laying its Foundation on such Principles, and organizing its Powers in such Form, as to them shall seem most likely to effect their Safety and Happiness.

The Founders chose *control of government by the people* [a republic with individual freedom and liberty rights]—*instead of control of the people by government* [collectivism].

The twentieth century gave the world a tragic history lesson on the basic differences between government structured to control the people [collectivism] and government structured to be controlled by the people. Collectivist systems in Europe and Asia caused the deaths of millions of people—ultimate confirmation of the failure [indeed, futility] of political systems based on control of the people by government.

In 1937, Walter Lippmann, founding editor of the *New Republic*, former advisor to Presidents Wilson and Franklin Roosevelt, reached the same conclusion. Hitler and Mussolini were on the march, the Czechs and the Austrians were in danger, and Poland was two years away from being carved up by agreement of two totalitarian leaders—Adolf Hitler and Josef Stalin.

Although the partisans who are now fighting for the mastery of the modern world wear shirts of different colors, their weapons are drawn from the same armory, their doctrines are variations of the same theme, and they go forth to battle singing the same tune with slightly different words. *Their weapons are the coercive direction of the life and labor of mankind. Their doctrine is that disorder and misery can be overcome only by more and more compulsory organization. Their promise is that through the power of the state men can be made happy.*

Throughout the world, *in the name of progress, men who call themselves communists, socialists, fascists, nationalists, progressives, and even liberals, are unanimous in holding that government with its instruments of coercion must by commanding the people how they shall live, direct the course of civilization* and fix the shape of things to come. . . . .

So universal is the dominion of this dogma over the minds of contemporary men that *no one is taken seriously as a statesman or a theorist who does not come forward with proposals to magnify the power of public officials and to extend and multiply their intervention in human affairs.* Unless he is authoritarian and collectivist, he is a mossback, a reactionary, at best an amiable eccentric swimming hopelessly against the tide.

But it is even more significant that in other lands where men shrink from the ruthless policy of these regimes, it is commonly assumed that the movement of events must be in the same direction. *Nearly everywhere the mark of a progressive is that he relies at last upon the increased power of officials to improve the condition of men. Though the progressives prefer to move gradually and with consideration, by persuading majorities to consent, the only instrument of progress in which they have faith is the coercive agency of government.* They can, it would seem, imagine no alternative, nor can they remember how much of what they cherish as progressive has come by eman-

122

cipation from political dominion, by the limitation of power, by the release of personal energy from authority and collective coercion. For virtually all that now passes for progressivism in countries like England and the United States calls for increasing ascendancy of the state: always the cry is for more officials with more power over more and more of the activities of men.

Yet *the assumptions of this whole movement are not so self-evident as they seem. They are, in fact, contrary to the assumptions bred in men by the whole long struggle to extricate conscience, intellect, labor, and personality from the bondage of prerogative, privilege, monopoly, authority. For more than two thousand years, since western men first began to think about the social order, the main preoccupation of political thinking has been to find a law which would be superior to arbitrary power.* Men have sought it in custom, in the dictates of reason, in religious revelation, endeavoring always to set up some check upon the exercise of force. This is the meaning of the long debate about Natural Law. This is the meaning of a thousand years of struggle to bring the sovereign under a constitution, to establish for the individual and for voluntary associations of men rights which they can enforce against kings, barons, magnates, majorities, and mobs. This is the meaning of the struggle to separate the church from the state, to emancipate conscience, learning, the arts, education, and commerce from the inquisitor, the censor, the monopolist, the policeman, and the hangman. . . . . . .

But *the burden of proof is upon those who reject the ecumenical tradition of the western world. It is for them to show that their cult of the Providential State is in truth the new revelation they think it is, and that it is not, as a few still believe, the gigantic heresy of an apostate generation.*[131]

Over the next eight years after Lippmann wrote this, Europe was engulfed in a war that spread across the globe, mobilizing more than 100 million military personnel. Between 50 and 70 million people died.

As Lippmann correctly predicted, the instigators of these conflicts, and of the forty-six-year Cold War that followed, wore different color shirts, shouted different slogans, and sang different battle songs. The weap-

---

131   Walter Lippmann, *An Inquiry into the Principles of the Good Society*, 1937.

ons, doctrine, promises were the same—ones the Founders rejected, but feared:

> *Their weapons [were] the coercive direction of the life and labor of mankind. Their doctrine [was] that disorder and misery can be overcome only by more and more compulsory organization. Their promise [was] that through the power of the state men can be made happy.*

The Founders of the American Republic would have recoiled in horror from events such as Stalin's forced starvation of the Ukraine in 1921, the Holocaust perpetrated by the National Socialist Party (NAZIs) in Germany, the Rape of Nanking in 1937, and the mass starvation caused by China's Great Leap Forward in 1958-61. They would *not* have been surprised that a government structured to control the people, rather than to be controlled by them, would be led by ambitious men "contending for pre-eminence and power."

> The latent causes of faction are . . sown in the nature of man . . A zeal for different opinions concerning religion . . government, and many other points[;] an attachment to different leaders ambitiously contending for pre-eminence and power; [have] . . divided mankind into parties, inflamed them with mutual animosity, and rendered them much more disposed to vex and oppress each other than to cooperate for their common good.[132]

As noted in Number 3, the *auxiliary precautions* Madison placed in the Constitution—and the *internal* and *external* controls—were to secure the public good and private rights against faction. Government *administered by men over men* was not to be perverted by the passions and self-interest of faction. Their solution: (a) establish a national government with limited, enumerated powers; and (b) confirm the police power to the States, where the mischief of faction could be separately and better managed by multiple state and local legislatures. Madison concludes *The Federalist Papers 10* this way:

> The influence of factious leaders may kindle a flame within their particular States but will be unable to spread a general conflagration through the other States. A religious sect may degenerate

---

132 Madison, *The Federalist Papers 10,* at p. 79.

into a political faction in a part of the [nation]; but the variety of sects dispersed over the entire face of it must secure the national councils against any danger from that source. A rage for paper money, for an abolition of debts, for an equal division of property, or for any other improper or wicked project, will be less apt to pervade the whole body of the Union[.] . . In the extent and proper structure of the Union, therefore, we behold a republican remedy for the diseases most incident to republican government. . . . [133]

Lippmann's 1937 assessment was right. The Founders reached the same conclusion one hundred and fifty years earlier.

Amicus

---

133   *Ibid*, at p. 84.

NUMBER 26.
Lippmann, Hayek, and Keynes Endorse Second Bill of Rights?

Here is the News Flash that might have been, had they lived to review *The Second Bill of Rights.*

New York. *Lippmann, Hayek, and Keynes Endorse The Second Bill of Rights*

Noted journalist Walter Lippmann today joined prominent economists F. A. Hayek and John Maynard Keynes in their endorsement of *The Second Bill of Rights*, proposed in 2012 as a set of amendments to the U.S. Constitution. Lippmann, Hayek, and Keynes reached this historic agreement in the wake of the death of more than 30 million people in World War II at the hands of centrally planned, totalitarian regimes. Walter Lippmann confirmed in an exclusive telephonic interview with the New York Sun that he had facilitated the merger of two ideas: (i) Hayek's view that "individual liberty and central planning [of whatever sort, left, right, or nationalistic] cannot co-exist" and (ii) Keynes' view that "clear lines had to be established defining the limit of government power to plan." Lippmann noted that the Founders of the American Republic had reached both of these conclusions in 1787—establishing a limited federal government with power in 18 enumerated areas, while individual liberty remained unreachable in all others. Lippmann confirmed that the proposed *Second Bill of Rights* would restore the balance the Founders originally established between the central power of the national government and the individual freedom of citizens.

The News Flash didn't happen. But, logic did not prevent it.

In 1931, F. A. Hayek arrived at the London School of Economics from Vienna, first as a lecturer on monetary theory, then as a visiting professor, and a year later as a chaired professor. The depression was deepening in England. A gold drain led to the collapse of the Labour government, the abandoning of the gold standard, and the imposition of protective tariffs.

After a 1931 intellectual spat with John Maynard Keynes over Keynes' new book, a *Treatise on Money*, Hayek opened a new topic in the inaugural lecture for his new chair—"The Trend of Economic Thinking." Hayek claimed public opinion was moving away from a theoretical approach to the social sciences and had undermined economic reasoning in general.

> [P]eople felt free to propose all manner of utopian solutions to the problem of the depression, solutions that any serious study of economics would show were infeasible.

Hayek's most famous political work,[134] *The Road to Serfdom*, began as an internal memo to the director of the London School of Economics. Published in 1938 as an article, Hayek believed he had found a fatal flaw in socialist planning—

> [it] "presupposes a much more complete agreement on the relative importance of the different ends than actually exists, and that, in consequence, in order to be able to plan, the planning authority must impose upon the people that detailed code of values which is lacking."[135]

Hayek worried that the success of centralized war planning within the UK economy to one purpose—winning the war—would be misused after the war to reorganize the government into a planned economy. One example was the Labour Party's 1942 pamphlet, *The Old World and the New Society*, which claimed the following:

- A planned society must replace the old competitive system
- The basis for our democracy must be planned production for community use . . .
- As a necessary prerequisite to the reorganization of society, the main Wartime controls in industry and agriculture should be

---

134 Hayek won the Nobel Prize in Economics. Most of his writings were in his professional field, and were widely read within that field.
135 F. A. Hayek, "Freedom and the Economic System" (1938), Vol. 10 of *The Collected Works of F. A. Hayek* (1997).

maintained to avoid the scramble for profits which followed the last war.[136]

Reacting to such proposals, Hayek extended his thoughts in *The Road to Serfdom*, which sold well in England, but was even more successful in the United States.[137]

The basic theme of *The Road to Serfdom* is that *all* attempts to use central planning to achieve outcomes in a free society cannot succeed at *both* producing the planned outcomes *and* maintaining the freedom of citizens. *Central planning and individual liberty cannot co-exist.* This was Hayek's view as a professional academic economist—verified from experience in his native Austria, in England, and while visiting totalitarian Germany, Italy, and USSR.

Hayek's 1944 words are relevant to today's federal legislation that seeks to plan outcomes in the financial, health care, and public infrastructure sectors.

> It is not difficult to see what must be the consequences when democracy embarks upon a course of planning which in its execution requires more agreement than in fact exists. The people may have agreed on adopting a system of directed economy because they have been convinced that it will produce great prosperity. In the discussion leading to the decision, the goal of planning will have been described by some such term as *common welfare*, which only conceals the absence of real agreement on the ends of planning.
>
> . . .
>
> The effect of the people's agreeing that there must be central planning, without agreeing on the ends, will be rather as if a group of people were to commit themselves to take a journey together without agreeing where they want to go; with the result

---

136 National Executive Committee of the Labour Party, Annual Conference, London, May 25-28, 1942.

137 F. A. Hayek, *The Road to Serfdom, supra.* Caldwell's 35-page introduction provides valuable context for the development of Hayek's views, alongside Lippmann and Keynes, and is well worth a careful independent read. This summary of Hayek's background relies heavily on Caldwell's introduction.

that they may all have to make a journey which most of them do not want at all.[138]

John Maynard Keynes read the book on the way to the Bretton Woods conference in 1944. He wrote to tell Hayek the following:

[M]orally and philosophically I find myself in agreement with virtually the whole of it; and not only in agreement with it, but in a deeply moved agreement.[139]

The *Road to Serfdom* is directly relevant to our discussion of *The Second Bill of Rights*. Washington, Madison, Franklin, Adams, and the rest of the Founders had already reached these same conclusions in 1787. The thirteen states confirmed these conclusions by ratifying the Constitution.[140] In the United States, *the national government would not be given power to centrally plan the individual lives of American citizens.* Rather, the national government would exercise its powers to centrally control ("plan") within its enumerated powers—i.e. war, peace, foreign affairs.

James Madison confirmed in *The Federalist Papers* that the Founders were 150 years ahead of Hayek, Keynes, and Lippmann (see Number 13, above).

The powers delegated by the proposed Constitution to the federal government are *few and defined.* Those which are to remain in the State governments are numerous and indefinite. The former will be exercised principally on external objects, as war, peace, negotiation, and foreign; with which last the power of taxation will, for the most part, be connected. The powers reserved to the several States will extend to all the objects which, in the ordinary course of affairs, concern the lives, liberties, and prop-

---

138 F. A. Hayek, *The Road to Serfdom, supra,* at pp. 103-104.

139 F. A. Hayek, *The Road to Serfdom, supra,* Introduction, at p. 23. Caldwell confirms that Keynes wanted more: "You admit that the line has to be drawn somewhere, and that the logical extreme is not possible. But you give us no guidance whatever as to where to draw it."

140 Hayek and Keynes were citizens of Britain, a country in which Parliament is a general legislature. Parliament can change its unwritten constitution, a set of principles rather than a document, a composite of concessions extracted from the monarchy, statutes, and the common law. Keynes suggestion that Hayek provide "guidance . . . as to where to draw [the line]" makes perfect sense in Britain. The United States had already done so in its written Constitution.

erties of the people, and the internal order, improvement, and prosperity of the State.[141]

In adopting the Constitution, the Founders did *not* embark upon a course of planning which in its execution requires more agreement than in fact existed. They defined the limits of their agreement on the powers that would be kept by the people and the States, and they enumerated a list of limited powers that would be granted the national government. They further separated these enumerated powers among the branches of the national government as a further precaution, and they barred the national government from changing this agreement.

Madison could have written Hayek's response to the collectivist's criticism of the Constitution.

> That our present society lacks . . . *conscious* direction toward a single aim, that its activities are guided by the whims and fancies of irresponsible individuals, has always been one of the main complaints of its socialist critics.

> [T]his puts the issue very clearly. . . . The various kinds of collectivism, communism, fascism, etc., differ among themselves in the nature of the goal toward which they want to direct the efforts of society. But they all differ from [editor's note: the old definition of] liberalism and individualism in wanting to organize the whole of society and all its resources for this unitary end and in refusing to recognize autonomous spheres in which the ends of the individuals are supreme. In short, they are totalitarian in the true sense of this new word which we have adopted to describe the unexpected but nevertheless inseparable manifestations of what in theory we call collectivism.[142]

Hayek's belief that central planning would destroy individual freedom fits with Madison's belief[143] in the need for internal and external precautions against arbitrary abuse in any government administered by men over men.

---

141 Madison, *The Federalist Papers 45*, at p. 292.
142 F. A. Hayek, *The Road to Serfdom, supra*, at p. 100.
143 See, Numbers 3, 4, and 6, above.

[D]elegation is usually justified by the technical character of the task. . . . *The objectionable feature is that delegation is so often resorted to because the matter in hand cannot be regulated by general rules but only by the exercise of discretion* in the decision of particular cases. In these instances delegation means that some authority is given power to make with the force of law what to all intents and purposes are *arbitrary decisions* (usually described as "judging the case on its merits").[144]

Lippmann, Keynes, Hayek, Washington, Madison, Franklin—peas in a pod—good company in support of *The Second Bill of Rights.*

Amicus

---

144 F. A. Hayek, *The Road to Serfdom, supra*, at pp. 106-107.

NUMBER 27.
The Common Law—Proven Principles of General Application

The Common Law in the Constitution

The Founders refer, in four (4) sections of the Constitution, to sources of law outside the document. These are references to the common law and to the process by which cases are duly decided—due process—in accordance with law.

First, the Fifth Amendment:

> No person shall . . . be deprived of life, liberty, or property, without due process of law;

Second and third, the Fourteenth Amendment:

> nor shall any State deprive any person of life, liberty, or property, without due process of law; nor deny to any person within its jurisdiction the equal protection of the laws.

Fourth, the Seventh Amendment:

> In Suits at common law, where the value in controversy shall exceed twenty dollars, the right of trial by jury shall be preserved, and no fact tried by a jury, shall be otherwise re-examined in any Court of the United States, than according to the rules of the common law.

The Founders knew the common law. The basic principles were common knowledge to non-lawyers. The English common law had its beginnings more than one thousand years ago, before the printing press. The common law developed from written decisions of impartial judges in real cases between English subjects, each represented by lawyers in an "adversary system." Each party presented its view of the facts and the law. In each case, the opposing parties presented facts to juries through witnesses and argued to the judge how the facts should be applied to the law established in prior decisions. From this adversarial process, a jury decided the facts, and an independent judge applied the law. Because the facts of each case differed, application of the law differed, too. Judges, lawyers, and the population learned to predict likely outcomes of cases, encouraging settlements. Numerous judges, attorneys, and parties were involved, with no connection whatever to other cases. The decisions by judges were viewed as independent, reasoned, and unbiased. The process led to steady development of *general rules applicable to all cases*—what the Founders knew as the common law.

The core principle of the common law—*general rules applicable to all cases*—is consistent with a constitutional republic based on individual freedom and liberty. Although not explicitly stated in *The Federalist Papers*, the common law—and its general principles—are yet another of the *auxiliary precautions* that stand in the way of factions in their attempts to manipulate government administered by some men over others. In the system of justice the Founders established, it is very difficult for factions to control the outcome of actual cases—in which impartial judges declare the law to the juries, and where independent juries are free to find facts and apply these facts to the law. It is more difficult, still, to control the development of general rules applicable within the common law when those rules relating to the police power are separately made in each of the States, and those applicable to the exercise of the enumerated powers of the national government are separately made by the federal judiciary. The common law, the Founders knew, would provide yet another powerful check on the exercise of arbitrary power by the national government over citizens in the federal sphere, and a similar check on arbitrary power by state governments.

Two examples illustrate the importance of the common law in the constitutional framework.

The first is one of the many rules of evidence—hearsay testimony in a trial. Should a common law judge allow a witness in court to repeat a statement made by another person when that other person is not present for cross-examination? In thousands of cases over hundreds of years, thousands of the English common law judges have developed rules of general application to answer this question in almost every conceivable factual situation. The answer is generally no, but there are more than two dozen exceptions to this rule—factual situations in which the answer is yes.

The second example is the definition of fraud, deceit, and misrepresentation, all wrongs recognized by the common law as the basis for a civil action by one person against another. In what circumstances would the common law provide a monetary recovery for fraud, for deceit, for misrepresentation? Long before the Congress, Executive agencies, and state legislatures began writing statutes or regulations about mislabeled products, false statements of manufacturers, or RICO, thousands upon thousands of common law judges have heard and evaluated opposing arguments by counsel. Judges developed rules of general application that defined fraud, deceit, and misrepresentation; described what needs to be proved in a civil action; and awarded damages for these wrongs.

The vast majority of America's legal principles come from this long process—the slow, steady, independent, reasoned development of principles of general application to all disputes among citizens, or between a citizen and the government.

On the Shoulders of Lord Coke; The Petition of Right

More than four hundred years ago, on November 13, 1608, Chief Justice Edward Coke of the Court of Common Pleas stood before his king, James I, in a debate with a bishop of the Church of England, head of the High Commission (an ecclesiastical or religious court). The High Commission was deciding cases on common law topics outside common law rules. Coke and his fellow judges had issued *prohibitions* banning the High Commission from each case.[145] Coke was at Whitehall Palace that day to defend the common law. England had no Bill of Rights. The common law stood between a citizen and encroachment by the king's claim of royal prerogative:

> The Bishop: [Judges are] delegates of the King, and the King may take what [cases] he shall please from the determination of the Judges and may determine them himself.

---

145 The exchange is described from several sources in *The Lion and the Throne*, Catherine Drinker Bowen, Little Brown & Co., 1957, at 302-06.

Coke: [B]y act of Parliament, . . the King cannot take any [case] out of any courts and give judgment upon it himself.

King James I: [The King] as supreme head of justice, would defend to the death his prerogative of calling judges before him to decide disputes of jurisdiction. Moreover he would ever protect the common law.

Coke: The common law protects the King.

King James I: A traitorous speech! The King protects the law, and not the law the King.

[Boswell's account]: . . . the Lord Coke humbly prayed the king to have respect [for] the Common Laws of his land. He [pleaded with] his Majesty to consider that the Ecclesiastical [law] was foreign. After which his Majesty fell into that high indignation [a rage] as . . . was never known in him, looking and speaking fiercely with bended fist, offering to strike him. . Which the Lord Coke perceiving, fell flat on all fours; humbly beseeching his Majesty to take compassion on him and to pardon him if he thought zeal had gone beyond his duty and allegiance. (Note: Old English spellings modernized.)

After this exchange, the king went off to hunt deer. The next day, undeterred, a new *prohibition* issued from the Court of Common Pleas to the High Commission, under Coke's seal.

Coke wasn't done. In 1610, Coke declared in *Dr. Bonham's Case*, 8 Co. Rep. 114, that the common law could declare even an act of Parliament void. A physician was imprisoned by the Royal College for practicing without a certificate from them, and the College took 1/2 of the fine. Coke cited the common law rule that one cannot be judge in his own case, set Bonham free, and voided the Act of Parliament that authorized the process with the following:

When an Act of Parliament is against common right and reason, the common law will control it and adjudge such Act to be void.

135

The King dissolved Parliament in February 1611 and attempted to rule the country by proclamation—(i.e., laws without Parliament). Coke was removed as Chief Justice of Common Pleas, recalled as Chief Justice of England, removed again, and imprisoned in the Tower. Later elected to Parliament, Coke was a principle author of the Petition of Right (June 1628), which preserved the privileges and immunities of English subjects everywhere (including the American colonies), with the protections of due process under the common law.

The Founders, Coke, and the Common Law

The privileges and immunities of Englishmen and the common law that protects them, were incorporated into state constitutions, and the American Constitution. Coke's words in *Bonham* were well known:[146]

> [They] echoed down the centuries . . . 1765, and a Stamp Act passes in Parliament. New England protesting. "An Act against natural equity is void!" shouted James Otis of Massachusetts, and from Boston to Virginia trumpets blew. Massachusetts Assembly declared the Stamp Act invalid, "against Magna Charta and the natural rights of Englishmen, and therefore, according to the Lord Coke, null and void."[147]

Judicial authority to declare void any federal legislation that was outside the Constitution lived on.[148] By adopting a written constitution, the Founders easily incorporated the result Coke reached under the English common law. In fact, the common law's principles of general application to all citizens provide the package of procedural protections that are at the crux of *due process of law* and *equal protection of the laws.*

The *Liberty Rights Amendments* renew and strengthen the vital connection between (i) the protection of liberty rights in a complex regulatory environment and (ii) common law principles of general application to all citizens—including due process and equal protection of the laws. Amendment 1 expressly includes the common law within the Rule of Law. Amendments 2 and 4 include a presumption of validity in a

---

146 Hamilton cited the Petition of Right in *The Federalist Papers 84*. Lord Coke's views came direct to America. He helped draft the charter of the Virginia Company, which included the rights of Englishmen and the common law.
147 *The Lion and the Throne, supra,* at pp. 315-16.
148 Hamilton confirms it in *The Federalist Papers 84.*

citizen's exercise of liberty rights, together with standards for how this presumption is rebutted, to be developed by the common law. Balance is restored, describing those circumstances in which a legislature may interfere with the liberty rights of citizens—directly or indirectly—by delegation. The common law—with independent judges and juries, appellate courts, recorded proceedings and written decisions—still serves the important function the Founders intended: to develop common law principles and rules of general application to all citizens in the day to day working of the Constitution, the police power of States, and the individual liberty rights of citizens. The performance of this function is still a key element in the continuing effort to scrape the self-interested, specialized barnacles of faction off the bottom of the U.S.(S.) Constitution.

Just as Coke tested the power of his King against the procedural protections of due process under the common law, the *Liberty Rights Amendments* re-establish the role of the common law in allowing citizens to have a fair opportunity to challenge the coercive power of government when it interferes with the exercise of liberty rights.

Amicus

NUMBER 28.
Continuity: Due Process, Equal Protection under the Rule of Law

Due process under the Rule of Law, equal protection of the laws, and prohibition against government discrimination on the basis of race, color, national origin, or gender, or on the basis of belief or non-belief in any creed or religion are bedrock principles upon which individual freedom and liberty rights rest. The protections in the first Bill of Rights were *auxiliary precautions* to protect citizens from government. The Thirteenth, Fourteenth, and Fifteenth Amendments extended these "precautions" to an entire class of freed slaves.[149]

The decision in *The Slaughterhouse Cases* brought the promise of a color-blind government to an unexpected end by 1876, not to be successfully revived until the Civil Rights movements of the 1950s and 1960s, and with the remarkable achievements of people like Thurgood Marshall and Martin Luther King, Jr. The legal setting was doubtful, because the constitutional ground of *privileges or immunities* of American citizens had been uprooted by the Court in 1873 in *Slaughterhouse*. Beginning in the 1950's, the Supreme Court tried to re-fill this ground with an equally tortured concept—*selective incorporation of rights from the Bill of Rights*, which were passed through the due process and equal protection clauses of the Fourteenth Amendment, one case at a time, and then imposed on States.[150] Every day, a first-year law student is confused. But for the decision in *The Slaughterhouse Cases*, the privileges and immunities clause would have provided a much more direct, more logical, and more durable solution.

The *Liberty Rights Amendments* in *The Second Bill of Rights* sort this out, and restore the Founders' framework. As noted in Number 17, the privileges and immunities of citizens are fully restored by Amendment 2, with the

---

149 See, Number 42, for the tortured path Congress took to achieve ratification of the Fourteenth Amendment.
150 See, Number 31, below.

auxiliary precaution of a presumption of validity in favor of the exercise of these rights by citizens.[151] *Slaughterhouse* is overturned, and the liberty rights of citizens are better protected from unprincipled power of either the national or state governments.

Amendment 3 completes the restoration of constitutional controls and precautions in favor of liberty rights, by expressly continuing and extending the protections of due process of law and equal protection of the laws. These principles are moved out of Section 1 of the 14th Amendment to stand on their own in *The Second Bill of Rights* Amendment 3, forever ending lingering confusion from the decision in *The Slaughterhouse Cases*, and making these principles even more prominent in the Constitution. Madison might well describe the application of due process, equal protection of the law, and prohibition of discrimination as yet *additional internal controls or auxiliary precautions* to protect citizens from government administered by men over men.

The text of Amendment 3 is simple and direct:

3. Due Process Under the Rule of Law, Equal Protection of the Law.
Neither Congress nor the Executive, and no State shall deprive any citizen of life, liberty, or property without due process in accord with the Rule of Law; nor deny to any citizen the equal protection of the laws; nor discriminate for or against any citizen on the basis of race, color, national origin, or gender, or on the basis of belief or non-belief in any creed or religion.

The due process and equal protection language is repeated, except that in *The Second Bill of Rights* Amendment 3, these protections apply *not only* against the States, but *also against* Congress and the Executive. Due process, equal protection, and protection against discrimination are extended beyond states to the legislative and executive branches of the federal government.

Due Process Protections Continue and Are Expanded

The new Amendment 3 begins more expansively: "Neither Congress, nor the Executive, and no state shall deprive any citizen of life, liberty, or

---

151 *The Second Bill of Rights*, Amendment 2, Section 4, and Amendment 4, Section 2.

property." And, the new amendment requires that the due process protections are "in accord with the Rule of Law," a term defined in Amendment 1, Section 1. The amendment does not authorize a regulatory process, run by the Executive, to deprive any citizen of life, liberty, or property. Instead, legislative and executive power may be challenged by a citizen through the independent judiciary guaranteed under the Rule of Law. The new amendment does not interfere with regulatory power properly delegated by the Congress in accord with the Rule of Law, but it does prevent purely administrative processes from interfering with the ordinary exercise of a citizen's liberty rights.

Equal Protection of the Law is Maintained, and Expanded

Similarly, the new Amendment 3 maintains, and indeed broadens, the principle of equal protection of the laws, as follows: "Neither Congress nor the Executive, and no State shall . . . deny to any citizen the equal protection of the laws." The equal protection of the laws remains as an important procedural and substantive safeguard for citizens—not only from state action, but from the legislative power of Congress and the regulatory power of the Executive. Laws and regulations will properly be scrutinized to determine whether they are of general application to all citizens—and therefore valid against the equal protection clause—or whether they are of impermissibly narrow application, neither justified (for the federal government) through an enumerated power, nor justified through the proper exercise of the police power of a state.

Specific Protection against Discrimination Added

The new Amendment 3 extends protections against discrimination *for or against any citizen* for prohibited reasons: "Neither Congress nor the Executive, and no State shall . . . discriminate for or against any citizen on the basis of race, color, national origin, or gender, or on the basis of belief or non-belief in any creed or religion." The new constitutional protection forbids discrimination by Congress, the Executive, and States for or against any citizen on the basis of race, color, national origin, or gender, a step long overdue in the long march forward for equal rights in the United States. The Amendment moves government from a partisan role for or against specifically named groups, back to a neutral position. Similarly, this same prohibition is extended to discrimination for or against any citizen "on the basis of belief or non-belief in any creed or religion." This language moves government from a partisan role for or against those who believe or who don't believe in any creed or religion—back to a neutral position. This portion of the amendment prevents Congress, the Executive or States from discriminating in favor of or against a particular religion, but also from discriminating in favor of or against non-belief in any religion. The Judiciary will no longer be under any constitutional requirement to default to either a particular religion or to atheism (non-belief). *The Second Bill of Rights* confirms that there is no particular creed or religion that is preferred by the Constitution. Non-belief is not preferred, either.

Dr. Martin Luther King, Jr. remains the most effective advocate of equal rights in our history. Each of the legacies of Lincoln, John Quincy Adams, and Douglass is blurred compared to that of Dr. King because of their roles in other activities and events. Dr. King's "*I Have a Dream Speech*" sets forth a view of emancipation, the Civil War Amendments, and civil rights that we hope is faithfully reflected in *The Second Bill of Rights* and in *The New Federalist Papers*.

Although numerous passages in Dr. King's speech track its principles, four excerpts have had special meaning in the framing of *The Second Bill of Rights*.

> In a sense we have come to our nation's capital to cash a check. When the architects of our republic wrote the magnificent words of the Constitution and the Declaration of Independence, they were signing a promissory note to which every American was to fall heir. This note was a promise that all men, yes, black men as well as white men, would be guaranteed the unalienable rights of life, liberty, and the pursuit of happiness.

> I have a dream that my four little children will one day live in a nation where they will not be judged by the color of their skin but by the content of their character.

> This will be the day when all of God's children will be able to sing with a new meaning, "My country, 'tis of thee, sweet land of liberty, of thee I sing. Land where my fathers' died, land of the pilgrim's pride, from every mountainside, let freedom ring."

> And when this happens, when we allow freedom to ring, when we let it ring from every village and every hamlet, from every

state and every city, we will be able to speed up that day when all of God's children, black men and white men, Jews and Gentiles, Protestants and Catholics, will be able to join hands and sing in the words of the old Negro spiritual, "Free at last! free at last! thank God Almighty, we are free at last!"

Valerius

NUMBER 29.
The Police Power of States—Amendment 4

The last of the four *Liberty Rights Amendments—Second Bill of Rights* Amendment 4—corrects another error in judgment introduced by the Supreme Court in *The Slaughterhouse Cases.*[152] The 5-4 majority in *Slaughterhouse* ruled, in effect, that states were not barred from interfering with privileges or immunities that belonged to citizens of the United States. The decision was devastating to newly emancipated slaves, and led to separate but equal, Jim Crow laws, state laws interfering with the right to vote, and so forth. Discrimination followed against other targeted groups.

The last of the four Liberty Rights Amendments restores the original principles at the Founding in four simple sections. Sections 1 and 2, discussed here, read this way:

1. The police power is reserved to each of the States under Amendment 10 and includes the power to promote the health, good order, morals, peace, and safety of citizens residing therein through laws of general application that preserve the common exercise of liberty rights.

2. The exercise by a citizen of liberty rights shall be presumed valid against any state law that denies or abridges such rights; Provided, that this presumption may be rebutted upon a showing by the state that such law could not achieve the purpose of the police power by other means not so restrictive of liberty rights.[153]

---

152 The impact of *Slaughterhouse* on the "privileges or immunities of citizens of the United States" language in the Fourteenth Amendment was described in Number 11 above.

153 As described in Number 18, Section 2 establishes a rebuttable presumption in favor of the exercise of a citizen's liberty rights when in conflict with a particular exercise of the police power by one of the several States.

The definition of the police power in Section 1 is simple and has long been recognized in both the common law and in constitutional jurisprudence. The first clause of Section 1 comes from the dissent of Mr. Justice Field in *Slaughterhouse.*

> The police power is reserved to each of the States under Amendment 10 and includes the power to promote the health, good order, morals, peace, and safety.[154]

This definition is consistent with the Founders' original framework. As noted in Number 13, Madison contrasted the role of States with the role of Congress.[155]

> The powers delegated by the proposed Constitution to the federal government are *few and defined. Those which are to remain in the State governments are numerous and indefinite.* The former will be exercised principally on external objects, as war, peace, negotiation, and foreign; with which last the power of taxation will, for the most part, be connected. *The powers reserved to the several States will extend to all the objects which, in the ordinary course of affairs, concern the lives, liberties, and properties of the people, and the internal order, improvement, and prosperity of the State.*

The rest of Section 1 confirms that the police power is to be exercised over citizens residing in each of the respective states "through laws of general application that preserve the common exercise of liberty rights."

Many constitutional academics have [wrongly] advanced the argument in the twentieth century that the first eight amendments in the Bill of Rights contain the liberty rights (including the privileges and immunities) of American citizens, and that the Supreme Court has been slowly, over the course of more than one hundred years, applying these protections against the States. The argument is then advanced that because of these developments, the Ninth and Tenth Amendments in the Bill of Rights are of reduced importance, or of no importance at all. This argument is entirely circular—and has never made any sense. Amendment

---

154 See, Dissent of Mr. Justice Field, in *The Slaughterhouse Cases*, 83 U.S. 36, at 87 (1873).
155 Madison, *The Federalist Papers 45*, at p. 292.

10 of the original Bill of Rights was an integral part of the Founders' framework. It was a shorthand method of confirming that the States would mediate and resolve nearly all of the day-to-day interactions of a free people—exercising their liberty rights as inhabitants of each State.

After *Slaughterhouse*, the fears of three of the four dissenters were realized with the oppression by state legislators of former slaves and their Republican supporters in the readmitted States—through voting laws, firearms laws, and the entire apartheid apparatus of Jim Crow. The Civil Rights Acts of 1866 and 1875 were gutted under the authority of *Slaughterhouse*. When the presidential election of 1876 was decided by a special electoral commission, in which the House of Representatives accepted Hayes instead of Tilden (through political compromise), the remaining federal troops enforcing civil rights were withdrawn from Southern states. The Supreme Court had judicially erased the "privileges or immunities" clause from the Fourteenth Amendment. States were free to misuse the police power to interfere with these privileges in favor of preferred groups and against targeted groups.

The purpose of Amendment 4 of *The Second Bill of Rights* is to return to the first principles of the Founders—updated by the result of the Civil War—and to restore the police power to its original role of neutral mediator among free citizens in the common exercise of their liberty rights.

From the most basic example, to the most complex, a state's exercise of the police power must be through laws of general application that preserve the common exercise of liberty rights—an express rejection of that aspect of *Slaughterhouse* that allowed a State to arbitrarily pick and choose among groups or individuals for favorable or unfavorable treatment.

As a simple example, two people cannot occupy the same spot on a public sidewalk, yet each has a liberty right to occupy any particular spot. The police power surely extends to mediate and resolve any disputes among citizens as to who stands where and for how long.

As a more complex example, the practice of a profession, such as structural engineering, is typically a matter of individual accreditation within a State. The safety of the public in the occupation of a high-rise steel building is at stake. Surely, the police power extends to a confirmation of the qualifications of an engineer to hold himself or herself out as a professional engineer within the State, licensed to prepare structural designs. Yet the police power relating to the qualification of professional engineers ought to be exercised through laws of general application that preserve the common exercise of liberty rights. A State does not have the power to interfere with the accreditation of professional engineers on the basis of race, gender, religion, non-religion, or hair color. This kind of legislative interference would not be of general application and would directly impinge on the common exercise of liberty rights.

States were sovereign republics at the time the Constitution was adopted, with general legislative powers that were limited by State constitutions to protect individual rights. The police power was one of the auxiliary precautions Madison relied upon in the Constitution, as noted in Numbers 3 and 4 above. These precautions, that is, the internal and external limits and controls on each level of government, were to reduce the *great object* of preserving individual liberty to a manageable one. Madison's solution was: (a) to establish a national government with limited, enumerated powers; and (b) to confirm the police power [i.e., management of everyday affairs] to the States, where liberty rights were already protected and the mischief of faction could be separately and better managed.

Madison concludes *The Federalist Papers 10* this way:

> *The influence of factious leaders may kindle a flame within their particular States but will be unable to spread a general conflagration through the other States.* A religious sect may degenerate into a political faction in a part of the [nation]; but the variety of sects dispersed over the entire face of it must secure the national councils against any danger from that source. *A rage for paper money, for an abolition of debts, for an equal division of property, or for any other improper or wicked project, will be less apt to pervade the whole body of the Union* . . . In the extent and proper structure of the Union, therefore, we behold a republican remedy for the diseases most incident to republican government. . . .

That *republican remedy* was confirmed in the Tenth Amendment to the original Bill of Rights, part of the mutually supportive limitations and allocations of power in the Constitution to protect each of us in the common exercise of our privileges, immunities, and rights—our liberty rights—as Americans.

146

The terrible decision in *Slaughterhouse*, and the century old effort by subsequent justices of that Court to minimize or avoid the effect of that decision is a poor substitute for the more direct fix contained in Sections 1 and 2 of Amendment 4 of *The Second Bill of Rights.*

Amendment 4 repairs the damage done by *Slaughterhouse*, and restores the central role of the States in the common exercise of liberty rights through laws of general application that protect such rights in accordance with the Rule of Law.

Valerius

NUMBER 30.
To Control Factions, End Federal Bullying of States

Madison confirmed in *The Federalist Papers 10* that the police power, separately exercised within each of the States, was THE "internal control" that the Founders believed would protect citizens from the destructive self-interest of factions. *Federal power*—limited to the enumerated powers listed in Article I—*did not overlap with the police power.* Day to day interaction of citizens—at home, at work, at school, in commerce—remained a local matter. The common law, supplemented by legislation consistent with state constitutions, protected all citizens in the common exercise of their liberty rights. This was the *police power*—and it was left with States.

Nowhere is the genius of the Founders more evident than in the division between state and federal power. Because federal power was fundamentally different from each state's police power—the Founders avoided the risk that two levels of government would claim overlapping power, would compete with, or would vilify one another. And, because the people of each state would enact slightly different laws in exercising the police power, factions would be hard pressed to spread their destructive influence from one state to another, from one state to the federal government, or from the federal government to a State.

The influence of factious leaders may kindle a flame within their particular States but will be unable to spread a general conflagration through the other States. A religious sect may degenerate into a political faction in a part of the [nation]; but the variety of sects dispersed over the entire face of it must secure the national councils against any danger from that source. A rage for paper money, for an abolition of debts, for an equal division of property, or for any other improper or wicked project, will be less apt to pervade the whole body of the Union[.] . . *In the extent and proper structure of the Union, therefore, we behold a republican remedy for the diseases most incident to republican government. [. . .]*

Amendment 4 of *The Second Bill of Rights* confirms the police power of the States, subject to each citizen's common exercise of liberty rights. Section 3 of Amendment 4 stops federal bullying of States, by preventing the national government from making any law, rule, or order requiring a State to exercise its police power in a specific way as a condition of receiving federal largesse.

> 3. Neither Congress nor the Executive shall make any law, rule, or order requiring a State to exercise the police power in a specific manner as a condition of receiving grants, appropriations, funds, or benefits from, or avoiding penalties imposed by, the federal government. All such conditions shall be held illegal and void.

The purposes of Section 3 are (i) to minimize the overlap between a State's police power and imagined (but not enumerated) federal power;[156] and (ii) to break the influence of factions (special interests) in Washington DC over police power issues in the States. In essence, Section 3 represents a return to Madison's model for appropriately managing factions. First, isolate the issues associated with exercising the police power from the enumerated powers assigned to the national government, and, second, separate the location where the police power is exercised—state capitals—from the nation's capital, Washington DC.

Why did the country move away from Madison's structure of non-overlapping federal and state power? How did we reach today's situation, in which the federal government asserts overlapping control of everything with States, and in which federal and state governments compete with, frustrate, and vilify one another? This transformation began as the Civil War ended. The Civil War Amendments banned slavery (the Thirteenth), created new U.S. citizens (the Fourteenth) and granted the right to vote (the Fifteenth) to former slaves. No longer property, former slaves were U.S. citizens.

Yet, equal rights (both economic and civil) for all citizens, black and white, did not flow naturally or smoothly from the ashes of war. A newly reconstituted legislature in Mississippi re-opened the political conflict in May 1865

---

156 See, Numbers 12 and 13 for a discussion of the Founders' concept of a limited federal government, with enumerated powers, and a discussion of the sweeping clause (now called the *necessary and proper* clause).

by enacting the Black Codes. Other states followed. Congress responded first with the Civil Rights Act of 1866, and next in March 1867, with the first of the Reconstruction Acts. Congress declared that no legal legislature existed in ten of the Southern states. These states were placed under military jurisdiction in five districts. Because its constitutional power was uncertain, Congress decided that the text of each of the Civil War Amendments would give Congress enforcement power inside the States.[157] Congress then passed the Fourteenth Amendment, and required each Southern state to ratify it as a condition of re-admittance to the Union. With this new legislative power, Congress could, for the first time, assert itself in matters affecting racial equality,[158] as it had already tried to do in 1866:

> [Black citizens] shall have the same right, in every State and Territory in the United States, to make and enforce contracts, to sue, be parties, and give evidence, to inherit, purchase, lease, sell, hold, and convey real and personal property, and to full and equal benefit of all laws and proceedings for the security of person and property, as is enjoyed by white citizens, and shall be subject to like punishment, pains, and penalties, and to none other, any law, statute, ordinance, regulation, or custom, to the contrary notwithstanding. [Excerpt, Civil Rights Act of 1866]

Madison's means for managing factions—sturdy separation of each State's police power from the enumerated powers of the national government—had been overridden with respect to racial equality.[159] But, what about the remaining police power of States—the everyday functions of state law that didn't involve racial equality? Would Madison's

---

157 See, Number 10, above, generally, for a discussion of the constitutional contradictions Congress faced at the end of the Civil War. Each Civil War Amendment contains language giving Congress enforcement power.

158 Before 1866, the police power resided exclusively in states.

159 It is hard to see how Congress might have acted differently. Congress did not yet know that the Supreme Court would discard the privileges or immunities clause from the Fourteenth Amendment in the *Slaughterhouse Cases*. It did not yet know that *Slaughterhouse* would "discover" two different classes of citizenship, or that Jim Crow, and *separate but equal* would follow. With reason, Congress had little faith in state legislatures, state courts, and the Supreme Court: 620,000 Americans had died in the Civil War, more than all losses in all American wars. Congressional Republicans were intent on obtaining and exercising power (the "means") to secure freedom, including economic and civil rights for former slaves (the "end") in the face of any contrary power.

concept survive as a curb on factions if federal power expanded still further into the realm of the police power of states?

A firm answer did not come until the 1930's—in the New Deal. Congress enacted legislation that authorized a federal agency to control the crops that could be grown within the States, down to individual farms. It relied on *both* the third of the eighteen enumerated powers in Article I, Section 8—*to regulate commerce among the States*—and on the last of the eighteen—the *necessary and proper* clause (known by the Founders as the *sweeping clause*).[160] In *Wickard v. Filburn,* the Supreme Court let the law stand in a 5-4 decision. Federal power had been permitted to substantially overlap the police power of states.[161] The control Madison placed in the Constitution to curb factions through distributed exercise of the police power was turned off. Factions quickly learned how to end-run the States by heading for Washington, where the disruptive effects of faction have been magnified ever since.[162] With the Founders' original curb on factions dismantled, interest group lobbying before Congress and the Executive is commonplace, relentless. Madison's great fear has been realized—that *government administered by men over men* might not be able *to control itself* in the face of factions.

The National Maximum Speed Law (NMSL)

In response to the Arab Oil Embargo in 1973, Congress enacted the Emergency Highway Energy Conservation Act, which gave States a *choice* in the exercise of their police power with respect to traffic speed—either adopt a uniform 55 mph speed limit or the Secretary of Transportation would disapprove funding for all that state's highway projects within the national system of interstate and defense highways.[163] States *chose* to *obey*. The NMSL was very unpopular, with modest gains in fuel economy.

---

160 See, Number 13, above, for a discussion of the *exhaustive list* of powers in the Constitution.

161 See, Number 19, above. Filburn set aside eleven acres of wheat for his own consumption on his own farm—yet the Court held that the power to regulate commerce among the states was so broad that Congress could prevent him from growing more wheat than the Department of Agriculture had authorized him to grow. In Madison's day, what a farmer grew on his own land for his own consumption was not a federal matter.

162 Indeed, political scientists began to call the new clash of factions "Interest Group Liberalism."

163 Bill Summary & Status, 93rd Congress, Public Law 93-239, Library of Congress (Thomas).

And, it conflicted with common-sense exercise of state police power! Speed limits in Nebraska need not be the same as in New York City! Non-compliance rates were above 82 percent in New York, Connecticut, and Texas. South Dakota's Highway Patrol director asked the following:

> Why must I have a trooper stationed on an interstate, at 10 in the morning, worried about a guy driving 60 mph on a system designed [for] 70 mph? He could be out on a Friday night watching for drunken drivers.[164]

Factions railed at one another in Washington over safety, fuel economy, and enforcement, while drivers ignored the law and police uncomfortably looked the other way. After several small retreats, all federal speed limits were lifted in 1995.[165]

Right Turn on Red

Young Americans have no memory of another federal-state power struggle. The issue: would drivers be allowed to turn right on a red light in Massachusetts? Massachusetts was the last of the fifty states to enact federally required legislation adopting a right on red law. Failure to comply with the federal requirement for such a state law by January 1, 1980, would result in loss of $1.4 million in U.S. Department of Energy funding for state projects.

Citizens in Massachusetts saw an unusual flurry of activity in the last days of 1979. Approximately 10,000 "No Turn on Red" signs were erected at more than 90 percent of the state's 3,100 intersections. The state was entitled to reimbursement from the U.S. DOT of 75 percent of the $470,000 cost for these signs. State officials made a strict interpretation of the federal "Manual on Uniform Traffic Control Devices for Streets and Highways" to decide that essentially all of the intersections should be marked "No Turn on Red." Federal officials promised to investigate state and local officials for an overly strict view of the federal manual. *The final scorecard in this round of federal/state foolishness*: the U.S. Department of Energy got its state legislation; Massachusetts got its $1.4 million;

---

164 See, *www.wikipedia.org*—under Emergency Highway Energy Conservation Act.
165 In 1979, the National Highway Traffic Safety Administration issued regulations telling car manufacturers what speedometers should look like, with emphasis on 55 mph and a max speed of 85 mph shown. This regulation, too, quietly disappeared, after factions churned the issue round and round in Washington DC.

10,000 signs went up for which the federal government got the bill; and lots of DPW holiday overtime was paid. Oh! On Massachusetts roads—not much changed.[166]

Federal/state competition over who controls the police power continues today, from roads, to signs, to water, wastewater, schools, and even the air we breathe. Congress uses a carrot and stick to reward states that do what it wants and punish states that don't. Funding reductions, denial of or delay in permits, approvals, and waivers provide the day-to-day battleground for new episodes of government vs. government. Factions in Washington press on for even greater overlap of federal power with that of states, reaching across the entire society, creating confusion and contradictions in law, and pitting group against group.[167]

Controlling Factions by Ending Divisive Competition among Governments

No one in 1868 could foresee that the relationship between Congress and the States would evolve well beyond racial equality to a competition over duplicative power, with rewards [carrots] to states who accept federal to-do lists; and punishment [sticks] to states that resist.

Section 3 of Amendment 4 minimizes the wasteful, unproductive game of federal vs. state government. Section 3 bans federal conditions—carrots and sticks—when the subject of the carrot or stick is the exercise of state police power. Section 4 of the Amendment assigns disputes over any such conditions to the courts of the several States, reviewable by the U.S. Supreme Court with due deference to each State's exercise of its police power.

Government vs. government, funded by taxpayers, is a game Madison never intended be played. To control factions in Washington, the feds needs to stop bullying States. *The Second Bill of Rights* restores Madison's model for durable restraints on the destructive power of factions.

Atticus

---

166 *Boston Globe* articles: two on January 3, 1980; one on March 27, 1980;

167 The most recent examples include: President Bush's "No Child Left Behind" Educational Program; President Obama's "Race to the Top" Educational Program; The Patient Protection and Affordable Care Act, enacted in January 2010 (Obama Care), and The Dodd-Frank Wall Street Reform and Consumer Protection Act of 2010.

NUMBER 31.
Cases and Controversies Involving the Police Power

As noted in Number 28, the decision in *Slaughterhouse*, and the century-old effort by subsequent justices of that Court to minimize or avoid the effect of that decision, are poor substitutes for the more direct fix contained in Sections 1 and 2 of Amendment 4. But, the tortured reading of the Fourteenth Amendment by the Court in *Slaughterhouse* cuts much more deeply. As the reality of Jim Crow was understood, beginning in the Court's 1954 decision in *Brown v. Board of Education*, federal courts have been slicing away at this aspect of the *Slaughterhouse* decision.

We can't go back to travel the very different road the country would have taken if the Court in *Slaughterhouse* had instead confirmed that the vocation of black, white, Republican, and Democrat butchers—an economic liberty right—was protected from destruction by the State, and, if taken by the State, required fair compensation. Instead, the Court wrote the privileges or immunities clause out of the Fourteenth Amendment.

Reinterpretation of the Bill of Rights—originally intended to limit the power of Congress—into a judicially established limitation on State power, through the Fourteenth Amendment, is viewed as *heroic* by misinformed historians.[168] Through hundreds, indeed thousands of federal lawsuits, trials, appeals, and Supreme Court decisions, pieces of the Bill of Rights have been applied against the police power of the State—a process called selective incorporation in constitutional law.[169]

Very destructive patterns emerged as the federal courts found renewed courage at the end of the eighty-year hiatus between *Slaughterhouse* (1873) and *Brown v. Board of Education* (1954): (i) the conversion of state courts into bystanders in disputes between their citizens and their

---

168 That the effort to heal the wound of *Slaughterhouse* was only necessary because the Court had "shot the country in the foot" is conveniently overlooked.
169 Again, an effort made necessary from the wreckage of the *Slaughterhouse* decision.

States in the exercise of the police power; and (ii) growing disagreement among citizens whether federal courts were acting appropriately in the civil and economic rights areas. From one point of view, the federal courts allowed much of this debacle to occur in the first place over 80 years, because its ruling in *Slaughterhouse* created two classes of citizenship (state and U.S.), and allowed state interference with the economic rights of black citizens. There was a great deal of damage to repair in constitutional law, much of it self-inflicted, with solutions that were less than ideal. From the other point of view, rational citizens could conclude that since federal judges are not elected by voters and are not responsible to voters, they should have no authority to act as legislators rather than as judges, as usurpers of the police power rather than as judges, or as a national legislature forcing homogeneity in the exercise of the police power by States.

Amendment 4 in *The Second Bill of Rights* takes on the *Slaughterhouse* case directly, not by indirection—the Court's practice since 1873. Sections 1 and 2 restore a principled exercise of the police power to the States, with a presumption in favor of an individual's exercise of liberty rights (see Number 29). Section 3 stops congressional bullying of States in the exercise of their police power (See Number 30). Section 4 completes the restoration of the police power by confirming that each State's judges are on the front line in the protection of each citizen's liberty rights. The liberty rights of each citizen are set forth in Amendment 2. Requirements for due process under the Rule of Law and for equal protection of the laws, including protections against discrimination, are set forth in Amendment 3. The judges of each State, sworn to uphold the Constitution of the United States including the Rule of Law, are fully capable of handling cases arising under the police power.

Section 4 of Amendment 4 assigns such cases to the State courts, not the inferior courts of the federal judiciary.

> 3. All cases, in law and equity, arising under this amendment shall be heard in the courts of the several States. The Supreme Court may review such cases, with due deference to each State's exercise of the police power.

As an *auxiliary precaution* to protect the dividing lines among a citizen's liberty rights, a state's police power, and the enumerated powers of the national government, Section 4 confirms that the Supreme Court may review such cases,[170] but with due deference to each State's exercise of the police power. This limitation is to ensure that the states remain free to reach different conclusions in the exercise of the police power: for example, setting the driving age, setting the times for opening and closing of restaurants and bars, setting health standards, etc.

Amendment 4 is a direct fix to the wreckage caused by the decision in *Slaughterhouse*, relying on Amendments 1, 2, 3, and 4, together, to be successful.

With the liberty rights package in place, the competition between federal and state courts to protect liberty rights will end—the state judiciary can once again serve as a bulwark for liberty rights in the state's exercise of the police power, while the federal judiciary will once again serve in the same capacity with respect to the coercive power of Congress and the Executive. The Supreme Court can again serve *both* as a safety valve that allows differences in how the police power is executed within the States *and* as the bulwark for liberty rights against the national government. The legal nightmare of selective incorporation that has buried law students and professors, legislators, and citizens in confusion will also end, buttressed by a rebuttable constitutional presumption in favor of a citizen's exercise of liberty rights.

Slaughterhouse has never been expressly reversed by the Supreme Court. As of 2012, it is still of precedential value. The contortions of federal and state judges, Congress, and numerous state legislatures since 1873 need to stop. A simple, direct alternative is laid out in the *Liberty Rights Amendments* (1—4).

Valerius

---

170 The Court has always taken the view that it can review cases involving the rights of citizens.

NUMBER 32.
Timely Financial Statements of Use to
Voters before Federal Elections

The fiscal year of the United States ends on September 30, a month before [even-year] federal elections. The United States never balances its books! It does not prepare financial statements—for itself, Congress, or taxpayers. Amendment 5 imposes on the federal government the same general requirements the government imposes on state and local governments, and on private enterprises. It is well past time for the national government to prepare, keep, and maintain a set of accounting records that is intelligible to citizens. And, such information should be organized and distributed, just as the Securities and Exchange Commission requires for shareholders, at a time that is useful to American voters in national elections.

With the passage of the Securities Act in 1933[171] and the Exchange Act of 1934,[172] Congress did much to improve the collection and transmission of timely financial information about publicly held companies. Clearly *necessary and proper* in the exercise of its power to regulate commerce among the several states, the Securities and the Exchange Acts have served the nation well—not perfectly, but well. Both Acts recognize that investors in the stock and the bond markets are *voting*—with their decisions to invest, to elect members of boards of directors, and to elect officers. And, there is a clear federal role under the interstate commerce clause to ensure that stock transactions in the common market of the fifty states are based upon the availability of reasonably accurate, complete, and timely information.

A fundamental premise of both Acts is that actual shareholders and potential shareholders ought to receive the same financial information regarding the financial condition of a public corporation, and further,

---

171 May 27, 1933, Ch 38, Title I, § 1, 48 Stat. 74.
172 June 6, 1934, 48 Stat. 881.

that it ought to be accurate. Throughout our history, American investors, as investors across the world, have had to deal with manipulation of
stock and bond prices. In 1720, the South Sea Company bubble crashed
world-wide stock prices, and in particular, those in England.[173] The *Credit
Mobilier* scandal was a factor in the depression of 1873—a stock manipulation related to the construction of the transcontinental railroads.[174] In
the last century, a number of Americans became famous, indeed, notori-
ous, for fraudulent conduct in securities transactions: Charles Ponzi in
the 20s, Michael Milken in the 80s, and Bernie Madoff in 2008.[175]

The Securities and Exchange Commission knows how to evaluate the
completeness, accuracy, and timeliness of financial statements. The SEC
can bring enforcement actions on its own behalf. It approves registration statements in contests for control of public corporations. It investi-
gates allegations of insider trading—that is, the misuse of inside corporate information to manipulate stock or bond prices to the advantage of
the insider and the disadvantage of the public. In cooperation with the
Justice Department, it prosecutes violations of the securities law as felonies and has imposed both jail time and fines. In short, the SEC serves
as a state trooper on the highway of corporate transactions—ticketing
some, cautioning others, investigating others, and putting some people
out of the business of driving at all.

Congress has not stopped policing securities markets by establishing the
SEC. Congress has also authorized private suits by shareholders (and
other interested parties) against companies believed to have violated the
Securities Act or the Exchange Act. Every holder of a security (a share of
stock, a bond, or in some cases, an option) is a potential plaintiff—and
with all others, a powerful deterrent that far exceeds the staffing capac-

---

173 To refinance the debt incurred by the British Government during the War of
Spanish Succession, the Lord Treasurer of England (with the help of numerous members of Parliament) raised funds for the government by selling a trading monopoly in
South America (the "South Seas") to a new company, the South Sea Company. It was
allowed to raise capital to pay for the monopoly through the sale of stock throughout
England. The value of the stock was manipulated up by unfounded promises of high
returns on what turned out to be doubtful investments.
174 Credit Mobilier, holder of the federal concession to build the transcontinental
railroads, diverted resources away from the construction contractors (that they also
controlled). Many members of Congress were implicated in the resulting scandal, arising from manipulation of the amount of federal subsidies for the project.
175 See Number 46, below.

ity of the SEC to investigate. Every citizen with a 401(k) account or a pension account is part of the SEC's extended police force.[176]

These Acts require transparency (everyone gets the same information) in the securities market—protecting every potential or actual investor. The same information—accurate, complete, and timely—is prepared and made available to each participant. Individuals are then free to make their own choices regarding whether, where, and when to buy and sell in this market.

Section 1 of Amendment 5 requires government to act similarly. Like private sector participants in securities markets—government is a participant as well. Section 1 establishes new obligations upon the Executive to regularly prepare and present government-wide financial statements and to require that such information be presented to shareholders (citizens) in time to be considered before election of the government's officers and directors (Congress and the Executive).

There are three distinct parts to Section 1. The first sentence of Section 1 changes the fiscal year to begin on April 1 and end on March 31. This gives the Executive six (6) full months from the close of a fiscal year to prepare the required financial for presentation to Congress.

The second sentence of Section 1 requires that the President prepare and present to Congress before October 1 government-wide financial statements in the same general format imposed by the Government Accounting Standards Board (GASB) upon state and local governments.[177] The timing of the President's submittal to Congress is to provide time-

---

176 The SEC, the Department of Justice, and individual shareholders bringing suits under these Acts may seek to set aside any election of directors and officers of companies that have not complied with requirements to prepare and distribute, well in advance of the election, financial statements that are current, accurate, and reasonably complete. The purpose of these Acts is basic: to encourage completeness, accuracy, and timeliness of the information distributed and to deter fraudulent conduct in the management of American businesses.

177 GASB is an independent entity that prepares standards that state and local governments must meet. It is not part of the Executive branch or Congress, nor should it be. The requirements imposed by *GASB Statement No. 34—Basic Financial Statements—and Management's Discussion and Analysis—for State and Local Governments* are not as stringent as those imposed on private entities by FASB or by Congress. GASB standards have been successfully applied by thousands of state and local governments.

ly information to citizens before their vote in federal elections. Those citizens with an interest, and the media, will have a full month before federal elections to review financial statements prepared by their government, and to use this information in determining how to vote for candidates for the House, the Senate, and for President and Vice President. Financial information for the past year must be presented in comparison to the two prior years, and must include management discussion and analysis, a mechanism proven by seventy-five years of SEC practice to highlight important trends, disclose key assumptions, identify missing information, and provide corrections to previously reported data.

The third sentence of Section 1 requires the President to submit to Congress before October 1 his recommended budget for the next fiscal year, in a format consistent with government-wide financial statements. The timing of the President's submittal to Congress of a budget for the next fiscal year is the same, to give voters a chance to examine and consider the financial performance of the last three years and the President's proposed budget for the next year in casting their votes in federal election years.

In its entirety, Section 1 reads as follows:

1. The fiscal year for the federal government shall begin on April 1 and end on the following March 31. Before October 1, the President shall present to Congress government-wide financial statements in accord with generally accepted government accounting principles for the previous fiscal year with comparisons to the prior two fiscal years, and which shall: include a statement of net assets and a statement of activities; report all of the assets, the condition thereof, current and future liabilities, revenues, expenses, gains and losses of government; distinguish between governmental and business-type activities; and include discussion and analysis. Before October 1, the President shall present to Congress his recommended budget for the next fiscal year, in a format consistent with the government-wide financial statements, with projected revenues, expenses, gains, and losses, changes in assets and the condition thereof, current and future liabilities, along with discussion and analysis.

Voters are hungry for timely information regarding the current financial status of the national government, compared to the prior two years and compared to the budget proposed for the next year. This situation is little different from that facing a shareholder asked to vote for a new board of directors, for a merger, or for an acquisition. Voters in federal elections would like to make an informed choice among candidates, one element of which may be the financial condition of the government, and each candidate's positions relating to policies and programs that affect it.

The voter who is a shareholder faces the same problem: how to make an informed decision on the matter at hand. The shareholder must rely in part on the information provided by the company's management. In the private sector, Congress has made it a civil wrong (with fines and civil penalties) or a felony (with prison and criminal penalties) not to provide timely, accurate, and complete information to the private sector shareholder or bondholder.

"Do what I say, not what I do!" is simply no longer acceptable in a period of record debt, record deficits, the looming retirement of baby boomers, and change in international markets. Amendment 5 in *The Second Bill of Rights* takes a giant step toward fiscal and electoral transparency and accountability.

Amicus

NUMBER 33.
A Funny Thing Happened on the Way to the Bank—
the Dollar Went Away

A funny thing happened on the way to U.S. banks in March, April, May, and June of 1933.[178]

Before we turn to 1933—imagine you signed a construction contract as an American company with the government of Argentina in 1981, during its period of hyperinflation. Over the two year term, everyone expects prices for equipment, material, and labor to rise between 30% and 200% per year. At the time of your bid, a fair price is 10 million Argentine pesos. But you fear that with prices inflating between 30% and 200% each year—payment of only 10 million Argentine pesos will bankrupt your company and you!

What to do?

In 1981, the solution was simple—your contract with the Argentines must require payment in US dollars. Then, the Argentine government bears the risk of inflation. It must acquire whatever pesos are necessary—at the exchange rate in effect when payment is made—to convert to US dollars. Assume in 1982, when you are half complete, a new Argentine law states that any contract requiring payment other than in Argentine pesos is against public policy. Inflation reaches 35+% per year. Your company is paid 10 million pesos. The work costs 20 million pesos. You're bankrupt! [Remember your interest in a stable U.S. dollar as we move on.]

---

178 *A Funny Thing Happened on the Way to the Forum* was a 1962 Broadway musical with music and lyrics by Stephen Sondheim. According to Wikipedia: The book was inspired by the farces of the ancient Roman playwright Plautus (251–183 BC) and tells the bawdy story of a slave named Pseudolus and his attempts to win his freedom by helping his young master woo the girl next door. The book upon which the musical was based was written by Burt Shevelove and Larry Gelbart.

Without a stable US dollar, the world's commerce would be tentative and more expensive. Your 1981 solution in Argentina –payment in U.S. dollars—has been *THE* solution to worldwide currency concerns since World War II. The US dollar is the world's go-to medium of exchange for goods and services, for oil and natural gas, precious metals, and commodities.

Let's move forward to 2012. You are about to sign a contract with the U.S. government to construct a building over four years for $100 million U.S. dollars. This time, you are worried about U.S. inflation. Assume (*although this won*'t happen) that the government will pay the $100 million price—adjusted for inflation. If inflation is 20 percent in each of the four years, the price would be adjusted upward to $120 million after year one, $144 million after year two, $172.8 million after year three, and $207.36 million after year four.

With 1981 Argentina and 2012 United States in mind, let's go back to March-June 1933.

On Saturday, March 4, 1933, Franklin D. Roosevelt was inaugurated as the 32nd President of the United States, the last President inaugurated on March 4.

FDR got busy!

On Monday, March 6, the President declared a bank holiday until March 9,[179] closing banks across the nation. On the same day, with FDR's approval, the Treasury Secretary instructed the Treasurer to make no payments of U.S. obligations in gold unless the payee had a license issued by the Secretary.

During the bank holiday, on Thursday, March 9, Congress passed the "Emergency Banking Relief Act," which confirmed what the President had already done without legislative authority, and which authorized the President to investigate, regulate, or prohibit "any transactions in foreign exchange, inter-bank transfers, and export, hoarding, melting, or earmarking of gold or silver coin or bullion or currency by any person." The Act authorized the Secretary to require all Americans to deliver

---

179 Facts taken from the decision of the U.S. Supreme Court in *Norman v. Baltimore & O.R. Co. United States et al v. Bankers Trust Co. et al*, 294, U.S. 240 (1935).

"any or all gold coin, gold bullion, and gold certificates owned by them to the Treasurer of the United States."

On March 10, one day after passage of the Act, the President authorized banks to reopen, but prohibited removal of gold coin, gold bullion, or gold certificates except as authorized by the Secretary. Instead, all gold and gold certificates were to be turned in before May 1, 1933.

In four days, gold was illegal to hold as an investment.[180]

On May 12, 1933, in a provision of the Agricultural Adjustment Act, the President was authorized to "fix the weight of a gold dollar in grains nine tenth fine . . . at such amounts as he finds necessary . . . but in no event shall the weight of the gold dollar be fixed so as to reduce its present weight by more than 50 per cent . ." Congress authorized the President to pay [in devalued currency] 50 percent of what the government had previously promised to pay its creditors.[181]

Take a breath! Consider events in 1933. For one hundred years prior to March 4, 1933, innumerable citizens had entered into contracts protecting lenders from the effects of inflation. Private lenders could agree with debtors to take payments in gold, silver, or in inflated equivalent dollars. Within six days of FDR's inauguration, it was against public policy to sign a contract requiring payment in gold or silver and illegal to hold gold or silver. Within two months, debtors could clear their debt by paying only 60 percent of their obligations with deflated currency.

A funny thing DID happen on the way to the bank in 1933! Forty percent of the dollar went away.

We can best imagine the reaction by considering what would happen if U.S. banks were told by the government to reduce every American's 401(k) account by 40 percent after a bank holiday. Some holiday!

---

180 Quite a contrast from what the Founders envisioned. *The Coinage Act of 1792* pegged the value of the U.S. dollar to a specific quantity and purity of gold, and encouraged citizens to bring the gold they held in for coinage.
181 On January 30, 1934, after a great commotion, Congress and the President agreed to limit this confiscation to 40 percent of the value of the dollar in gold (rather than 50 percent). Gold Reserve Act of 1934.

A thin 5-4 majority of the Supreme Court chose not to invalidate these shenanigans in *Norman v. Baltimore Co United States v. Bankers Trust Co,* 294 U.S. 240 (1935). Mr. Justice McReynold's dissent (in which Justices Van Devanter, Sutherland, and Butler joined) is blistering.

[We] conclude that, if given effect, the enactments here challenged will bring about confiscation of property rights and repudiation of national obligations. Acquiescence in the decisions just announced is impossible; the circumstances demand statement of our views. 'To let oneself slide down the easy slope offered by the course of events and to dull one's mind against the extent of the danger, . . . that is precisely to fail in one's obligation of responsibility.'

Just men regard repudiation and spoliation of citizens by their sovereign with abhorrence; but we are asked to affirm that the Constitution has granted power to accomplish both. No definite delegation of such a power exists; and we cannot believe the farseeing framers, who labored with hope of establishing justice and securing the blessings of liberty, intended that the expected government should have authority to annihilate its own obligations and destroy the very rights which they were endeavoring to protect. Not only is there no permission for such actions; they are inhibited. And no plenitude of words can conform them to our charter [the Constitution]. . .

The dissenters were troubled by government interference with private contractual rights in corporate bonds.

The gold clauses in these bonds were valid and in entire harmony with public policy when executed. They are property. . . To destroy a validly acquired right is the taking of property. . . . They established a measure of value and supply a basis for recovery if broken. Their policy and purpose were stamped with affirmative approval by the government when inserted in its bonds.

. . .

The purpose of section 43 [of the Agricultural Adjustment Act] . . . *was clearly stated by the Senator who presented it.*[182] *It was the destruction of lawfully acquired rights.*

. . . [I]f this power exists Congress may readily destroy other obligations which present obstruction to the desired effect of further depletion. The destruction of all obligations by reducing the standard gold dollar to one grain of gold, or brass or nickel or copper or lead will become an easy possibility. Thus we reach the fundamental question which must control the result of the controversy in respect of corporate bonds . . . We think that in the circumstances Congress had no power to destroy the obligations of the gold clauses in private obligations. . . [T]o do this was plain usurpation, arbitrary, and oppressive.

Since 1935, Congress has increasingly deferred to the Federal Reserve System, its chairman and its constituent bank presidents, to manage the value of gold against the U.S. dollar. In sum, Congress has delegated its enumerated power over coinage and currency to a third party.

Amendment 5, Section 2, restores the Founders' view that a stable currency is only possible if Congress *alone* is responsible to voters for its equivalent value in gold coin.

Congress shall by law establish the number of grains of gold nine-tenths fine that shall be the standard unit of value equivalent to the U.S. dollar, which standard shall thereafter be adjusted only through legislation originating in the House of Representatives, and passed by three fifths of both the House of Representatives and the Senate. All forms of money issued or coined by the United States shall be in parity with this standard. Congress shall not delegate the setting or adjustment of this standard to anyone, including the Executive.

---

182 He said: "It will be my task to show that if the amendment shall prevail it has potentialities as follows: It may transfer from one class to another class in these United States value to the extent of almost $200,000,000,000. [$200 billion]. This value will be transferred, first, from those who own the bank deposits. Secondly, this value will be transferred from those who own bonds and fixed investments." Cong. Record, April, 1933, pp. 2004, 2216-19.

Congress *alone* will take future decisions to confiscate the property of American citizens through currency deflation, rather than hidden policies of the Federal Reserve, the Executive, or unnamed officials.

Amicus

NUMBER 34.
No Department of Circumlocution!

On February 17, 2009, the Senate and the House passed, and the President signed, H.R. 1—the American Recovery and Reinvestment Act of 2009 (ARRA or the Stimulus Act). Division A of the Act appropriated $787 billion to recovery and reinvestment, including federal funding for many hundreds of *projects* that politicians described as *shovel ready*—that is, *ready to go*. The Act requires listing of such projects within forty-five days, and completion within one year.

Section 5 declares all expenditures an emergency—exempting the $787 billion from "pay-as-you-go policies" enacted in the prior Congress. The President repeated the claim that hundreds of *shovel ready projects* were waiting for funding under the Act, would keep unemployment under 8%, and would begin a *summer of recovery* by 2010. Factions convinced the President to make the following public statements, both before and after passage of the Act:

Dec 7, 2008
> I think we can get a lot of work done fast.
> When I met with the governors, all of them have projects that are shovel ready.

Dec 15, 2008
> We've got shovel ready projects all across the country.

Dec 16, 2008
> Shovel ready projects, rebuilding our roads, our bridges.

March 3, 2009
> We are seeing shovels hit the ground.

May 8, 2009
> Shovels are breaking ground and cranes dot the sky

July 15, 2009
> Shovels will soon be moving earth and trucks will soon be pouring concrete

August 15, 2009

There are almost a hundred shovel ready projects already approved in Colorado which are beginning to create jobs. [183]

By mid-2010, the *summer of recovery* had not appeared, unemployment had exceeded 10 percent (then settled around 9 percent), and cranes did not dot the sky.

October 13, 2010

The *New York Times* magazine, quoting the President.

[The President] realized too late that "there's no such thing as 'shovel ready projects' when it comes to public works."

June 13, 2011, Jobs Council Meeting

'Shovel ready' was not as 'shovel ready' as we expected.

The Stimulus Act is classic verification of the evils of faction (Madison's great fear) in the administration of government. No federal employee turns a shovel, prepares a plan, checks a design, or operates a machine used in construction.[184] Very few state or local government employees turn a shovel, prepare a plan, check a design, or operate a machine used in construction.[185] Virtually all significant public works projects at the state and local levels—highways, roads, water, sewer, bridges—are designed in the private sector and built by privately owned general contractors—after years of advanced preparation.

To anyone even remotely familiar with the construction industry, the notion that thousands of *shovel ready projects* worth half a trillion dollars could be listed in forty-five days and completed in one year is silly! *Yes*, local governments can place a top coat of paving on sub-surfaces that would need more than a year to properly repair—in effect, throwing the top coat away after a few years. *Yes*, towns can paint or make cosmetic fixes to public infrastructure, without improving long term condition. *No*, you can't spend $500 billion dollars wisely on public infrastructure in one year. Silly—disgustingly silly!

---

183 Search YouTube on the Web for "shovel-ready projects."

184 We ignore military construction, a tiny portion of which may be done by uniformed personnel.

185 A small portion of state and local public works expenditures is through directly performed labor.

At best, the President and the Congress were misinformed by the factions clamoring for funds in favor of particular industries, companies, and unions, at the expense of all Americans. Even more preposterous are the spend-it-or-lose-it provisions of the Act. *FAST* is the criteria that Congress favored.[186] State and local governments were told to spend money quickly—be a spendthrift—if you want part of the $787 billion in ARRA funding, *or lose it*. No parent gives money to children with a requirement to spend it all, or return it! Congress does this routinely.

Will your Town repave roads with ARRA money even if they don't need repaving? Good!

Does your Town have a sinking fund for a high school in 5 years? Bad, no ARRA $$ for you!

The limited government Washington, Madison, Adams, Franklin, and Hamilton established had no power to enact any bill for the purpose of spending. At its core, ARRA consists of a congressional desire to spend tax money quickly. The specifics don't matter, where doesn't matter, what doesn't matter—just quickly! Factions promoting the Act know how to win the race to the $787 billion. Outsiders (the rest of us) are too late! Elected officials unfamiliar with construction are sufficiently naive to believe that stimulus will work and that administrators will fairly spend $787 billion, yet they are unable to even write the law without input from the tiniest of factions within the industry to openly earmark the legislation. The ARRA is a model of how *not* to spend half a trillion dollars.

How not to do it! was the subject of an amusing chapter in one of Charles Dickens' novels, *Little Dorrit*.[187] The characters in the novel are continually frustrated by the Department of Circumlocution (circular motion), an aggregation of the ministries within the British government. Dickens' description is well worth a careful read today: a 150-year-old reminder that Dickens and the Founders all understood the difficulties inherent in *any government administered by men over men*.

---

186 Fear for reelection might have been a motivator behind FAST.
187 Chapter 10—*Containing the Whole Science of Government.* (Monthly Serial, December 1855 to June 1857).

The Circumlocution Office was (as everybody knows without being told) the most important Department under Government. No public business of any kind could possibly be done at any time without the acquiescence of the Circumlocution Office. Its finger was in the largest public pie, and in the smallest public tart. It was equally impossible to do the plainest right and to undo the plainest wrong without the express authority of the Circumlocution Office. . . . . .

Whatever was required to be done, the Circumlocution Office was beforehand with all the public departments in the art of perceiving—HOW NOT TO DO IT.

. . . . .

It is true that HOW NOT TO DO IT was the great study and object of all public departments and professional politicians all round the Circumlocution Office. It is true that every new premier and every new government, coming in because they had upheld a certain thing as necessary to be done, were no sooner come in than they applied their utmost faculties to discovering HOW NOT TO DO IT. It is true that from the moment when a general election was over, every returned man who had been raving on hustings because it hadn't been done, and who had been asking the friends of the honourable gentleman in the opposite interest on pain of impeachment to tell him why it hadn't been done, and who had been asserting that it must be done, and who had been pledging himself that it should be done, began to devise, HOW IT WAS NOT TO BE DONE. It is true that the debates of both Houses of Parliament the whole session through uniformly tended to the protracted deliberation HOW NOT TO DO IT. It is true that the royal speech at the opening of such session virtually said, My lords and gentlemen, you have a considerable stroke of work to do, and you will please to retire to your respective chambers and discuss, HOW NOT TO DO IT. It is true that the royal speech, at the close of such session, virtually said, My lords and gentlemen, you have through several laborious months been considering with great loyalty and patriotism, HOW NOT TO DO IT, and you have found out; and with the blessing Providence upon the harvest (natural and political), I

171

now dismiss you. All this is true, but the Circumlocution Office went beyond it.

Because the Circumlocution Office went on mechanically, every day, keeping this wonderful, all-sufficient wheel of statesmanship, HOW NOT TO DO IT, in motion. Because the Circumlocution Office was down upon any ill-advised public servant who was going to do it, or who appeared to be by any surprising accident in remote danger of doing it, with a minute, and a memorandum, and a letter of instructions that extinguished him. *It was this spirit of national efficiency in the Circumlocution Office that had gradually led to its having something to do with everything.*

The Constitution was structured by the Founders to prevent the federal government from engaging in the endless circular motion (the agitation) caused by factions in Congress or the Executive. The Constitution is unique—exceptional—in that it enumerates in writing the powers the States and the people conferred on the government. Within this limited range—Congress is free to discover *how to do it!* or *how not to do it!* Outside this limited range, such decisions are left to the states or the people. With the *Liberty Rights Amendments* (1—4) of *The Second Bill of Rights* in place, the Founders' structure preventing circumlocution orchestrated by the federal government will be restored.

Valerius

NUMBER 35.
The Greedy Hand of Government

Amity Shlaes opens her 1999 book *The Greedy Hand*, with a quote from Thomas Paine:

> If, from the more wretched parts of the old world, we look at those which are in an advance stage of improvement, *we* still find *the greedy hand of government thrusting itself into every corner and crevice of industry*, and *grasping the spoil of the multitude. Invention* [creativity] *is continually exercised, to furnish new pretenses for revenues and taxation. [The Greedy Hand] watches prosperity as its prey and permits none to escape without tribute.*

Download a copy of the current edition of Title 26 of the United States Code (the Internal Revenue Code or the Code) from *http://uscode.house. gov/download/title_26.shtm*. The unformatted file is 28.3 megabytes. Converted to standard PDF format, 8 ½ x 11 inches in size, Title 26 is 7,947 pages long. Regulations implementing the Code are much longer. The Code is 2 1/2 times as long as Leo Tolstoy's *War and Peace* (2,882 pages, 5.7 megabytes),[188] and *10+ times longer than the King James version of the Bible* (742 pages, 2.6 megabytes).[189]

Since 1939, the federal government has moved past revenue into social engineering. The Code influences every citizen's life differentially— pushing, pulling, warning, and rewarding—depending on whether the choices we make are favored or disfavored in the Code. The Code drives gambling and bartering—and it drives the underground economy. The Code affects: your clothes, your work, your marriage, your house, your baby, your school, your accountant, your success, your retirement, and your death.[190]

---

188 Usually described as the longest book in the world. *http://www.taybacuniversity.edu*
189 *http://www.bookbindery.ca/KJBIBLE.pdf*
190 *The Greedy Hand: How Taxes Drive Americans Crazy and What to Do About It,* by Amity

The Effect on Individuals—Are We a Nation of Scofflaws?

Need the kid down the street to mow your lawn? A baby sitter for Friday night? Someone to help with spring cleaning? Someone to walk the dog? Check Title 26, Subtitle C, Chapter 21, Subchapter C, Section 3121(d)(3)(C) to see if you have hired a *home worker performing work according to your specifications.* If so, you may have an *employee.*

Providing food to a *home worker* for your *convenience?* Check Title 26, Subtitle A, Chapter 1, Subchapter B, Part III, Section 119.

Taking your kid to a major league baseball game? If he catches a home run and gives it back to the hitter—does he owe the IRS a gift tax?[191]

Getting a sitter from a service? Check Title 26, Subtitle C, Chapter 25, Section 3506.

Setting up a real-estate brokerage business in your home town? Check Title 26, Subtitle C, Chapter 25, Section 3508 to see whether your brokers must be treated as employees.

Won a big personal injury suit? Check Title 26, Subtitle A, Chapter 1, Subchapter B, Part III, Section 104 to learn whether receipts are taxable. Better hire a lawyer and an accountant to *structure* your settlement to avoid or minimize tax.

Thinking about setting aside some money for your retirement (with your family medical history in mind)? The Code will tell you what you can do, when you can do it, and how you can get the money you've set aside.

Asked by your company to relocate? The Code tells you whether reimbursement for relocating to a house acceptable to your spouse and kids is income to you or a deduction to your boss.

Shlaes, Random House, New York, 1999, Table of Contents. *The Greedy Hand* is a sobering reminder how subtly, yet pervasively, the federal government has crawled deep into the lives of individuals Americans.

191 In September 1998, the IRS took this position regarding the soon to be hit 72nd home run by Mark McGwire. If a fan returned the ball to McGwire—worth $1,000,000 on the street—a gift tax of $145,000 would be *due from the fan.* Congress moved to undo these threats before the hit. The IRS backed off, as long as the ball was instantly given to McGwire. *The Greedy Hand, supra,* at p. 11.

Sixty-five years old, but want to work longer because inflation has re-duced the value of your nest egg? How much can you earn before you lose social security benefits? Check the Code.

Built a business yourself? Own the family farm? Inherit the family cot-tage? Can you afford to *both* pay a 50+ percent estate tax and pass the business, the farm, or the vacation home down to your children? You'll need to understand how Chapters 1 (Income Taxes and Surtaxes), 11 (Estate Tax); 12 (Gift Tax); and 13 (Tax on Generation-Skipping Trans-fers) work, and you'll need expert advice on whether you should buy expensive life insurance and establish multiple trusts to have a realistic hope of passing a business, farm, or cottage down to your family.

The income, estate, and gift taxes—Title 26 of the United States Code—are the weapons Congress uses to micromanage the daily lives of Ameri-can citizens.

The Effect on Businesses—a Cesspool of Differential Treatment

The effect of the Code on American business is both disgusting and ab-surd. Thousands upon thousands of differential tax benefits and treat-ments have been (1) written into the Code by the tiniest of *factions* [using Madison's term], (2) inserted into legislation by cooperative members of Congress or Executive officials, (3) bundled with similar insertions by other factions through other members of Congress, (4) passed into law, and (5) signed by the President.

The energy exerted by factions to gain tax preferences is breathtaking! Millions of busy bees working 24x7, 365 days each year. Title 26 is an-other flagship of Dickens' Department of Circumlocution—*how not to do it!* Thousands of factions have created extraordinary complexity, denied equal protection of the law, and interfered with the ordinary exercise of liberty rights by citizens. Use the Find function to confirm that the Greedy Hand of Government actively promotes [or crushes] even the tiniest piece of American society.[192]

Search the Code for basketball. Special language in Section 1317(S) provides tax exempt bonds for a $225 million facility if:

---

192   Only a few of many, many examples are set forth below.

(i) such facility is to be used by both a National Hockey League team and a National Basketball Association team, (ii) such facility is to be constructed on a platform using air rights over land acquired by a State authority and identified as site B in a report dated May 30, 1984, prepared for a State urban development corporation, and (iii) such facility is eligible for real property tax (and power and energy) benefits pursuant to State legislation approved and effective as of July 7, 1982.

Congress has no courage to name the facility, but courage enough for special legislation earmarked to benefit a private sector interest. No ordinary American can get such a preference.

Search for curling—a game pushing weights along an icy surface with brooms. In 1965, Congress removed a 10 percent tax on curling equipment—but kept it in place for fishing equipment. Curling got a boost—fishing didn't.

Search for borough—and you find a special rule for certain tax exempt bonds:

(6) Special rule for certain high cost housing area
In the case of a project located in *a city having 5 boroughs and a population in excess of 5,000,000,* subparagraph (B) of paragraph (1) shall be applied by substituting "25 percent" for "40 percent."

Congress has no courage to name New York as the only such city, but this provision allows a different percentage of apartment buildings in New York to be subsidized by tax-exempt financing. Too bad if you are trying to get the same treatment elsewhere!

Search for pests and you will learn that Section 263A(d) of the Code gives farmers whose edible crops have been destroyed by pests favorable treatment if he or she replants the same type of crop either on the same land or on other land of the same acreage. Different crop? Different acreage? Different tax result! Government knows more than farmers what to plant!

When in a Hole—Stop Digging!

None of this—*none of it*—would be possible without the Code itself, and the opportunity it provides for differential treatment of citizens and businesses. Since 1939, when the Code was enacted, Congress has been unable to *perfect* the language. Supposedly *deceitful* citizens adjust to avoid taxation and create *loopholes, forcing factions* to push a *reluctant* Congress to establish ever more complex *fixes*. Lawmakers lament its imperfections, and perennially run for election on the conceit that perfect words will be found to *reform* the Code. Congress just hasn't yet found the right words and the right 7,947 pages to produce the perfectly fair income, estate, and gift tax code.[193]

All of this is pretense! Nonsense! Decades of experience confirms a simple truth:

1. Factions have succeeded in lobbying Congress and the Executive to add millions of barnacles into the Code, favoring some individuals and businesses over others.

2. Factions use the coercive power of government to pick winners and losers—just what Madison feared from "any government administered by men over men."[194]

3. The tax code is a major divider of Americans, so absurdly detailed that all Americans, in one way or another, are technically tax scofflaws.

The very notion that 537 elected Americans[195] have *both* sufficient mental capacity and sufficient knowledge to write and implement this complexity is absurd—silly on its face.[196]

---

193 As Shlaes notes in *The Greedy Hand, supra,* at chapter 4, it is not possible to write the income tax to simultaneously support the family, keep progressivity, and lower rates for a second family earner.

194 See Numbers 3, 4, and 5, *supra.*

195 435 members of the House, 100 members of the Senate, and the President and Vice President.

196 See Number 5, specifically, the economic analysis of Hayek.

The Second Bill of Rights Amendment 6 proposes to abolish the income, estate, and gift taxes in their entirety in favor of a consumption tax closely modeled on The Fair Tax. As a backup to this proposal, *The Second Bill of Rights* Alternate Amendment 6 proposes a dramatically simplified income tax with constitutional protections against the abuse of factions in its administration.

Amicus

NUMBER 36.
One Consumption Tax In Place of Income, Estate, and Gift Taxes

The monstrosity that has become the Tax Code provides one of the best examples why the barnacles that have attached themselves to the hull of the U.S.(S.) Constitution need to be scraped clean. The 8,000-page Code is Exhibit A in demonstrating how factions have taken control from Congress, the Treasury Department, and the IRS of a system that is now so complex, so divisive, and so absurd that reforming it makes no sense.

The fault is not with the framework the Founders established. The Founders' aim was to prevent the use of its taxing authority to micro-manage the lives of citizens or to favor or disfavor personal choices made in their daily lives.

Instead, the Founders established a republic with a Rule of Law that is unique in the history of mankind. External and internal controls in the Constitution prevented runaway complication of federal law. Power was allocated among the people, the states, and the national government by a written Constitution. Broad liberty rights were retained by the people. States kept the police power, to preserve the common exercise of liberty rights. The people granted limited, enumerated powers to the national government. The national government's powers were separated among Congress, the Executive, and the Judiciary. Outside this framework, as a further check on it, the Founders made sure the common law could develop through an independent state and federal judiciary.[197]

The U.S. Tax Code is merely a symptom of the great problem on which the Founders focused—how to oblige any government administered by some over others to control itself.[198]

---

197 These principles are collected and given greater prominence as the first of the Liberty Rights Amendments to *The Second Bill of Rights* (Amendment 1).
198 "[T]he great difficulty lies in this: you must first enable the government to

The language coming out of Washington DC to describe how the Code can be *reformed* is nonsense. For example, *deductions* available under the Code are called *tax expenditures* by the talking heads in DC. A tax deduction is called a *tax expenditure* by some in Congress, because Congress receives less money from taxpayers if taxable income is reduced. Read that again, if it doesn't make sense! It still won't make sense until you begin with the proposition that every dollar every American earns is the government's dollar—to be taken or not at the discretion of members of Congress who are influenced by the factions that support them.

According to the Tax Foundation, the IRS estimates Americans spend 6.6 billion hours per year filling out tax forms—1.6 billion hours on the 1040 form alone.[199] The cost of tax compliance is estimated to have grown from $79+ billion in 1990 to $243+ billion in 2004, and projected to grow to $482+ billion in 2015.[200] Most astounding is that the cost of compliance is expected to rise from 14 percent of total revenue collected to more than 20 percent of total revenue.

Is there a better use for 6.6 billion hours of American brainpower per year? Is there a better use for $482+ billion dollars of taxpayer money each year? Is the machinery for collecting a tax too complex when those who pay have to spend an additional 20 percent to just comply?

It is not surprising that costs of compliance with the U.S. Tax Code is driving up the cost of goods made in the United States and driving business units overseas.

A Consumption Tax in Place of the Income, Estate, and Gift Taxes

The Tax Code doesn't need to be reformed; it needs to be replaced. Nearly a century of factions *perfecting* its language, its rates, and its details have only led to more complication and greater intrusion into the everyday lives of Americans. The American taxpayer just can't handle any more *help* from factions in *perfecting* the Income Tax code.

---

control the governed; and in the next place oblige it to control itself." Madison, *The Federalist Papers 51*, at p. 322. See Number 2, above.
199   *http://www.taxfoundation.org/research/topic/96.html*
200   "The Rising Cost of Complying with the Federal Income Tax," *Tax Foundation Special Report No. 138* (January 2006).

A century of bad results from the work of "factions" in Washington to "fix" the U.S. Tax Code has run its course—and failed. Adoption in the Constitution of a consumption tax on the retail sales of new goods and services, with a uniform exemption from personal expenditures paid monthly to every American citizen will move the nation back to the system envisioned by the Founders—a limited government, funded by consumption-type taxes. Amendment 6 to *The Second Bill of Rights* (the second of the *Finance and Revenue Amendments*) eliminates the estate, gift, and income taxes, and the excise tax on wages from daily life in America.[201]

The idea of a consumption tax on the retail sales of new goods and services is not new. A version of just such a tax, the so-called Fair Tax, has been pending in Congress since 1999, and has attracted more support as the enduring flaws of the Code become ever more obvious. The consumption tax is applied only once, never on resale of goods.

The consumption tax is an attractive substitute for the Code for many reasons beyond time and compliance cost savings:

- Every wage and salary earner takes home all of his pay, free from any federal taxes.

- The tax will not fall *at all* on the poor—because the monthly exemption will eliminate any tax on expenditures below the poverty line. (See Number 37, below, for a more detailed explanation).

- The tax promotes upward mobility of hard-working Americans, who can more freely choose where and how to spend disposable income, including savings.

- The tax will fall more heavily on big spenders. There just won't be a way to avoid paying taxes on expensive purchases—the yacht, the plane, front-row seats at the Lakers, a dress for the Oscars, a diamond tiara, the limousine, the fancy lawyer or accountant . . .

---

201 One exception relates to those citizens, between 45 and 64 years of age, who elect to continue to pay social security and medicare taxes to the Federal government and to receive benefits provided under current law at age 65. See, *The Second Bill of Rights*, Amendment 11, Section 2.

- Foreign visitors (legal and illegal) pay the consumption tax on retail sales of new goods and services, but only citizens and permanent residents will receive exemption payments. The perception that illegal aliens are getting services but not paying taxes (true or not) will end. The incentive to become a citizen or legal resident will be strong.

- The cost of manufacturing in the United States (at home) will go down, as the cost of tax compliance goes down. Foreign imports become sales to which the consumption tax applies. The relative advantage of low-wage manufacturing overseas will be reduced.

- Governments, including federal, state, and local, pay the consumption tax on retail purchases of new goods and services, which will level the competitive playing field between government enterprises and private companies.

- Trillions of dollars of profits previously made abroad in foreign subsidiaries of American companies, now overseas, should find their way back to the United States, for further investment in manufacturing and construction here, at home.

The Fair Tax is pending in Congress as HR25.[202]

The principles set forth in the Fair Tax are aligned with the Constitution and *The Second Bill of Rights.* Section 1 of HR25 is set forth in the notes.[203]

---

202 Also introduced in the Senate as S13. The economics and the politics of the Fair Tax have been described in numerous studies, books, and papers. *The Fair Tax Book,* Neal Boortz and John Linder, 2005, HarperCollins Publishers; See the materials describing the proposed legislation at *www.fairtax.org.*
203 SEC. 1. PRINCIPLES OF INTERPRETATION.
(a) IN GENERAL.—Any court, the Secretary, and any sales tax administering authority shall consider the purposes of this subtitle (as set forth in subsection (b)) as the primary aid in statutory construction.
(b) PURPOSES.—The purposes of this subtitle are as follows:
(1) To raise revenue needed by the Federal Government in a manner consistent with the other purposes of this subtitle.
(2) To tax all consumption of goods and services in the United States once, without exception, but only once.
(3) To prevent double, multiple, or cascading taxation.
(4) To simplify the tax law and reduce the administration costs of, and the costs of compliance with, the tax law.

To produce an equivalent amount of overall federal revenue, the initial rate for the consumption tax is expected to be 22-23 percent. *But,* this is *not* an additional tax, but a substitute for income, estate, gift, social security, and medicare taxes. *And,* this 22-23 percent tax is paid by foreign visitors, illegal aliens, and foreign companies selling goods manufactured overseas—all of which provide a cushion (a subsidy) that favors the American taxpayer, rather than foreign producers and foreign visitors. *And, every single citizen and permanent resident receives monthly payments that produce a complete exemption from the consumption tax below the poverty line.* The Fair Tax is entirely consistent with constitutional principles of equal protection of the laws and protection from the abuse of government power in favor of some over others.

There is little to dislike about the Fair Tax.

Section 2 of Amendment 6 restores the Constitution to the position established by the Framers—before the addition of the 16th Amendment in 1913.[204]

> 2. Congress shall have no power to levy federal taxes on income, estates, and gifts; no power to lay or collect a Value Added

---

(5) To provide for the administration of the tax law in a manner that respects privacy, due process, individual rights when interacting with the government, the presumption of innocence in criminal proceedings, and the presumption of lawful behavior in civil proceedings.

(6) To increase the role of State governments in Federal tax administration because of State government expertise in sales tax administration.

(7) To enhance generally cooperation and coordination among State tax administrators; and to enhance cooperation and coordination among Federal and State tax administrators, consistent with the principle of intergovernmental tax immunity.

(c) SECONDARY AIDS TO STATUTORY CONSTRUCTION.—As a secondary aid in statutory construction, any court, the Secretary, and any sales tax administering authority shall consider—

(1) the common law canons of statutory construction;

(2) the meaning and construction of concepts and terms used in the Internal Revenue Code of 1986 as in effect before the effective date of this subtitle; and

(3) construe any ambiguities in this Act in favor of reserving powers to the States respectively, or to the people.

204 The excise tax on employees, measured by wages, is a separate tax on employers, and on the self-employed, measured by wages (or salary). See, *Chas. Steward Mach. Co. v. Davis,* 301 U.S. 548 (1937).

Tax; and no power to levy any excise tax measured by wages. The sixteenth article of amendment to this constitution is repealed

The Estate Tax (and Its Sibling, the Gift Tax) Can Never Be Consistent with Liberty

The estate tax (and its sibling, the gift tax) impose unacceptable hardships on families forced to sell the farm or business as the only means of raising the cash necessary to pay the estate tax. Small businesses have long been the lifeblood of the American economy in terms of employment, wealth creation, and innovation. Abolition of any federal power to levy an estate or gift tax will go far in protecting the family farm, and the family business from destruction and sale upon the death of a parent.[205]

Valerius

---

205 The *Constitution of the United States*, including *The Second Bill of Rights*, is set forth in the Appendix.

NUMBER 37.
A Uniform Cost of Living Exemption Paid to Each Citizen

One aspect of the consumption tax proposed in Amendment 6 requires special discussion, because it has been a source of confusion in the debates surrounding the Fair Tax.

Amendment 6 to *The Second Bill of Rights*, at §1, contains an important proviso that mandates the inclusion of uniform rebates for adults and for children, indexed for inflation and deflation, in legislation implementing the tax to shield basic household necessities[206] from the tax.

> Provided, that Congress shall at the same time establish uniform rebates for adults and for children, indexed for inflation and deflation, to shield basic household necessities from such consumption tax, paid monthly to each citizen, legal resident, or the guardian thereof, by the State in which they then reside that

Every citizen and permanent resident, *every one*, receives the same uniform rebate.

- The president of Microsoft receives the same uniform rebate as the retired teacher.
- The most famous movie star receives the same rebate as the part-time movie employee.
- The basketball player in the NBA receives the same rebate as the ticket taker.

---

206 "Basic household necessities" represents the base-line cost of life in the United States: food, clothing, shelter. It is similar to the poverty level, but is focused on the essentials of running a household in the United States. The amendment requires that once Congress sets this amount, it will be indexed for inflation and deflation.

- Every minor child receives the same rebate, though different from adults in amount.

The uniform rebate would be paid monthly to each citizen and permanent resident, in an amount sufficient to shield all from the cost of basic household necessities.

The practical effect of this rebate is to encourage savings and, at the same time, to allow freedom in how individuals and families allocate their resources.

An example of how the uniform exemption works may help.

Assume that the average cost of basic retail purchases of food, clothing, and shelter set by Congress is $30,000 per adult and $15,000 per minor child. If the consumption tax is 20 percent on retail sales, each adult would be paid $6,000 per year ($1,500 per quarter, or $500 per month). A family of four (two adults/two children) would have a uniform exemption of $90,000 ($60,000 for the adults plus $30,000 for the children), and would receive $18,000/year (20 percent of $90,000), or $4,500 per quarter, or $1,500 per month.

The consumption tax proposed in Amendment 6 is regressive, *in favor of the needy,* but does not interfere with the choices each citizen makes on how to spend his or her income or rebate. This is left to the individual, based on his or her own needs and preferences, and consistent with liberty.

Valerius

NUMBER 38.
Can Americans Live without the Internal Revenue Service?

It is a significant, if little-noted, fact of American social history that nearly every sitcom since the invention of television has featured an episode involving an IRS audit. Jack Benny, Mary Tyler Moore, Oscar Madison, even Homer Simpson have faced the feds.

In a 1952 episode of *The Honeymooners,* the rotund Ralph Kramden (Jackie Gleason) sought the advice of his dim-witted friend, Ed Norton (Art Carney) in going over his tax return. Norton reads out a six-digit number and asks what income it refers to.

> "That's not any income, that's my social security number," Ralph declares.
> "I thought maybe it was your weight," Norton responds.

An easy fat-joke for 1952, when everyone would recognize the absurdity of having to declare one's weight to the IRS. But who would be surprised today if Congress used the tax code to combat obesity? A form for a carbohydrate tax offset is too easily imagined.

Nobody likes to pay taxes, but everyone recognizes the need to do so. As John Locke, the principal philosophical source for the Founders, noted: "[i]t is true, governments cannot be supported without great charge, and it is fit everyone who enjoys his share of the protection, should pay out of his estate his proportion for the maintenance of it."[207] Even if the federal government is restored to proper constitutional limits, there will be plenty for it to do, and it will need revenue.

---

207 John Locke, *Two Treatises on Government,* Book II, Chapter XI. Of the Extent of the Legislative Power, Section 140, Editor, Thomas Hollis, published by A. Millar et al., London, 1764.

But we clearly have an overly complicated and frequently perverse system of internal taxation, one that goes far beyond the Constitution's grant of power to Congress "to lay and collect taxes, duties, imposts, and excises, to pay the debts and provide for the common defense and general welfare of the United States."

The code is so complex that our Secretary of the Treasury was unaware that he had to pay self-employment taxes on several hundred thousand dollars of income he earned when working for the International Monetary Fund. The chairman of the House Ways and Means Committee, the principal tax-law writer in Congress, also claimed that he could not understand his tax liability for a vacation home in the Caribbean.

We're all familiar enough with IRS horror stories—that's what makes them such regular sitcom fodder.

The fundamental problem is that Congress uses the tax code to promote or discourage all sorts of activity, like buying homes, insulating homes, drilling for oil, or purchasing health insurance. Most of these are only remotely related to the Constitution's stated end, "to pay the debts and provide for the common defense and general welfare of the United States."

For a century and a half, it was agreed that taxing and spending for the general welfare was defined by the seventeen specific, enumerated ends that followed this taxing-and-spending power in Article I, Section 8—to raise armies, for example, or to establish post offices. Not until 1936 did the Supreme Court revise this understanding, and hold that the general welfare clause was a grant of power separate from the enumerated powers. Even so, the benefit provided had to be general—not limited to a particular interest group. Even this limitation broke down, and we have an incomprehensible system in which everyone seeks subsidies and tries to shift the tax burden onto everyone else.

The amendments in *The Second Bill of Rights* move a long way toward restoring the proper ends of federal action. Amendment 6 will help to restore the proper means of funding the federal government. The tax code will no longer encourage this or that particular activity, but will encourage productive activity by taxing consumption. There has never been a more opportune moment to make this shift, and it is a shift back to the founders' thinking.

Amendment 6 to *The Second Bill of Rights* repeals the Sixteenth Amendment. This raises the question of why we have a Sixteenth Amendment in the first place.

The Sixteenth Amendment, ratified in 1913, declares that "Congress shall have power to lay and collect taxes on incomes, from whatever source derived, without apportionment among the several states, and without regard to any census or enumeration." This amendment was necessary because the Supreme Court, in 1895, held that taxes on incomes were direct taxes, which had to be apportioned among the states according to population. That is to say, if New York had 10 percent of the country's population, its citizens would pay 10 percent of the total income tax, even if they had 50 percent of the nation's income. The citizens of another state with the same population would also pay 10 percent of the total income tax, even if they brought in only 1 percent of the national income. With the direct tax apportionment requirement, the Court defeated the principal purpose of the sponsors of the income tax. The sponsors wanted to reduce the tariff (a consumption tax) and make up lost revenue with high-income earners, concentrated in a few urban-industrial states.

The 1895 decision, *Pollock v. Farmer's Loan & Trust Co.,* is among the most controversial decisions in the Court's history. The fact that the Court in 1881 unanimously upheld a nearly identical income tax from the Civil War period was only one of its objectionable features. Most historians have concluded that the term "direct tax" was understood in 1789 to mean only taxes on people (a capitation tax) and real estate.

But the Court's decision was not wholly without merit. At the Constitutional Convention, Rufus King asked what was the precise meaning of direct taxation. James Madison's notes recorded that "No one answered." Hamilton defined indirect taxes as "duties and excises on articles of consumption."[208] He expected that the federal government would rely primarily on indirect taxes like the tariff. "The genius of the people will ill brook the inquisitive and peremptory spirit of excise laws," he

---

208 Hamilton, *The Federalist Papers* 36, at p. 219.

noted. "Taxation will consist, in a great measure, of duties which will be involved in the regulation of commerce."

The requirement of apportionment for taxes on real estate was meant to prevent one section of the country—populous but without much valuable land—from shifting the tax burden onto another section—less populous but with valuable land. And this has been the tendency of the income tax. Initially, it meant to shift the tax burden from consumers (who paid higher prices for imported goods) onto a small number of high-income individuals in the growing cities of the Northeast. The income tax did not become a mass tax until the Second World War. In recent decades, the proportion of the population paying income taxes has fallen to barely half of the population.

All of this indicates that the Supreme Court in Pollock had an inkling of the unfairly redistributive tendency of the income tax—one that the Founders shared and one that ought to concern us as well. Despite the opposition to the *Pollock* decision, it was never overruled. Congress did not enact another income tax to get the Court to overrule its decision in Pollock. The Sixteenth Amendment confirmed that the Court's decision was correct. To abolish the income tax, we need only repeal the Sixteenth Amendment.

A common criticism of the pre-income tax era, when the federal government derived most of its revenues from the tariff, was that the tariff was regressive, that it burdened all consumers equally, rather than imposing a heavier burden on the more affluent. The uniform rebates provided for in Amendment 6 of *The Second Bill of Rights* will obviate this criticism.

The greatest advantage of replacing the income tax with a consumption tax is that it will encourage productive economic activity and provide incentives to curb excessive consumption. With consumption taxes, Hamilton observed, "The amount to be contributed by each citizen will in a degree be at his own option."[209] The extravagant will pay more, the frugal will pay less. The tax system will thus provide incentives to work, save, and invest. After the spending and consumption binge of the last few decades, this will be good for both the government and citizens.

---

209 Hamilton, *The Federalist Papers* 21, at p. 142.

Some fear that a consumption tax will be so easy to collect that it will produce a revenue windfall, leading only to more irresponsible spending. But consumption taxes are self-limiting, a feature Hamilton appreciated.[210] "It is a signal advantage of taxes on articles of consumption that they contain in their own nature a security against excess. They prescribe their own limit . . " If they are too high, they become prohibitive, and produce less revenue.

Finally, Amendment 6 is not overly restrictive in setting a limit to consumption tax rates. This protects us in case of emergencies like wars.[211] Because we cannot know the threats that the country might face in the future, the power of taxation should not be unnecessarily limited by the Constitution.

Prosperus

---

210 *Ibid.*
211 Hamilton, *The Federalist Papers* 31, at p. 193. Hamilton cautioned that "there ought to be no limitation of a power destined to effect a purpose which is itself incapable of limitation."

NUMBER 39.
The Innovative Nature (Technological and Otherwise) of a Mobile Citizenry

Citizens in possession of individual freedom, each with unique talents, experiences, and preferences, will make slightly different choices in the exercise of their economic and civil rights—together, their liberty rights.

As noted in Number 3, some citizens will become *explorers* feverishly pursuing their unusual individual talents with astonishing results. Most of us become *balancers*—of work, family, and our more mundane talents and preferences, trying to pursue each as best we can. Many of us will be forced by the choices we've made, by genetics, by our health, or by fate, to become the *competent* or the *flexible*, re-directing our lives in small, or in more significant ways.

With freedom and liberty come (i) choices and (ii) consequences, known and unknown. Free people choose in an uncertain environment—they take calculated risks. In a free society, some things are left to chance—including the interplay of each person's choice with that of others.

Can any government administered by some men and women over others plan or control results for each citizen? Even if angels were found to accomplish the task, could it be done without substantial interference with individual freedom and the exercise of liberty rights? The Founders were sufficiently humble to say *No* to both questions. Economists as diverse as Adam Smith, F. A. Hayek, Walter Lippmann, and J. M. Keynes also said *No!*[212]

Instead of trying to fashion a government that would centrally plan how each citizen pursues happiness, the Founders focused on a different solution. They structured the Constitution to abolish the primary means of central planning—privilege conferred on some men and women

---

212 See, Numbers 25 and 26, above.

ahead of others. In its place, the Founders put individual freedom and equal rights under the common law—a structure that values hard work, mutual respect, and personal integrity (merit).

The Constitution bans the creation of privilege from the power of government—favoring some over others. For example, the authority to interfere with personal liberty—through criminal charges or assertions of treason—is dramatically curtailed.[213] As citizens move across State boundaries, their privileges and immunities travel along.[214] The national government cannot suspend the writ of habeas corpus,[215] pass bills of attainder[216] or ex post facto[217] laws.[218] Titles of nobility are banned.[219] States, too, may not pass bills of attainder, ex post facto laws, or laws impairing the obligation of contracts, and they cannot grant titles of nobility.[220] And, quite importantly to the establishment of America as the most prolific nation of inventors in history, the Founders charged the government with protecting authors and inventors through patent, trademark, and copyright laws.[221]

Two hundred and twenty-five years after the Founding, the profound step of abolishing privilege seems unimportant. Yet, the Founders' success—a mobile citizenry—is all around us. The path to a career in the

---

213 See Article III, which established an independent judiciary, trial by impartial jury, and a narrow definition of treason. See Amendments 4, 5, and 6 in the first Bill of Rights, which requires due process of law, and Amendment 14, which adds equal protection of the laws.
214 See Article IV, Section 2, paragraph 1.
215 Holding a citizen without bail, and without appearance before an independent judge so that the accused could hear the charges against him, and receive the assistance of counsel.
216 A most hated practice of the Crown at the time of the Revolution, punishing the family—husband, wife, father, mother, sons, or daughters—for the crime of a relative. This practice was completely banned. In the United States, the "sins of the father were [never to be] visited upon the son."
217 Another legislative practice in Britain at the time, which was abhorrent to the Founders. Ex post facto [after the fact] laws punished acts that had already taken place or interfered with contracts that had already been signed—that were not prohibited when the acts took place or the contracts signed.
218 See, Article I, Section 9, paragraphs 2 and 3.
219 See, Article I, Section 9, paragraph 8.
220 See, Article I, Section 10.
221 Article I, Section 8, paragraph 8 reads: To promote the Progress of Science and useful Arts, by securing for limited Times to Authors and Inventors the exclusive Right to their respective writings and Discoveries.

skilled trades is not barred to any citizen willing to learn and work at it. The path to college is not barred, because of what a person's parents do or did, or the level of their income. The path to a career in the military is open. The path to a career requiring unique talent—singer, musician, professional athlete, or inventor—is not barred by status, privilege, or birth. The path to a career as mother or father, raising children, is open. The Founders succeeded in a most fundamental task—that of creating a durable foundation for fellow citizens to develop their own unique plan—not a *central* plan from government, but a plan *centered* on their own situation, free from government.

In every sense of the word—*America is the most mobile society ever seen on the planet*. Physically, citizens are free to move and live throughout the nation, free to seek and obtain different employment, across state lines, without interference by government. Citizens are free to seek different forms of education and training—book-based or practical—and to apply what they've learned in the pursuit of their own plan for happiness.

We all learn from experience that our vision of happiness evolves—and its principle components change. The value we place on friendship, family, health, and love, for example, change throughout our life, especially in relation to the value of money and possessions. Few mature Americans would exchange good health, good friends, strong family, or the love and respect of others for money or stuff.

Yet, money has been the means by which free people throughout history have been able to pursue their own individual plans—their own happiness—in concert with fellow citizens. It is through the common exchange of money that the electrician is able to convert his skills into the money he or she needs to buy bread, milk, and eggs from the grocer, whose skills as a merchant are used by various farmers to convert their work into money needed to grow food. And, on and on. While the need to earn money may be viewed by leaders of some factions as bad, it would be more accurate to say that the temporary possession of money[222] is the means by which each of us is free to pursue happiness with liberty.

Although annual income may not be a perfect, or even a good, measure of happiness, and though income level is often used by factions to vex

---

222 None of us can take it with us.

and divide us,[223] a series of studies by the U.S. Treasury Department confirm that America remains an economically mobile society.[224] The major findings are the following:

> There is considerable income mobility of individuals in the U.S. economy over the 1996 through 2005 period. More than half of taxpayers . . . moved to a different income quintile between 1996 and 2005. About half . . . of those in the bottom income quintile in 1996 moved to a higher income group by 2005.

> Median incomes of taxpayers in the sample increased by 24 percent after adjusting for inflation. The real incomes of two-thirds of all taxpayers increased over this period. Further, the median incomes of those initially in the lowest income groups increased more in percentage terms than the median incomes of those in the higher income groups. The median inflation-adjusted incomes of the taxpayers who were in the very highest income groups in 1996 declined by 2005.

> The composition of the very top income groups changes dramatically over time. Less than half . . . of those in the top 1 percent in 1996 were still in the top 1 percent in 2005. Only about 25 percent of the individuals in the top 1/100 percent in 1996 remained in the top 1/100 percent in 2005.

> The degree of relative income mobility among income groups over the 1996 to 2005 period is very similar to that over the prior

---

223 As Madison noted in the Federalist No. 10, differences among citizens in income and possessions offer the ambitious leaders of factions a ready opportunity to "divide . . mankind into parties, inflame . . them with mutual animosity, and render . . them much more disposed to vex and oppress each other than to co-operate for their common good."
"But the most common and durable source of factions has been the various and unequal distribution of property. Those who hold and those who are without property have ever formed distinct interests in society. Those who are creditors, and those who are debtors . . . A landed interest, a manufacturing interest, a mercantile interest, a moneyed interest, with many lesser interests, grow up of necessity in civilized nations, and divide them into different classes, actuated by different sentiments and views."
224 *Income Mobility in the U.S. from 1996 to 2007,* Report of the Department of the Treasury, November 13, 2007 (Typographical revisions, March 2008). See p. 4. The Treasury Department's report summarizes similar results for the period from 1967 to 1976.

decade (1987 to 1996). To the extent that increasing income in-equality widened income gaps, this was offset by increased abso-lute income mobility so that relative income mobility has neither increased nor decreased over the past 20 years.

In the simplest of terms—the report confirms what we see around us.

The identity of the people inside each of the income ranges is chang-ing regularly. High tech startups succeed, new products emerge, and the newest set of inventors and innovative manufacturers are rewarded with rapid increase in income. New consumer products emerge, along with new outlets for highly valuable new products, with similar results. New medical technologies emerge, saving, extending, or improving the conditions of life—along with similar results in the practice of medicine. New companies are formed in the construction, manufacturing, and service industries—offering differing products, services, and benefits, along with similar results in the establishment of new business leaders.

Young people entering the work force see their income rise over their working lives. Over each ten-year period, more than half move out of the lowest quintile of income into one of the top four quintiles. The median income of more than 2/3rd of taxpayers is *increasing*—while the median income of the top quintile *declines* as citizens reach and pass retirement age.

While the media, and factions, focus heavily on the increasing ratio be-tween average earning at the top and at the bottom of the society—little attention is given to the fact that *the people inside both groups*—at the top and at the bottom—*are constantly changing*. Citizens are consistently moving up within the income distribution of all citizens, while others are (as a mathematical necessity) moving down.

Beneath the rhetoric of factions, beneath the barnacles that have at-tached themselves to the U.S. Constitution, the platform established by the Founders for a mobile citizenry remains intact.

- Physical and economic mobility, based on merit, and never on privilege;
- Citizens fully invested in the pursuit of their individual plans for happiness;

- Individual merit driving innovation in technology, manufacturing, and services;
- All in an environment based on individual freedom and liberty.

The package of Amendments in *The Second Bill of Rights* aims to re-energize the innovative nature inherent in a mobile American citizenry. It is a task no central planner can ever achieve.

Valerius

NUMBER 40.
Alternative Amendment 6—
a Flatter, Fairer, Simpler Income Tax

As described above,[225] Amendment 6 to *The Second Bill of Rights* eliminates the income, estate, and gift taxes; repeals the Sixteenth Amendment; and precludes the national government from adding a value added tax (VAT). In their place, Amendment 6 gives Congress power to impose a consumption tax, with a uniform rebate, as described in Numbers 36 and 37 above.

Ending a system in which every American is a tax scofflaw and substituting one in which individuals earn and take home their pay, free from federal tax, would represent a major infusion of freedom and liberty in the entire society. Other benefits of ending the income, estate, and gift taxes would be substantial, tending to restore a more dynamic, even more mobile, society that is free to innovate and adapt in a changing world, with reduced cost of tax compliance, competitive rates of business taxation in world markets; and broad incentives to save, to invest, to produce, and to consume more wisely. The incredibly complex income tax code now encourages all sorts of aberrant behavior—buying losses to offset profits, corporate re-organizations to avoid tax, and conduct aimed not at being productive or competitive but at avoiding or minimizing tax.

But, but . . .

Despite nearly one hundred years of partisan failure in perfecting the language of the income tax, the preference of the American people might yet be to take one more stab at income tax reform.

Alternate Amendment 6 contains recommendations for reform of the power now contained in the Sixteenth Amendment to levy a tax on the

---

225 In particular, Numbers 35 through 39.

basis of income.[226] The advantages of Alternative Amendment 6 go far beyond huge savings in compliance costs for individuals and businesses.

Section 1 sets maximum rates and discourages future divisiveness caused by the incessant tinkering of factions and their lobbyists.[227] Only one tax on the income of individuals may be imposed—just one. Only one tax on the net income of business entities may be imposed—just one. The net income of business entities is to be determined in accordance with generally accepted accounting principles under the common law—no longer in accord with thousands of pages of regulations produced through factions lobbying Congress and the Executive. The accounting profession, good business practices, and the applicable corporate law will reassert prior common law governing these issues, eliminating the labyrinth of loopholes, special rules, and arbitrary results that now characterize regulations implementing the income tax.

The second sentence of Section 1 formally establishes a fixed ratio of two (2) between the maximum and minimum rate of tax imposed on ordinary income of individuals, and sets the highest rate that Congress might impose on ordinary income at thirty percent (30 percent). Were Congress, by law, to subsequently set this rate at 30 percent, the lowest rate would then be fixed at 15 percent. Were Congress to set the highest rate at 28 percent, the lowest rate could not be lower than 14 percent. These provisions strike a balance between retaining some progressivity

---

226 Alternate Amendment 6 includes variables to be set by Congress so that enactment of the amendment can be revenue neutral. But, the number of variables is dramatically reduced. These variables are designed to send most tax lobbyists packing and to reduce or eliminate instances throughout the system where particular conduct, individuals, or industries gain "privileged status" at the relative expense of other conduct, individuals, or industries.

227 1. Congress shall have no power to levy other than a single tax on the income of individuals, and a single tax on the net income of business entities determined in accordance with generally accepted accounting principles under the common law. The highest rate of tax imposed on ordinary income shall not exceed thirty percent and shall not exceed two times the lowest rate so imposed. The rate of tax imposed on income from (i) property held for one year or more, including property so held by or on behalf of individuals for retirement; (ii) the domestic manufacture of durable goods for sale; and (iii) the design, construction, repair, maintenance and operation of domestic infrastructure facilities (including water supply and treatment, energy supply and generation, road, port, airport, rail, transit, and such other facilities as may be identified by Congress) shall not exceed one-half of the lowest rate of tax imposed on ordinary income.

in the rates set by Congress on ordinary income, and relentless partisan bickering among factions, their leaders, and political leaders in the setting of rates applicable to the ordinary income of individuals. Congress would still have authority to establish the brackets of income to which the rates apply, but within the top and bottom parameters established in the Amendment.

The third sentence of Section 1 formally establishes a lower rate of tax—one-half (1/2) of the lowest rate imposed on the ordinary income of individuals—to be imposed on three different classes of income. The three classes of income are the following:

(i) property held for one year or more, including property so held by or on behalf of individuals for retirement;
(ii) the domestic manufacture of durable goods for sale; and
(iii) the design, construction, repair, maintenance and operation of domestic infrastructure facilities (including water supply and treatment, energy supply and generation, road, port, airport, rail, transit, and such other facilities as may be identified by Congress).

For example, if Congress sets the maximum rate of tax on an individual's ordinary income at 30 percent, the minimum rate of tax on individual ordinary income would be 15 percent, and the maximum rate of tax imposed on these three classes of income would be 7.5 percent.

The reasons for setting this lower rate in this fashion are to encourage savings and investment (capital gain), encourage domestic manufacturing, and encourage renewal and reconstruction of the infrastructure platform on which the American economy runs—roads, ports, bridges, water, sewer, and energy networks. Continuation of lower tax rates for capital investment promotes long-term savings and investment. Deterioration of the domestic manufacturing basis has been a difficult problem for skilled American workers, who find it increasingly difficult for domestic employers to compete with low-paying competitors in foreign countries with low corporate tax rates. As recent Congresses have learned, repair and renewal of domestic infrastructure facilities takes years, along with a sustainable commitment to constantly work on maintenance, repair, replacement, and expansion. The costs of maintaining the nation's infrastructure base should not be artificially raised by high taxes on business entities that design, build, maintain, repair, and operate such facilities.

The third sentence of Section 1 solidifies a durable domestic tax environment encouraging savings and investment by individuals, domestic manufacturing, and a public infrastructure base supporting expansion in manufacturing and services here, in the United States.

Section 2 formally establishes three specific exemptions and one specific deduction for individuals against the income tax on ordinary income.[228] Again, a principle goal is to stop the unending partisan bickering that has led to unintelligible complexity in the current provisions of the Code, and to reduce the opportunity for the leaders of various factions to inflame citizens against one another. Each adult and dependent child is entitled to a separate personal exemption. Each adult is also entitled to an exemption of up to 20 percent of gross income for funds actually set aside by the taxpayer for retirement. Each adult and dependent child who has contracted for basic health care coverage, as defined by the state in which the taxpayer resides, is also entitled to a separate exemption; and each taxpayer is entitled to a deduction of not more than 20 percent of adjusted gross income for funds actually contributed to charitable organizations during the year. That is it. No more exemptions or deductions!

The third sentence of Section 2 requires that exemptions be indexed for inflation and deflation, eliminating so-called bracket-creep.

The fourth sentence of Section 2 precludes any other adjustment to income or to tax on income that is dependent on a taxpayer's level of

---

228 2. Congress shall establish for individuals: (i) separate personal exemptions from gross income uniformly applicable to each adult and dependent child; (ii) a separate maximum exemption uniformly applicable to each adult deferring from gross income funds actually set aside by the taxpayer during the year for retirement, but not in excess of 20% of gross income; (iii) separate exemptions from gross income uniformly applicable to each adult and dependent child who has contracted for basic health care coverage, as defined by the state in which the taxpayer resides; and (iv) an annual deduction not in excess of 20% of adjusted gross income uniformly applicable to each taxpayer for funds actually contributed to charitable organizations during the year. Exemptions shall be indexed for inflation and deflation. No other adjustment to income or to tax on income shall depend on a taxpayer's level of income, value of assets held, or applicable rate of tax.

income, value of assets held, or applicable rate of tax. This provision re-establishes equal protection of the laws for each taxpayer—and expressly forbids Congress' present practice, for example, of granting a deduction for mortgage interest paid, on the one hand, but limiting the availability of that deduction on the basis of level of income. The fourth sentence precludes such conduct going forward. While Congress retains flexibility to set rates, it can no longer treat taxpayers differently on the basis of economic status.

Section 3 of Amendment 6 eliminates the authority of Congress to levy estate and gift taxes, and also eliminates the authority of Congress to levy the current tax on businesses and the self-employed known as FICA. This is technically an excise tax on employees measured by wages and imposed on wage earners and businesses, collected and paid by businesses.[229]

Section 4 confirms that Congress has no power to add a VAT or a consumption tax on top of the income tax, as revised by Alternative Amendment 6 of *The Second Bill of Rights*.[230]

Amicus

---

229 3. Congress shall have no power to levy any excise tax on employers measured by wages and no power to levy any tax on the estates of, or on gifts made by, citizens and residents of the United States. Gifts and bequests shall not be income to recipients.
230 4. Congress shall have no power to lay or collect a Value Added Tax or a Consumption Tax.

NUMBER 41.
A Regular Process for Naturalization and Residence—
Amendment 7

Fouled by factions, current controversy regarding citizenship, naturalization, and permanent residence have deep roots in the history of slavery. And, most regrettably, these issues provide an enticing modern opportunity for

> leaders [to] ambitiously contend . . for pre-eminence and power, . . divide . . mankind into parties, inflame . . them with mutual animosity, and render . them much more disposed to vex and oppress each other than to co-operate for their common good.[231]

Amendment 7 to *The Second Bill of Rights* moves away from the flames of animosity engendered by faction toward a workable solution in which Congress has a clear, ongoing, duty to act fairly and promptly. A durable process for naturalization of citizens and for establishment of permanent residency has been part of the Founders' vision for the nation since the Constitutional Convention in 1787[232]:

> "[t]o establish an uniform Rule of Naturalization . . . throughout the United States."

Immigration and naturalization have been fertile ground for factions for more than 150 years.[233] The present debate centers on place of birth and on the meaning of the first sentence of the Fourteenth Amendment.[234]

---

231 Madison, *The Federalist Papers 10, supra,* at p. 79. See, Number 6, above.
232 One of the enumerated powers in Article I, Section 8, at paragraph 4.
233 In chapters now repealed, this Title 8 of the U.S. Code previously limited alien ownership of land, excluded the Chinese from citizenship, regulated the (sp) "Cooly Trade," and provided for Alien Registration.
234 This same sentence is the subject of a different discussion in Number 11, related to classes of citizenship.

Amendment 14 (Section 1, first sentence.)
All persons born or naturalized in the United States and subject to the jurisdiction thereof, are citizens of the United States and of the State wherein they reside.

Just who are *persons born or naturalized in the United States and subject to the jurisdiction thereof?* The definition of two words, the conjunctions "or" and "and" are critical. [O]r means the alternative—the sentence applies to either group of persons—those born in the United States *or* those naturalized in the United States. The next word, *and*, means that in addition to a requirement to belong to one of these two groups, persons must, at the same time, be *subject to the jurisdiction of the United States* to be citizens under this sentence.[235]

The language is curious. Why is it there? What was its purpose when enacted?

To answer these questions, a review of the Civil War Amendments, the Civil Rights Act of 1866, the Reconstruction Acts, and part of the *Slaughterhouse* decision, is necessary to understand the constitutional context in which factions have so successfully inflamed all sides of today's immigration debates. Current animosity originates with slavery, not immigration.

The Civil War Amendments, the Civil Rights Act of 1866, and the Reconstruction Acts

The 1864 federal election not only gave Abraham Lincoln a second term as President, but returned a 70+ percent Republican majority to the House of Representatives. Those states that formed the Confederate States of America had no voting members in the Senate or the House. Their absence, the addition of Senators and Representatives from West Virginia (admitted in 1863, from territory carved out of Virginia), and Nevada (admitted in 1864) provided just enough votes—just enough—to ensure passage (by 2/3 of both the House and Senate) of the Thirteenth Amendment, banning involuntary servitude in the United States.[236]

---

235 Foreign diplomats and heads of state, visitors, military personnel, and even Soviet spies captured during the Cold War have always been considered to be not "subject to the jurisdiction of the United States." See, *The Second Bill of Rights*, Amendment 1, Section 2. The publicly known meaning of these words at the time the Amendment was adopted is what matters.
236 The amendment cleared the Senate in April 1864, the House in January 1865.

The words "subject to their jurisdiction" entered the Constitution in the Thirteenth Amendment.

Amendment 13

1. Neither slavery nor involuntary servitude, except as a punishment for crime whereof the party shall have been duly convicted, shall exist within the United States, or any place *subject to their jurisdiction.*

2. Congress shall have power to enforce this article by appropriate legislation.

On April 9, 1866, led by moderate Republicans like Lyman Trumbull, Congress enacted the *Civil Rights Act of 1866,* over the veto of President Andrew Johnson. Section 1 declared, in the part relevant to citizenship, naturalization, and residency:

> That all persons born in the United States *and not subject to any foreign power,* excluding Indians not taxed, are hereby declared to be citizens of the United States . . .

On June 13, 1866, the 39th Congress proposed the Fourteenth Amendment.[237] The first sentence of Section 1 addresses citizenship:

Amendment 14 (Section 1, first sentence.)

All persons born or naturalized in the United States, and *subject to the jurisdiction thereof,* are citizens of the United States and of the State wherein they reside.

The 14th Amendment was approved by two-thirds of the Senate and House[238] *before* the eleven states of the Confederacy were readmitted.[239] When it was sent to all thirty-seven states for ratification, *all* of the legis-

---

Lincoln signed and sent the Thirteenth Amendment to the states for ratification in February, 1865, two months before his assassination. It became effective on December 6, 1865 when ratified by 3/4 of the States (then represented in the Union).

237 As noted in Number 11, above, Congress was concerned that the privileges and immunities in the Civil Rights Act of 1866 (just legislation) be raised to a higher status—written Constitutional protection.

238 Every Democrat seated in both Houses voted against the amendment, and against the 1866 Civil Rights Act.

239 Alabama, Arkansas, Florida, Georgia, Louisiana, Mississippi, North Carolina, South Carolina, Tennessee, Texas, and Virginia.

latures of the Southern States, except Tennessee, refused. The Amendment was stuck. Ten states rejected it. Ratification by 3/4 of States was impossible.[240]

The Reconstruction Act of March 2, 1867.

Congress then declared that state governments in these ten states were not legal, there was no "adequate protection for life or property" in these states, and that they would be divided into five districts under military authority "until loyal and republican[241] State governments can be legally established."[242] Under the Act, military rule would not end and each state would not be represented in Congress until (i) male citizens of all races had drafted and voted to approve new state constitutions, (ii) these constitutions had been approved by Congress; and (iii) *newly formed state legislatures had ratified the Fourteenth Amendment.*

Ratification of Amendment 14.

Between June 1868 and July 1870, these ten states were *reconstructed*, new constitutions put in place, new legislatures elected, and the Fourteenth Amendment ratified by each of the new legislatures. Once the required 3/4 majority of the States had ratified, the Fourteenth Amendment became effective.[243] These actions were seen by many as both high-handed

---

240 The legal structure of "old South slavery" did not go down quietly at the end of the Civil War. In May, 1865, one month after Lincoln's assassination, Mississippi's then legislature enacted the first set of state laws now known as the Black Codes. Most southern states quickly followed suit. The *Mississippi Black Codes* are tough reading for any living American. These laws reinstituted the unlimited indentured service of blacks in place of slavery, with severe restrictions on their economic, political, and civil rights across the "free" South.

241 This is not a reference to a party but to the form of government adopted by the Founders. The U.S. has never been a "democracy." Rather, it is a "democratic republic."

242 March 2, 1867, 39th Congress, Session II, Chapter 153, passed over the President's veto. On July 19, 1867, Congress extended and confirmed these powers, 40th Congress, Session I, Chapter 30. Military power for the removal of state and local officials was confirmed. The military commander in each district was ordered to protect all persons and their property, to suppress insurrection, and to preserve the peace. As decided by the commander, military commissions would take the place of the state courts.

243 Even this was controversial, as Ohio had rescinded its ratification in the meantime. During military rule over these States ("reconstruction"), the Fifteenth Amendment, guaranteeing the vote to males of all races also passed Congress, and was ratified by the States. For example, a new Texas legislature ratified the Fourteenth and Fifteenth amendments before being readmitted.

and un-constitutional. To others, they produced bi-racial voters, bi-racial legislatures, black governors, and black Representatives and Senators. Underneath, resentment, fear, and hatred seethed.

The Slaughterhouse Cases confirm that the history and purpose of the Civil War Amendments[244] were to secure individual freedom and liberty rights for former slaves:

> We repeat, then, in the light of this recapitulation of events, almost too recent to be called history, but which are familiar to us all; and on the most casual examination of the language of these amendments, *no one can fail to be impressed with the one pervading purpose found in them all, lying at the foundation of each, and without which none of them would have been even suggested; we mean the freedom of the slave race, the security and firm establishment of that freedom, and the protection of the newly-made freeman and citizen from the oppressions of those who had formerly exercised unlimited dominion over him. It is true that only the fifteenth amendment, in terms, mentions the negro by speaking of his color and his slavery. But it is just as true that each of the other articles was addressed to the grievances of that race, and designed to remedy them as the fifteenth.*
> [Excerpts from the next paragraph of the Court's decision are in the footnotes.][245]

> The first section of the fourteenth article, to which our attention is more specially invited, opens with a definition of citizenship—
> . . . [I]t had been held by this court, in the celebrated *Dred Scott* case, only a few years before the outbreak of the civil war, that a man of African descent, whether a slave or not, was not and could not be a citizen of a State or of the United States. This decision . . . had never been overruled; and if it was to be accepted as

---

244 *The Slaughterhouse Cases*, 83 U.S. 36, 71-72 (1873).
245 We do not say that no one else but the negro can share in this protection. Both the language and spirit of these articles are to have their fair and just weight in any question of construction. Undoubtedly while negro slavery alone was in the mind of the Congress which proposed the thirteenth article, it forbids any other kind of slavery, now or hereafter. If Mexican peonage or the Chinese coolie labor system shall develop slavery of the Mexican or Chinese race within our territory, this amendment may safely be trusted to make it void. And so if other rights are assailed by the States which properly and necessarily fall within the protection of these articles, that protection will apply, though the party interested may not be of African descent . . .

a constitutional limitation of the right of citizenship, then all the negro race who had recently been made freemen, were still, not only not citizens, but were incapable of becoming so by anything short of an amendment to the Constitution.

To remove this difficulty primarily, and to establish a clear and comprehensive definition of citizenship which should declare what should constitute citizenship of the United States . . . *the first clause of the first section was framed.*

. . . It declares that persons may be citizens of the United States without regard to their citizenship of a particular State, and it overturns the *Dred Scott* decision *by making all persons born within the United States and subject to its jurisdiction citizens of the United States.* That its main purpose was to establish the citizenship of the negro can admit of no doubt. *The phrase, 'subject to its jurisdiction' was intended to exclude from its operation children of ministers, consuls, and citizens or subjects of foreign States born within the United States.*

What does the first sentence of the Fourteenth Amendment have to do with birth citizenship of aliens who are not citizens or permanent residents?? *Nothing!*[246]

Amendment 7 of *The Second Bill of Rights* charts a durable, middle course forward: a predictable process in law for non-citizens to make application for citizenship or residency, for clear standards and prompt review, and upon approval, for an applicant to thereby become subject to the jurisdiction of the United States as a citizen or as a resident. Children born of citizens or permanent residents who are already subject to such jurisdiction have citizenship at birth.

Valerius

---

246 This sentence overturned *Dred Scott*, and retroactively declared that former slaves born here and already subject to the jurisdiction of the United States, were citizens. The inclusion of "and subject to the jurisdiction thereof" simply confirmed the obvious—the Amendment did not change the status of aliens, whose nationality or allegiance remained elsewhere. The notion that the child of persons who are not subject to the jurisdiction of the United States is a citizen by birth, from a tourist to a visiting head of state, makes no sense.

NUMBER 42.
Proven Technology Meets Gerrymandering—and Wins!

Elbridge Gerry (1744–1814), was a member of the Constitutional Convention. He later served in Congress, and as Governor of Massachusetts. In 1812, Governor Gerry signed a bill into law that redistricted his state in congressional district to benefit his Democratic-Republican party (the Jeffersonians) against the Federalists. Gerry was packaging voters across congressional districts to manipulate the likely result of the upcoming election. A cartoon in the Boston Centinel on March 26, 1812 ridiculed the bizarre shape of a district in Essex County as a dragon.[247] The painter, Gilbert Stuart, likened it to a salamander. The editor, Benjamin Russel, advised "Better say a Gerrymander." The name stuck.

In 1981, after the 1980 U.S. Census, Massachusetts lost one of its congressional seats. The state had to be redistricted. There were eleven Democrats and one Republican (Margaret Heckler) in the House of Representatives.[248] One of these Democrats was Barney Frank, a maverick in the delegation. To arrange that Frank and Heckler would oppose each other in the next election, the Massachusetts legislature gerrymandered the Commonwealth of Massachusetts to establish a district in which they both lived and Frank could win, stretching from Newton to Fall River, often only a town wide. Heckler was defeated.

Many Congressional districts are routinely manipulated by factions to accommodate the wishes of incumbents of both major parties, often as

---

247 The cartoon can be seen on the Web at http://en.wikipedia.org/wiki/Gerrymandering.

248 Massachusetts has been losing seats in the House since 1820, when four (4) of its twenty (20) seats were lost to the new state of Maine as part of the Missouri Compromise. In 2013, Massachusetts will have only nine seats in the House. This time, the entire Congressional delegation is Democrat. There is no opponent to gerrymander out. The legislature's hope that an incumbents would announce his retirement came true—Barney Frank did—just before this book went to press. Otherwise, a federal cabinet or ambassador post might have been needed.

a compromise between multiple factions. Search the Web for U.S. Congressional District Maps. Here is a list of the worst: Illinois 1st, 4th and 17th; Maryland 2nd, 3rd, and 4th; Massachusetts 4th and 7th: New Jersey 6th and 7th, New York 8th, 9th, 12th, 15th, 22nd, 27th, and 28th; North Carolina 12th; Pennsylvania 12th and 18th; Tennessee 3rd; and Texas 29th. Maryland 3rd is laughable; Illinois 4th and New York 8th preposterous; Pennsylvania 12th obviously designed in coordination with Pennsylvania 18th.

Beginning with Elbridge Gerry, the factions Madison and the Founders feared have been very busy playing math games with elections. It no longer matters who is allowed to vote.[249] In the twenty-first century, factions now seize on how to package votes to get the outcome they seek.

To illustrate, let's play math games, too. Imagine a state with one thousand (1000) actual voters and ten (10) Congressional Districts—five hundred (500) Red voters and 500 Blue voters. If the Blues have power to draw ten (10) district lines with one-hundred (100) voters in each district—the Blues can always achieve a nine (9)-district to one (1)-district result. It is easy! Just gerrymander *one* district to have a supermajority of one-hundred (100) Red voters—*every other district* can then be gerrymandered to have a statistical majority of Blue voters. In our state of 1000 actual voters—evenly split—gerrymandering produces nine (9) Blue members of Congress and one (1) Red. The Blues have conceded one seat to the opposition. Not to worry! The Blues will put the one Red on the worst committees in Congress, ignore the one Red, and vote against him or her. Stories in the media will report that the one Red is not an effective member of the House. In the five elections before the next census, the Blues might pick up that last seat.

In *Gary v. Sanders*, 372 U.S. 368 (1963) Justice Douglas wrote "the conception of political equality from the Declaration of Independence, to Lincoln's Gettysburg Address, to the Fifteenth, Seventeenth, and Nineteenth Amendment can mean only one thing—one person, one vote." Elected and appointed officials have long cheered for "one person, one vote"—a principle that now includes citizens eighteen years and older.

---

249 Leave aside, for now, pre-civil rights strategies of legislative barriers to voting, based on race, age, or gender.

Four amendments since the Civil War have forbidden the federal and state governments from interfering with who can vote: Amendment XV relates to race, color, or previous condition of servitude; Amendment XVIII to sex [gender]; Amendment XXIV to poll taxes; and Amendment XXVI to age. But, the stream of cases about districting confirms that "one person—one vote" is no longer the issue—the issue is gerrymandering. The battlefield has shifted from who can vote to how to package voters together into voting districts. And the battle has raged for decades.

In *Wesberry v. Sanders*, 376 U.S. 1 (1964), the Supreme Court held "that as nearly as is practicable one man's vote in a congressional election is to be worth as much as another's." In 1966, The Supreme Court ruled in *Burns v. Richardson*, 384 U.S. 72, 89 (1966), in a case coming out of Hawaii that "the fact that district boundaries may have been drawn in a way that minimizes the number of contests between present incumbents does not alone establish invidiousness." In *Thornburg v. Gingles*, 476 U.S. 30 (1986) the Supreme Court entered the argument under the Voting Rights Act about voter packaging and race. Is there a right for minority groups to participate equally in the political process and to elect candidates of their choice? Which groups? Who defines them? In *Davis v. Bandemer*, 478 U.S. 109 (1986), the Court held "that political gerrymandering cases are properly justiciable [suitable for decision] under the Equal Protection Clause. We also conclude, however, that a threshold showing of discriminatory vote dilution is required for a prima facie case of an equal protection violation."

In *Shaw v. Reno*, 509 U.S. 630 (1993), the Court opined that "Racial gerrymandering, even for remedial purposes, may balkanize us into competing racial factions; it threatens to carry us further from the goal of a political system in which race no longer matters—a goal that the [Civil War] Amendments embody, and to which the Nation continues to aspire. It is for these reasons that race-based districting by our state legislatures demands close judicial scrutiny."

Fortunately, technological innovation offers a ready solution—in the form of geocoding of addresses (Google® or their competitor maps). Amendment 8 in *The Second Bill of Rights* does away with congressional gerrymandering by requiring states to establish substantially different districts after each enumeration, and to construct these districts in shapes that are as close to squares as reasonably practicable. Voters are not to be packaged on the basis of race, color, gender, creed, religion, or party affiliation. And, in states with multiple districts, after every census, congressional districts will be substantially redrawn.

Amendment 8, Section 1.

> . . . Based upon each Enumeration, every State with more than one district shall establish district boundaries for the House of Representatives that are substantially different from the preceding Enumeration, without regard to race, color, gender, creed, religion, or party affiliation of persons therein. Each district shall comprise an area that is contiguous and not of unusually irregular shape. The quotient obtained from dividing the sum of the outer circumference of each district by the square root of the area of the district shall be as close as reasonably practicable to that obtained for all other districts and as close as reasonably practical to four—that of a square. Boundaries with other States and with navigable waters may be approximated by straight lines. The cognizant United States Court of Appeals shall have original trial jurisdiction in an action by a citizen to enforce this Amendment for a district in which the citizen resides.

Madison describes in *The Federalist Papers 55—58* why he expected the House could be trusted with the people's business.

> I will add, as a fifth circumstance in the situation of the House of Representatives, restraining them from oppressive measures, that they can make no law which will not have its full operation on themselves and their friends, as well as on the great mass of the society. This has always been deemed one of the strongest bonds by which human policy can connect the rulers and the people together. It creates between them that communion of interests and sympathy of sentiments of which few governments have furnished examples; but without which every government degenerates into tyranny. If it be asked, what is to restrain the House . . . from making legal discriminations in favor of themselves and a particular class of the society? I answer: the genius of the whole system; the nature of just and constitutional laws; and above all, the vigilant and manly spirit which actuates the

people of America—a spirit which nourishes freedom, and in return is nourished by it.

If this sprit shall ever be so far debased as to tolerate a law not obligatory on the legislature, as well as on the people, the people will be prepared to tolerate anything but liberty.[250]

How far the House has fallen from Madison's hopes! The House of Representatives has a lower turnover rate than the British House of Lords. It is an "imperial" club of incumbents, protected from competing with one another, or with newcomers, through gerrymandering. Factions have captured the election process for the House—creating a political class immune from voters. Amendment 8 to *The Second Bill of Rights* fixes this, simply and permanently.

Congressmen whose districts adjust with each required census every ten years may well have to compete with one or more of their incumbent colleagues, before a different mix of constituents. Districts will emerge in which there is no incumbent. Candidates for the House will actually have to run on the merit of the ideas and policies they advocate, rather than on mirroring the factions their districts have been configured to protect. The result is what Madison hoped for, a prudent, responsive, substantive Congress.

Amicus

---

250 Madison, *The Federalist Papers 51*, at pp. 341-361. The quoted passages are at pp. 352-353.

NUMBER 43.
Representation of Washington City, MD—Amendment 8

Many Americans have visited Washington DC, first as high school students or young men and women engaged in monument hunting, and later as business men and women to meet with members of Congress, their staff, officials in the Executive departments, or with businesses there. Washington is a marvelous city, full of sites chronicling the development of the United States, and with an interesting history itself.

The concept of a capital city originated during the Constitutional Convention, over which George Washington presided as President between May and September, 1787. See Number 13, *supra*. In choosing the District of Columbia, the Founders found an acceptable compromise to the competing interests of New York and Pennsylvania in "hosting" the new nation's capital.

The seventeenth (17th) of the eighteen (18) enumerated powers granted to Congress in Article I, §8 of the Constitution provides for a new seat of government (a capital city).

> To exercise exclusive Legislation in all Cases whatsoever, over such District (not exceeding ten Miles square) as may, by Cession of particular States, and the acceptance of Congress, become the Seat of the Government of the United States . . .[251]

The new States of Maryland and Virginia later jointly agreed to cede an area ten miles square on both sides of the Potomac River. The Maryland portion of the original grant is now the District of Columbia, or Washington DC.[252]

---

251 The thirty-one square miles of the District contributed by Virginia was retroceded (returned) in 1847.
252 So named to honor George Washington, the most famous American, "first in the hearts of his countryman," member of the Continental Congress, Commanding

Visitors to Washington DC also encounter a curious symbol of the ongoing frustration among city officials and the exclusive Legislative power given to Congress over the District. Residents in the city pay U.S. federal income tax on income. The city's license plate reads "Washington DC. Taxation Without Representation," showing city officials' dry sense of humor over the fact that the District of Columbia is not a State, and does not have the same representation in either the House or the Senate as do citizens of the Several States.

Amendment XXIII, ratified by the States in 1961, gives the District of Columbia the same number of electors in the electoral college as the least populous state—namely three (3). But, it is not a State, and is not fully represented in Congress. The license plates still read "Taxation Without Representation."

Amendment 8, Section 2, of *The Second Bill of Rights* solves this issue in a way similar to the treatment of the Virginia portion of the original land area in 1847—the people of the United States should give the vast majority of the area back to the State of Maryland. Section 2 establishes Washington City, Maryland, comprising virtually all of the areas of the district in which voters reside. Only the immediate area surrounding the Mall, and major federal buildings and monuments are retained as Washington DC. Washington City, MD, and its citizens will be restored to full representation in the Senate and the House, and will fully participate in the selection of Maryland's representatives in the Electoral College. Section 2 reads as follows:

> 4. One year after the effective date of this amendment, the Seat of Government—Washington DC—shall be limited to the land now comprising the National Mall with its museums and libraries, the Lincoln and Jefferson Memorials, the Houses of Congress and their existing office buildings, the Supreme Court, Lafayette Park and its existing office structures, the White House, and such other immediately adjacent facilities as Congress shall identify prior to such date by legislation. The rest of the District of Columbia shall be returned to Maryland as Washington City,

---

General of the Continental Army, President of the Constitutional Convention, and first President of the United States.

and its citizens part of the enumeration for Maryland. Amendment XXIII is repealed.

It is long past the time for the uneasy relationship between Congress and the elected representatives of what is now Washington DC to end amicably; for residents of Washington City, MD, to be fully represented in the legislature of Maryland and in the House and Senate of the United States, and for an appropriate change in those license plates.[253]

Amicus

---

253 The *Constitution of the United States*, including *The Second Bill of Rights*, is set forth in the Appendix.

NUMBER 44.
Commerce among the States—Amendment 9, Sentence 1

The Founders perceived one *great difficulty* before them in 1787, the same *great difficulty* Americans have faced since the Founding and will continue to face as long as free men and women continue to enjoy liberty in the constitutional republic the Founders established.

> [T]he great difficulty lies in this: you must first enable the government to control the governed; and in the next place *oblige it to control itself*.[254]

To accomplish the first task of this "great difficulty," the Founders gave the national government specific, enumerated powers in which federal power prevails—to defend the nation, to conduct international relations, and to establish what amounts to a "free trade zone" for commerce among the States. In addition, the Founders acknowledged the prevailing role of sovereign States under the police power to manage common exercise by all citizens of their liberty rights.

To accomplish the second task of this *great difficulty*—that is to oblige the government to control itself—the Founders recognized the liberty rights already held by citizens of the several States under the Confederation and confirmed that it was a free people who established not only the new Constitution but the national government. The Founders placed both *internal* and *external* controls, as well as *auxiliary precautions* in the Constitution to distinguish the powers granted to the national government from the police power retained by the States, and from the liberty rights reserved by citizens. In essence, the Founders established a constitutional definition of the Rule of Law[255] that would oblige the government to control itself.

---

254 Madison, *The Federalist Papers 51*, at p. 322. See Numbers 2 and 36, above.
255 A rule of law clear from the entire document, but made explicit in Amendment 1, *The Second Bill of Rights*.

The natural equilibrium embedded in the Constitution was pure genius, with the advantage of hindsight. Throughout our 225-year history, the *controls* and *precautions* in the Constitution have pushed factions—bent on destroying this equilibrium—back! Back toward the original, stable, constitutional, middle ground. The competing interests of individual freedom and liberty rights; mutual exercise of these rights under the police power; and protection of the republic were present at the Founding, have existed from 1787 to 2012, and will remain in the future.

There *must* be some limit to federal power, or the Rule of Law in the United States[256] could not exist. The national government would steadily and systematically encroach on the police power of States[257] and on the individual freedom of citizens in the exercise of the liberty rights.[258]

Similarly, there *must* be some limit to the power of States, or the Rule of Law could not exist. One or more of the States would steadily and systematically interfere with matters entrusted to the national government by the Constitution, such as the free trade zone established by the commerce clause among the States,[259] or the control over navigable rivers flowing among the States.[260]

There *must* be some limit on the power of citizens as well. Otherwise, individuals might contend that in the exercise of their liberty rights, they need not comply with the laws of the United States.[261] Without such lim-

---

256 As defined in *The Second Bill of Rights* Amendment 1.

257 The national government would dictate road speeds when driving next to the corn fields of Nebraska, or regulate how ladders must be positioned in preparation for cleaning, stripping, and re-painting wood siding.

258 The federal government might attempt to dictate whether a citizen must purchase and consume items in commerce, such as medical insurance, life insurance, or [iron-rich] broccoli.

259 Nevada might establish prohibitive tolls on the movement of goods in commerce across its roads, choking interstate shipment of goods across the nation. Or South Carolina might differently regulate the width of trucks allowed on its roads, with similar interference in the movement of goods in interstate commerce. See, *South Carolina State Highway Department v Barnwell Bros.*, 303 U.S. 177 (1938).

260 An upstream state—such as Colorado—could dam and take all the water out of the Colorado River. New York could do this with the Delaware River, Pennsylvania with the Ohio, and Minnesota with the Mississippi.

261 Shay's Rebellion in Western Massachusetts and the Whiskey Rebellion in Western Pennsylvania against the collection of federal excise taxes on alcohol were both put down by President Washington.

its, the Rule of Law could not exist.[262] Neither anarchy nor the broadest imaginable definition of individual freedom—no role for government— has ever been recognized as part of the Rule of Law in the United States.

The first sentence of Amendment 9 in *The Second Bill of Rights* restores the Founders' original grant of power to Congress with respect to commerce among the several States. These are the words the Founders used, in Article I, Section 8, paragraph 3:

> To regulate Commerce with foreign Nations, and among the several States, and with the Indian Tribes;

From 1787 until 1942, this language was construed to mean the transportation or movement of goods and services from within the nation to foreign nations, and among the several States. This language was not intended by the Founders to give power to the national government to regulate the manufacture of goods within a State—which was the province of the liberty rights of citizens under the police power. And, this language was certainly never intended to reach the creation of goods or growth of food by a citizen for his or her own consumption in a single state on his own land. Yet, this result was reached by the Supreme Court in *Wickard v. Filburn.*[263]

In that case, the Court applied its new *rational basis* test, created in 1934 by the Court in *Nebbia v. New York.*[264] The Court declared that it would not look behind Congress' assertion that the national government had the power, under a combination of the commerce clause and the *necessary and proper* clause, to control whether an individual farmer could grow wheat on his own farm to make his own bread for his own consumption.

---

262 Each citizen exercises his or her liberty rights in common with other citizens. Two people can't stand in the same place on a public sidewalk, yet each has a right to stand on a public sidewalk. Two people can't exclusively own the same smart phone, yet each has a right to own a phone. No citizen can unreasonably interfere with the liberty rights of another. Thus, liberty rights must be exercised subject to the Rule of Law, as defined in Amendment 1 to *The Second Bill of Rights.* Specific (non-criminal) disagreements among individuals (now more than three hundred million citizens) can only be properly handled by an independent judiciary using rules of general application developed by the common law, always under the Rule of Law.
263 317 U.S. 111 (1942)
264 See Number 23, above.

The first sentence of Amendment 9 reverses the result in *Wickard*, and restores the original equilibrium among the liberty rights of citizens (to grow or make, and consume on their own); the police power of the States (to manage common exercise of these rights); and national power to regulate commerce among the States. The first sentence of Amendment 9 reads:

> Congress' power to regulate Commerce among the several States shall only extend to transportation, trade, or exchange of goods and services in such Commerce.

The Founders knew that for any government to itself be subject to the Rule of Law, limits to federal power had to be set forth in the Constitution. The Founders certainly did not intend that Congress have power to tell any of us whether we might grow tomatoes, beans, potatoes, or carrots in our back yard, or whether we should or should not plant flowers instead.

The Supreme Court's decision in *Wickard* was a limitless expansion in federal power that has led to other attempts by Congress to exert federal power not consistent with the Founders' notion of a government obliged to control itself.

Congress was given power to protect a free trade zone among the States—an idea later copied from the Framers by the European Economic Community, and now the European Union. But this limited power is not consistent with claims by collectivist factions that the power to regulate the movement of goods and services among the States is the same as within each State, or provides any basis for central planning of the entire economy. The words *economics* and *economy* do not appear in the powers enumerated to Congress.

What the words "regulate commerce among the several States" meant in 1787 has been successively changed, not by constitutional amendment, but by the pressure of factions and self-interest, all in violation of the Founders' vision. These same words are now contended to mean the regulation of all aspects of the *economy*—a concept that the Founders, Smith, Hayek, and Lippmann would have viewed as arrogant, impossible, silly, and in the end, self-defeating.

In the years since *Wickard*, Congress has claimed that the original language of the Founders can reach beyond your back-yard garden, into the flower garden in your front yard, your bedroom, your doctor's office, your retirement plans and insurance contracts, and your private papers. These assertions are the basis for an unreasonably expansive, [collectivist] view of the power of the national government to plan the U.S. economy. This view was expressly rejected by the Founders,[265] is inconsistent with logic, and is destined for failure.

We already see symptoms of this failure: (i) in social services, unsustainable promises associated with social security, medicare, medicaid, drug benefits, and a national requirement to purchase healthcare, all in a context of increasing unfunded future liabilities and decreasing contributions;[266] (ii) in the public infrastructure sector, unsustainable promises to build new networks—road, port, airport, water, sewer, and energy—in a context that neither recognizes nor adequately funds ongoing maintenance, operations, or replacement of existing networks.[267]

The Founders knew what Hayek made explicit—collectivist (socialist) governments cannot plan a complex economy without substantially interfering with individual freedom and the exercise of liberty rights.

Europe, and in particular Greece, Spain, Portugal, and Italy face the results of centrally planned economies today. Britain has been dealing with the financial, social, and economic effects of central planning by collectivist governments for nearly forty years. Margaret Thatcher, then Prime Minister of Britain, concluded the following in 1976:

> [S]ocialist governments traditionally do make a financial mess. They always run out of other people's money. [268]

---

265 See, Numbers 10 and 19, above.
266 Against an unfunded liability of $114 trillion dollars in 2011, the government faces the impossible demographics of a dramatic rise in retirees and a reduction in working Americans over the next decades.
267 Against $7 trillion dollars of infrastructure holdings in 1991, the federal government spent $50 billion, a drop in the bucket, incapable of meeting any commitment by government to sustain current networks.
268 Wiki Answers, television interview for Thames TV *This Week* on February 5, 1976. This has been popularly paraphrased as: "The trouble with socialism is that eventually you run out of other people's money."

The purpose of the first sentence of Amendment 9 is not only to allow Americans to grow tomatoes in their back yard and flowers in the front yard, without interference from the national government, but to stop Congress from relying on a tortured meaning of the commerce clause— Article I, §8, clause 3 as the basis for destroying the equilibrium the Founders established among the national government, the States, and the liberty rights of citizens.

Valerius

NUMBER 45.
Economic Liberty to Plan for Retirement— the Balance of Amendment 9

Even a squirrel has the freedom, in the spring, summer, and fall each year to plan for the lean months of winter that are sure to come. Each squirrel finds or builds an appropriate nest, and collects and stores an appropriate supply of nuts, mushrooms, and other edibles for its own survival and that of its descendants. Squirrels have the sense to understand the difference between a long winter in northern Minnesota, a more mild winter in the hills of Tennessee, and almost no winter in the middle of Florida.

Just as nature gives squirrels the sense to evaluate and prepare for winter differently from North to South across the United States, human beings have sufficient capacity to appreciate their own circumstances and make rational decisions about what preparation is appropriate as each of us moves from youth (spring) to adult (summer) to middle-aged and retirement (fall) to old-age, and death (winter). The Founders understood that each citizen might and likely would come to different conclusions as to what these preparations should be! To the Founders, the individual right to evaluate our own talents, preferences, and tastes, and to make our own decisions to pursue one, none, or all of these, based on our own individual circumstances, was the essence of individual freedom and liberty.

Imagine for a moment, that your son or daughter and his or her spouse, both 30 years old, have asked for your advice regarding their financial situation and a set of decisions they are about to make. Here is the factual scenario they describe.

We own the largest family-owned summer camp in America, with hundreds of small buildings scattered across thousands of acres of mortgaged land in various states of repair, including our home. We have current annual income of $2,318 dollars, but have been spending $3,622 dollars each year on expenses. We're spending $1,304 more each year than we take in. The mortgage on the camp and our house is $15,179 and we pay $221 in interest on the mortgage each year. We actually owe $117,065 to prior campers and their children, who we allow to come to camp for free after their third year. The banks might take the house, particular parcels of land, or one or more of the small buildings scattered over the camp. Our cost of living and the cost of running the camp have been going up, particularly for gas and food, at a rate of 8% per year. Our individual medical insurance costs are going up more quickly than inflation—but so far we are healthy. The cost of raising our two small children and sending them to college is also going up at a rate higher than inflation.

We don't have any money to put away for our retirement or old age. We're thinking of having more children, expanding the camp business, and incurring more debt.

What do you think?

Is there a parent in the United States who wouldn't advise his or her child to stop spending! Stop giving away free camp! Work harder! Consider selling assets! Consider running a smaller camp! Don't take on any further liabilities until your income is sufficient to cover existing and future liabilities! The advice would be hard to give and difficult to accept, but it would be necessary.

Convert the numbers above from dollars into billions of dollars and your children would be describing the current financial state of the United States government.[269]

The long-term financial situation of the United States has reached the level of Alice in Wonderland—including political, but not binding, promises of the New Deal, when the number of contributors to social security outnumbered the number of beneficiaries by **42 to 1**, which have been made preposterous since 1937 by the ambitions of factions and the desire for political support by incumbents in the House and the

---

269 As of January 1, 2012. See *US Debt Clock* on the Web for current figures.

Senate. The ratio of contributors to beneficiaries has fallen from 159 to 1 in 1940 to 2.9 to 1 in 2010, and is expected to fall further to 2.7 to 1 by 2015, and 2.5 to 1 by 2020.[270] Benefits have gone up and coverage has been extended, fueled by factions. In the meantime, retirees are living much longer.

The problem is *not* that Congress just hasn't found the right words or level of taxation yet, after eighty (80) years of experimentation. The problem *is* that no set of humans ever born—including the current members of the House and the Senate—can successfully plan for the retirement, old age, and care of a free society of more than 300 million citizens. This fatal conceit has been demonstrated again and again for one hundred years. Factions have led the way. The Founders never intended that the national government micromanage how 300+ million citizens planned for their retirement, old age, and death. There are at least 300+ million different strategies for successfully doing so—and none of these need originate with the national government. Instead of allowing a free citizenry to make their own decisions about these matters, and only after the Supreme Court discarded 150 years of jurisprudence during Roosevelt's New Deal, Congress has employed the income tax, the estate tax, the gift tax, along with the social security, medicare, and medicaid systems to substantially interfere with the everyday exercise of each citizen's rights to plan for his or her own retirement, old age, and death.

The combination of federal tax law and social safety net legislation has at least two irrational effects on the exercise of liberty rights by every American. First, these systems assume that each American is in the same situation with the same needs—an assumption preposterous on its face. The father with a family history of heart disease and early death is *not* in the same position as another father with a family history of ancestors living into their 90s. A family with five young children is *not* in the same position as another family with no children. A family living on their 10,000-acre farm in Indiana is *not* in the same position as another family living in Detroit with parents working in the U.S. auto industry. *Our prospects, our situations, our interests, our talents, our preferences, and our chances differ.* In a nation of free people, with broad liberty rights, we all have options, choices, and the freedom to pursue our own course and our

---

270 2011 Social Security Trustees Report, Table IV.B.2 Covered Workers and Beneficiaries, Calendar Years 1945-2085.

own lives—maybe in the hope of bettering our own situations, but more frequently in the hope of improving the options, choices, and freedom of our children and their children.

With the advantages of freedom and the power to exercise liberty rights comes the responsibility to make our own choices, to pursue our own talents and preferences, and but for exceptional circumstances, to accept the results of the choices we've made. The second and third sentences of Amendment 9 of *The Second Bill of Rights* restore the original vision of the Founders, in which the right and responsibility of freedom remained with individual citizens, mediated by the police power of the States, and free from micro-management by the national government.

> Congress shall have no power to require any citizen, resident, or legal entity to engage in such commerce. Congress shall have no power to require any citizen, resident, or legal entity to participate in or contribute to any retirement, annuity, insurance, medical, disability, or similar plan established, managed, or controlled by the United States.

Most baby-boomers[271] that I know have assumed, since the early 1970's, when the demographics of the baby boom generation were first understood, that social security, medicare (and later, medicaid) would not and could not exist as centrally planned when our generation retired. Factions have convinced many that a fix to the financial silliness of $114 trillion dollars in unfunded mandates is the third rail of politics. We suspect that more citizens than elected officials might admit came to a more sober conclusion three decades ago—social security, medicare, and medicaid simply won't (and can't) exist in the same form when the bulk of baby-boomers retire.

The second and third sentences of Amendment 9, together with the provisions of Amendment 11, Section 2, provide transitional power to Congress and a rational way forward. Commitments to those already over sixty-five (65) years of age and dependent on these benefits must be met in full, and an option provided to those between forty-five (45) and sixty-four (64) years of age to either proceed with the current system

---

271 Citizens born in the fifteen years following the end of World War II, from 1945 to 1960.

or to escape from it. Congress is given transitional power to provide for reduction in the timing, amount, and extent of benefits using a means test of general application to all citizens.[272]

Valerius

---

272 See, Number 48, below.

NUMBER 46.
Charles Ponzi, Bernie Madoff and Social Security

In December, 1919[273] the citizens in Boston were given a rare opportunity—one too good to be true—earn a 50 percent profit on every investment of $100 in just 90 days. From $100 on day 1, to $150 after 90 days, to $225 after 6 months, to $337.25 after 9 months, to $506.25 in one year. Turn $100 into more than $500 in one year! Charles Ponzi had entered the business of investing in the City of Boston. The U.S. Supreme Court described his work this way:[274]

> The litigation grows out of the remarkable criminal financial career of Charles Ponzi. In December, 1919, with a capital of $150, he began the business of borrowing money [in exchange for] his promissory notes. . . . He borrowed the money on his credit only. He spread the false tale that on his own account he was engaged in buying international postal coupons in foreign countries and selling them in other countries at 100 per cent profit, and that this was made possible by the excessive differences in the rates of exchange following the war. He was willing, he said, to give others the opportunity to share with him this profit. By a written promise in 90 days to pay them $150 for every $100 loaned, he induced thousands to lend him. He stimulated their avidity by paying his 90-day notes in full at the end of 45 days, and by circulating the notice that he would pay any unmatured note presented in less than 45 days at 100 per cent of the loan. Within eight months he took in $9,582,000, for which he issued his notes for $14,374,000. He paid his agents a commission of 10 per cent. With the 50 per

---

273 Woodrow Wilson was President, World War I had ended, Boston had gotten past the flu epidemic of 1918, and the Boston Police strike. The top income tax rate had been raised during his Presidency from 7 percent in 1913 to 73 percent in 1919. Ponzi's fraud took place before withholding and before the introduction of Form 1099. The Securities Act (1933) and the Exchange Act (1934) were not yet in place.
274 *Cunningham v. Brown et al*, 265 U.S. 1 (1924). Mr. Chief Justice Taft delivered the opinion of the Court. Decided April 28, 1924.

cent promised to lenders, every loan paid in full with the profit would cost him 60 per cent. He was always insolvent, and became daily more so, the more his business succeeded. He made no investments of any kind, so that all the money he had at any time was solely the result of loans by his *dupes.*

After eight months, it all came crashing down. Ponzi had committed the most basic common law fraud—intentionally misrepresenting what he was doing and how he was doing it for the purpose of stealing money from silly investors—thousands of "dupes," as Chief Justice Taft rightly described them. There were no postal coupons, no differences in exchange rates, no profits, only worthless promissory notes signed by Ponzi to repay contributed investments with 50 percent interest. Dupes either took their losses and went away, or hired attorneys to chase (i) third party commission agents who, the dupes argued, should have seen through Ponzi's schemes and (ii) lucky early investors who had been repaid in full with the 50 percent profit as well.[275] A number of cases related to Ponzi's bankruptcy reached the state and federal courts.

Although the details are yet to fully emerge, Bernie Madoff began a similar, but more toney, scheme in the 1970s to defraud thousands of investors. Madoff's fraud is believed to have lasted for more than 30 years, ensnaring the most sophisticated individual investors in America, along with their financial advisors. More than $18 billion in losses are estimated.

Just as with Ponzi's dupes, Madoff's dupes either took their losses and went away, or hired attorneys to chase third parties. Just as with Ponzi, numerous cases related to Madoff's fraud will reach the state and federal courts.

Ponzi's and Madoff's schemes relied on a key misrepresentation—that investor's money was sufficient, *and would be used,* to purchase something of value (coupons by Ponzi, securities by Madoff), which Ponzi, or Madoff, respectively, held within his control. Ponzi and Madoff instead used the money invested to pay the promised high returns to early investors—using the illusion of high payouts to attract more investors. When

---

275 Part of Ponzi's scheme was to pay early investors back with the interest, stimulating more investors to play. Some of these dupes later sought to recover the 50 percent interest earned by early investors.

Ponzi's game of musical chairs suddenly stopped—those remaining had no chairs, and were left with the scraps. Ponzi's stunning success was given his name—the "Ponzi scheme." Madoff is just one of Ponzi's many subsequent admirers, able to duplicate Ponzi's feat.

Is the Social Security Act of 1935 a Ponzi Scheme? Similar to One? You Make the Call!

Three similarities and two differences are cause for alarm when comparing Ponzi's scheme with the logic of the national government's flagship social program—Social Security.

A First Similarity: Take from Some the Amount Needed to Pay Others.

The Social Security program relies on the practice of taking enough money from covered workers—citizens and residents under sixty-five (65) years old—to pay what has been promised to beneficiaries—citizens and residents over sixty-five (65) years old. Money must keep going out—to preserve confidence. If *either* the inflows are too low or the outflows are too high, covered workers must pay more, since early beneficiaries are unwilling to take less.

A Second Similarity: There are No Assets Assigned to Each Contributor.

The money contributed by covered workers for Social Security is not separately housed for contributors within the government. There is no money in an account with each taxpayer's name on it.[276] Excess money is actually not in this trust fund—but in special issues of the U.S. Treasury (i.e. securities payable upon demand by the trustees).[277]

---

276 "The money you pay in taxes is not held in a personal account for you to use when you get benefits. Your taxes are being used right now to pay people who now are getting benefits. Any unused money goes to the Social Security trust funds, not a personal account with your name on it."
"When you work, 85 cents of every Social Security tax dollar you pay goes to a trust fund that pays monthly benefits to current retirees and their families and to surviving spouses and children of workers who have died. The other 15 cents goes to a trust fund that pays benefits to people with disabilities and their families." Social Security web site, *http://ssa.gov*.
277 Social security website. Trust fund facts. *http://www.ssa.gov/oact/progdata/fund-FAQ.html*.

A Third Similarity: Early Participants Thrive.

Early participants—those who become beneficiaries first through retirement—receive more than complete repayment of their contributions.[278] The demographics of baby boomers will alter the future of social security. The ratio of covered workers to beneficiaries has dropped from 41.9 to 1 in 1945 to 2.9 to 1 in 2010, and is expected to drop further to 2.3 to 1 by 2025.

An Important Difference: Ponzi's and Madoff's Investors Could Stop Investing.

Social security is not voluntary, and Congress claims power to require every "covered worker" to participate. The only escape is: death before sixty-five (65); reduced benefits and early retirement; or retirement. In contrast, Ponzi and Madoff convinced thousands of their dupes to choose to participate, based on false promises of high and quick returns. Ponzi's and Madoff's investors were free from any legal obligation to continue investing. Ponzi never had the coercive power of government backing him. Ponzi's and Madoff's victims could stop!

Another Important Difference: No Actual Obligation to Pay Particular Benefits.

Since 1935, Congress has structured Social Security in such a way that Congress must appropriate funds from tax receipts for the payment of Social Security benefits. Congress is free to change the amount and timing of benefits, as well as the rate of the social security excise tax that generates payments by covered (working) persons.

When the Justice Department defended the constitutionality of the Social Security Act before the Supreme Court, the briefs filed in the case and the Supreme Court's decision confirm that Social Security is an excise tax measured by the wages payable by an employer during the calendar year. *The social security tax did not include a legislative commitment to pay even a single dollar in benefits to anyone.*[279]

---

278 Ida May Fuller, the first U.S. recipient of monthly Social Security benefits, paid a total of $24.75 in Social Security taxes over her last three years of work before retirement but received a total of nearly $23,000 in benefits before her death. *The Fair Tax Book*, at p. 127.

279 *Chas. C. Steward Mach. Co. v. Davis*, 301 U.S. 548, at 574 and at 577 (1937). Mr. Justice Cardozo's summarized the relevant portions of the Social Security Act (42 U.S.C.A §§301-1305) this way:

Reasonable people can rationally debate whether the Social Security program, and its siblings Medicare, Medicaid, and the new Health Care program, bear close or no resemblance to the schemes of Charles Ponzi and Bernie Madoff. Regardless of your opinion, these programs are clearly not sustainable as structured. The changing demographics of covered workers and beneficiaries cannot work, without steep changes *up* in contributions and steep changes *down* in benefits. Like those who invested late with Ponzi and Madoff (just before they were caught), it will hurt not to be an early participant in these federal programs.

The second and third sentences of Amendment 9 of *The Second Bill of Rights* confirm there is no federal power to direct whether or how citizens engage in commerce and plan for retirement and economic security. Each citizen is free to make their own plan, such as setting aside real or other property; establishing annuities or pensions; or contracting for health, disability, life, long-term care, or other insurance.

To fulfill previous commitments to persons over sixty-five (65), and to provide an option to persons between forty-five (45) and sixty-four (64) years of age, Section 2 of Amendment 11 to *The Second Bill of Rights* gives Congress the power to convert the nation's prior moral commitments to social security and medicare into a legal one.[280]

Amendment 11 restores the income tax-free status of social security and medicare payments. Congress is also given power to establish a means test of general application to effectively apply trust funds to beneficiaries who need them and who are counting on receiving them.

Planning for retirement and economic security are matters of individual choice that seventy years of experience confirms cannot prudently be controlled by the national government. Both Congress and the Executive have been unable to resist relentless pressure from factions to ex-

---

"The tax begins with the year 1936, and is payable for the first time on January 31, 1937. During the calendar year 1936 the rate is to be 1 per cent., during 1937 2 per cent., and 3 per cent thereafter. The proceeds, when collected, go into the Treasury of the United States like internal revenue collections generally. Section 905(a), 42 U.S.C.A. §1105(a). *They are not earmarked in any way* . . .
No present appropriation is made to the extent of a single dollar. All that the title (the Act) does is to authorize future appropriations."
280 See, Number 48, below.

pand benefits and coverage (mission creep), and have had no courage whatsoever to maintain financial stability as life expectancy increased dramatically and as the ratio of covered workers to beneficiaries fell dramatically. Elected and appointed officials much prefer unbalanced budgets, deficit spending, and "Alice in Wonderland" accounting to admitting to citizens that the social programs they asserted were self-sustaining are not in fact so, and cannot become self-sustaining without massive interference with individual freedom and liberty rights. Competing factions continue to churn these issues in Congress and the media while the status quo moves the nation toward bankruptcy.

Amicus

NUMBER 47.
The Judiciary as Bulwark for Liberty—Amendment 10

Amendment 10 to *The Second Bill of Rights* makes technical changes with respect to the Judiciary to reinforce its intended role as bulwark in defense of liberty rights within the Rule of Law. The Amendment contains five sections, each of which is described in turn.

Second Bill of Rights 10. [38. The Judiciary; Appointments; Jurisdiction.]
1. The Judicial power shall be exercised to preserve liberty rights, the Rule of Law, the police power of each of the several States, and the republican form of government. Section 2 of Amendments XIII, XV, XXIV, and XXVI; Sections 1 and 5 of Amendment XIV; and the second paragraph of Amendment XIX are repealed.

The first sentence of Section 1 confirms that the judicial power shall be exercised to preserve the constitutional framework—specifically, to preserve liberty rights, the Rule of Law, the police power of each of the States, and the republican form of government.

The second sentence of Section 1 restores balance between the power of the States and the power of the federal government to interfere one with the other, in their respective spheres. The enforcement language in several of existing amendments is repealed. State and federal courts can and will handle cases involving violations of the Constitution under the Rule of Law.[281]

---

281 For example, the Twenty-sixth Amendment states that citizens eighteen years and older may vote. The second paragraph gives Congress power to enforce this requirement. The second paragraph is unnecessary and redundant, and creates contention among States, the Congress, and the courts. The words in the Twenty-sixth Amendment are plain. The States understand these words, and can enact appropriate legislation under the police power, without congressional intrusion. And, most importantly, courts can enforce the Amendment. Congress need not divert attention from its

2. The President in nominating, and the Senate in advice and consent, shall consider the experience of each judicial nominee in the practice of the common law.

Section 2 of Amendment 10 adds a qualification to be considered by the President and the Senate when making and advising on appointments to the federal judiciary. The qualifications and the temperament required for great federal judges come from experience in the common law, and a working knowledge of the Rule of Law set forth in the constitution. Experience in the common law is most widely gained by attorneys with strong practices, background, and experience in the practice of law in the states. This is not the same in federal practice, where the issues are confined to the enumerated powers rather than to the broad range of topics typically arising under the police power and in the everyday exercise of liberty rights. The role of the Judiciary as bulwark for the protection of liberty rights is often not glorious, not overly spontaneous, and not an exercise in which the most unusual idea is typically best. Section 2 of Amendment 10 properly recognizes the importance of common law experience.

3. In all Cases before the Courts of the United States between Citizens of different States, the prevailing party or parties shall be awarded reasonable attorneys' fees, costs, and expenses.

In 1789, six Supreme Court justices and thirteen federal district judges managed the federal judicial system. By 1913, Congress had added federal circuit courts (thirty-two circuit judges) and expanded the number of judges to ninety-two. But, the court system was still compact.

No longer! Over the last century, Congress authorized a six-fold increase in circuit court judges and a seven-fold increase in the number of district judges.[282] The federal courts have been busy throughout this period. In

---

enumerated powers to hold hearings, meetings, and votes on this topic. The Executive need not worry about regulations enforcing this mandate. The entire group need not wait for others to act, creating still more confusion among federal, state, and local governments.

282 From thirty-two circuit judges to one hundred seventy-nine. From ninety-two district judges to six-hundred and sixty-seven. The 2010 caseload statistics and the historical statistics of authorized federal judges are available at http://www.uscourts.gov/ Statistics.aspx—the United States Courts website.

2010, 293,000 civil cases were commenced in federal district courts.[283] In 2010, 76,000 criminal cases were pending in the district courts. This caseload is surprising in the following two respects:

> Thirty-seven (37) percent of the 293,000 civil cases commenced in 2010 were private cases involving state law brought by citizens of different states (known as diversity of citizenship cases because the parties are from diverse states). More than 108,000 diversity cases were commenced in the federal courts in 2010.[284]

> The number of diversity cases commenced by private parties in the federal district courts in 2010—108,000—substantially exceeds all of the criminal cases commenced in the federal courts for the year ending March 2010—76,000.

Section 3 encourages citizens, when choosing between state and federal court in diversity cases, to consider the likelihood of success of their suits before consuming limited federal judicial resources. Limited federal judicial resources are more appropriately directed to cases—both criminal and civil—that directly relate to federal law.

To accomplish this, Section 3 adopts the common law rule from a growing number of States, and generally applicable in Australia, Canada, New Zealand, and Britain[285] to diversity cases before the federal courts.

---

283 The growth in civil cases, in particular, has been extraordinary. In 1940, the number of annual civil case filings and criminal case filings were approximately the same—averaging about 37,000 in each category. *Criminal Caseload in U.S. District Courts: More than Meets the Eye*, David L. Cook et al, The American University Law Review, Vol. 44: 1579 (1995). Cook and his colleagues note a 560 percent increase in civil case filings during the period from 1940 to 1994. The adverse effects on federal criminal dockets are described.

284 Since the first Judiciary Act in 1789, the trial courts of the federal government have been given the authority from Congress to hear civil cases between citizens of different states (diversity jurisdiction).. The basis for this special jurisdiction was to provide out-of-state parties with a federal court alternate forum, rather than an in-state forum, for the resolution of civil cases. The out-of-state party may elect to proceed in state court, but has the alternative to remove a case to the federal court instead. In diversity cases, the federal district court judge and the jury (if there is one) sit as a state court applying state law. No change in diversity jurisdiction is proposed.

285 Most of the world's common law countries switched to follow this rule in the 1830's.

Reasonable attorneys' fees, costs, and expenses are awarded to the prevailing party in diversity of citizenship cases.[286]

> 4. No inferior court of the United States shall have jurisdiction over: (i) any matter involving a uniformed military service, its policies and regulations, its personnel, its code of military justice, or the conduct of such personnel in military service; or (ii) any case or controversy which the President declares in writing involves terrorism with some foreign element. The President need not disclose specifics of such elements in the notice.

Section 4 of Amendment 10 removes the trial judges of the federal judiciary and the intermediate Courts of Appeals from the military justice system. At least seven (7) of the eighteen (18) enumerated powers in Article I, Section 8, deal with Congress' authority over the military. It is difficult to argue that Congress' control over the armed forces is not plenary, even though command of the armed forces is vested in the President.[287] Congress has expressly enumerated power to prescribe discipline. Congress has exercised this authority through legislation—the Uniform Code of Military Justice (UCMJ), including an entire disciplinary and punishment regime. Section 4 of Amendment 10 restores Congress' plenary control of this system, to be exercised without interference from the inferior courts of the United States. All the inferior courts of the United States are creatures of the Congress. Congress can limit their

---

286 In 2010, more than 44,000 civil cases were commenced in which the United States is a party. More than 140,000 cases were commenced in the district court involving questions of federal law. More than 76,000 federal criminal cases were pending as of 31 March 2010.

287 To define and punish Piracies and Felonies committed on the high Seas, and Offenses against the Law of Nations;

To declare War, grant Letters of Marque and Reprisal, and make Rules concerning Captures on Land and Water;

To raise and support Armies, but no Appropriation of Money to that Use shall be for a longer Term than two Years;

To provide and maintain a Navy;

To make Rules for the Government and Regulation of the land and naval Forces;

To provide for calling forth the Militia to execute the Laws of the Union, suppress Insurrections and repel Invasions;

To provide for organizing, arming, and disciplining the Militia, and for governing such Part of them as may be employed in the Service of the United States, reserving to the States respectively, the Appointment of the Officers, and the Authority of training the Militia according to the discipline prescribed by Congress.

jurisdiction.[288] Section 4 does *not* preclude the Supreme Court from review of cases heard in the military justice system. The UCMJ remains subject to congressional review and oversight.

> 5. Citizens accused of terrorism against the United States may be tried for treason in the Courts of the United States in accord with the Rule of Law.

Section 5 of Amendment 10 clears up one of the issues debated in the media and Congress following the attacks of September 11, 2001, regarding long-term confinement and trial of combatants captured overseas by the military forces of the United States who are U.S. citizens. Section 5 confirms that citizens accused of terrorism against the United States may be tried for treason in accord with the Rule of Law. Article 3, Section 3 of the existing Constitution expressly deals with treason against the United States, how it is to be proven, and how punished.

Valerius

---

288 Article I, Section 8, the ninth of the eighteen enumerated powers. "To constitute Tribunals inferior to the Supreme Court."

NUMBER 48.
Re-codification of Federal Statutes—Transition

The first ten amendments within *The Second Bill of Rights* contemplate an ordered repositioning of the relationship between American citizens and their government. Section 1 of Amendment 11 establishes a sense of deliberate urgency for Congress and the Executive to re-codify the Statutes of the United States. Once ratified by the States, Section 1 establishes a transition program under which: (i) the Executive stops enforcing inconsistent laws, rules, and orders and (ii) Congress promptly modifies the statutes of the United States.

> 1. From the effective date of Amendments 28 to 39 (the Second Bill of Rights), the Executive shall not execute or enforce any law, rule, or order, or make any new rule or order inconsistent with the Constitution, as amended. Congress shall promptly modify the statutes of the United States for an orderly transition to conform herewith.

Major portions of the existing statutes of the United States will not require change as a result of *The Second Bill of Rights*. These statutes can be reenacted as new law with no (or few) changes and with existing cross references eliminated or harmonized in a new version of the Code. Examples of existing statutes not likely to require substantial revision include the laws relating to the military services, federal criminal law, the SEC, the FBI, the U.S. Patent and Trademark (and Copyright) Office, export control, existing U.S. treaty obligations, and the laws relating to safety in interstate transportation of goods.

On several prior occasions, the statutes of the United States have been re-codified as a natural result of tinkering and wholesale changes made by successive sessions of Congress with portions of the U.S. Code. The Code is now nearly unintelligible, not only to typical citizens engaged in their own pursuits, but even to the most knowledgeable members of legislative staff.

Inherent in every prior re-codification of these statutes is simplification.

- Regular re-codification provides the opportunity to remove or harmonize conflicting and confusing language in the statutes of the United States.
- Regular re-codification provides the opportunity to re-confirm continuing support in the Congress (and in the general population) for existing federal law.
- Regular re-codification allows citizens, in the exercise of their liberty rights, to learn and then predict how federal statutes affect private choice, for themselves and their families.
- Simplification allows citizens to plan their affairs and conserve their resources, with corresponding benefits to enforcement by agencies and adjudication by courts.

Re-codification increases support for federal statutes—one key component of the Rule of Law.

To remove any doubt that Congress has the power to pass transitional legislation with respect to the payment of specific social security benefits, Section 2 expressly provides the following:

2. Congress may enact legislation that: (i) preserves social security payments and medicare benefits under current law, but free of income tax, for persons who at the date of this amendment are 65 years of age and older; (ii) gives the option to persons then between 45 and 64 years of age (a) to contribute to social security and medicare under current law and (b) at age 65 to receive such payments and benefits, free of income tax; and (iii) establishes a means test of general application to all persons for reductions, in whole or part, and in amount or time, with respect to one or more of these payments and benefits.

Section 2 exempts social security payments from income tax. Section 2 protects such payments for persons over sixty-five (65) years of age at the time of ratification, and authorizes Congress to provide the option to take such benefits for persons between forty-five (45) and sixty-four (64) years old at the time of ratification.

Section 2 authorizes Congress to establish a means test of general application to all persons for reductions, in whole or part, and in amount. Section 2 requires that any such means test be of general application— that is, logically based.

By way of example, Congress might provide the following as a means test of general application for social security benefits. A citizen with aggregate retirement assets greater than fifty (50) times the annual maximum social security benefit in a year for which he or she is otherwise entitled to a social security benefit might have his or her social security benefit reduced, in whole or part, with respect to that year.[289]

Congress might provide the following as a "means test" with respect to medicare benefits. A citizen with aggregate retirement assets in excess of $10 million (indexed from 2012 for inflation/deflation) in a year for which he or she is otherwise entitled to a medicare benefit is available might have his or her medicare benefits reduced, in whole or part, with respect to that year.

Valerius

---

[289] Note that Amendment 11 to *The Second Bill of Rights* does not relate to benefits earned as a result of service in the military of the United States.

NUMBER 49.
The Substance of Individual Freedom and Liberty Rights

Since the 1787 Constitutional Convention, judicial decision, technical advances in media, and the unlimited capacity of *factions* for self-promotion have attached algae and barnacles to the hull of the U.S. Constitution, tugging at the *controls* and the *precautions* the Founders employed to protect individual freedom and liberty from a coercive *government administered by men over men.* Madison placed these controls and precautions in the Constitution to allow a good scrubbing every once in a while, a written barrier to the inevitable abuse of government in favor of some at the expense of others. The written American constitution is still the first and best evidence of American exceptionalism.

The Founders were *not* able to agree on eradication of slavery—a major error in the identification of who was entitled to the benefits of individual freedom and liberty rights. *But, this was not an error in the description or the content of individual freedom and liberty.*

Although the Civil Rights Act of 1866 and the Thirteenth through Fifteenth Amendments were intended to fix this error, the fix worked in form only, *never* in substance. In form, all citizens were equal, but in practice they were separated and treated differently.[290]

With the Thirteenth, Fourteenth, and Fifteenth Amendments, a practice also began in which Congress was given power to implement amendments through legislation.[291] This practice arose from a basic distrust by Republicans in the post-Civil War Congress of political institutions across the defeated Southern states (historically Democrat) and the judiciary. These Republicans feared that factions hostile to the principles of

---

290 One purpose of *The Second Bill of Rights* is to solidify the liberty rights of every citizen—period. Further legislation with respect to liberty rights should be minimal.
291 Section 2 of Amendments XIII, XV, XXIV, and XXVI; Sections 5 of Amendment XIV; and the second paragraph of Amendment XIX.

the Thirteenth, Fourteenth, and Fifteenth Amendments would misuse the police power to circumvent the amendments after these states were readmitted, and the courts would do nothing about it. There was reason behind this fear, as shown by the decision in *The Slaughterhouse Cases* and the subsequent enactment of Jim Crow across the South. Pitting Congress against the Southern States may have been practical in 1866. But, at its heart, government vs. government has *not* worked, is in conflict with the Founders' federal system, and continues to provide combustible fuel for the divisive interests of factions.

A basic premise of the Founders in establishing our federal system was that States could be trusted to implement the police power in a reasonable and fair way, ensuring that all citizens may exercise their political, civil, and economic liberty rights in concert with fellow citizens under the Rule of Law. *The Second Bill of Rights* returns to this basic premise,[292] trusting States in the exercise of their police power,[293] *but with two new auxiliary precautions* to justify this trust: (i) a presumption in favor of a citizen's exercise of liberty rights,[294] and (ii) confirmation of the Judiciary's role in preserving liberty rights.[295]

Rather than pitting Congress against the States,[296] *The Second Bill of Rights* provides expansive, explicit protection for liberty rights[297] and establishes a presumption that a citizen's exercise of these rights is valid.[298] The burden is generally on the government to overcome the presumption, which is easily done when Congress is exercising an enumerated power, but more difficult when government is acting narrowly on behalf of some while interfering with the liberty of others.

Candidates for President and Congress, spurred by factions and the media, forever advance the fiction that wonderful results can be centrally planned and implemented by the national government. Too many citi-

---

292 *The Second Bill of Rights*, Amendments 1, 2, and 3.

293 *The Second Bill of Rights*, Amendment 4, Section 1.

294 *The Second Bill of Rights*, Amendment 4, Section 2.

295 *The Second Bill of Rights*, Amendment 10, Section 1.

296 The implementing provisions are repealed. *The Second Bill of Rights*, Amendment 10, Section 1, sentence 2.

297 *The Second Bill of Rights*, Amendment 2, Sections 2 and 3. See, Numbers 8 and 11, above.

298 With respect to: the national government, Amendment 2, Section 4; the States, Amendment 4, Section 2.

zens, the media, and most politicians have fallen (at least outwardly) for the hopeful, but silly, notion that 537 elected officials[299] are so smart they can agree on everything. With 537 angels placed in Congress and the White House, the Founders' fear of the evils of faction would evaporate!

Well-known examples include the fifty-year war on poverty, the forty-year war on drugs, innumerable national energy plans, "No Child Left Behind," and "Race to the Top."[300] Running for federal office now depends on drawing media attention to nonsensical assertions that while the most recent central plan failed this or that way, the next central plan will be even better. Not to worry!

Albert Einstein is reputed to have said:

> [t]he definition of insanity is doing the same thing over and over again and expecting different results.

Agreement on everything is not possible! Madison, Washington, Adams, and Franklin reached this conclusion in 1787, when they established a limited national government whose mandate extended only to reaching agreement on seventeen (17) items set forth in Article 1, Section 8. The Founders knew that *agreement on everything* was impossible, and they structured the national government *so it would never seek to do so.* The Founders left the police power to the States, so there would be room for differences, comparisons, experimentation, and opportunities for citizens to relocate. The Founders left the development of each individual's interests, capability, and preferences to citizens—the gift of freedom.

Hayek understood the flaw of central planning, a flaw admitted by leading advocates of collectivism.[301] Taking up the challenge of reaching *agreement on everything* is self-defeating for any republic—insane, to use Einstein's word. The pattern Hayek saw in the 1940's predominates in twenty-first century America—ever bigger failures in central planning lead to even bigger promises to get it right with the next, more comprehensive central plan. The unintended casualty is an increasingly cynical

---

299 435 members of Congress, 100 members of the Senate, the President and the Vice President.
300 But, the national government is engaged in many thousands of more routine national plans relating to ladders, cranes, hot drinks, trans-fats, sugar, and on and on.
301 See, Numbers 22 and 25, *supra.*

citizenry, ever more suspicious of government institutions that perennially promise—but can't achieve—*agreement on everything.*

It may be the unanimously expressed will of the people that its [legislature] should prepare a comprehensive economic plan, yet neither the people nor its representatives [can] agree on any particular plan. *The inability of democratic assemblies to carry out what seems to be a clear mandate of the people will inevitably cause dissatisfaction with democratic institutions.* [Legislatures] come to be regarded as ineffective "talking shops," unable or incompetent to carry out the task for which they have been chosen. The conviction grows that if efficient planning is to be done, the direction must be "taken out of politics" and placed in the hands of experts—permanent officials or independent autonomous bodies.[302]

A Substantive Path Forward

The Founders foresaw our current difficulty—an ever more officious national government intruding into the smallest nook and cranny of our individual lives, administered by less than angelic men over the rest of the citizenry. The Founders had faced an entrenched royal bureaucracy, writs of assistance, searches without warrants, and obstructions to liberty of all sorts by a royal government focused on maintaining a central hold on citizens. They rejected it!

The Founders created the structure to preserve individual freedom and liberty rights against such a national government. The structure is there—the principles remain. *The Second Bill of Rights* comprehensively redresses the twists and turns that have obscured these principles. Using the *USS Constitution* as a metaphor for the U.S. Constitution once again, the package of amendments in *The Second Bill of Rights* scrapes off the barnacles, repaints the hull, and re-floats the constitutional ship.

In one way or another, each amendment in *The Second Bill of Rights* returns to substance over form, and to Founding principles of individual freedom and liberty rights. The *Liberty Rights Amendments* (1—4) restore these principles to primary status and pave the way toward balanced confirmation of the mutual obligations of the government, states, and the judiciary to protect a people endowed with inalienable liberty rights.

---

302 F. A. Hayek, *The Road to Serfdom, supra,* at p. 104.

Amendment 5 requires the same transparency in financial matters government imposes upon public companies, in a manner that timely informs voters before elections. Amendment 5 also requires Congress to regain direct responsibility for a stable currency. Amendment 6 abolishes the income, estate, and gift taxes. A uniform consumption tax is authorized that exempts, through monthly rebates, every citizen from the tax up to the national poverty level. Amendment 7 provides for a statutory process for naturalization (citizenship) and for residency. Amendment 8 substantially eliminates gerrymandering of the House of Representatives and restores residents of the city of Washington DC to the State of Maryland with representation in the House. Amendment 9 confirms that the power to regulate interstate commerce is not without limit, and confirms that each of us is at liberty to establish his or her own plans for retirement and for economic security. Amendment 10 makes technical changes relating to the Judiciary to promote more active focus upon the common law, administration of civil litigation, preservation of individual liberty rights, the police power of the States, and the republican form of government. Amendment 11 provides for re-codification of the Statutes of the United States to conform with *The Second Bill of Rights*.

The effects of *The Second Bill of Rights* will be seen in the lives of millions of Americans riding in the *US(S) Constitution*, from the hold to the mast of the ship. Armed with a presumption of liberty, any six-year old kid can run a lemonade stand until a government proves otherwise to a court. What a very different, and very hopeful, lesson for the generations that follow Madison.

To extend and preserve the blessings of freedom and liberty for generations to come, *The Second Bill of Rights* tinkers with the Founders' structure[303] and adds several "auxiliary precautions" to safeguard citizens in the exercise of liberty rights, always under the Rule of Law defined in the Constitution.

Valerius

---

303 The *Constitution of the United States*, including *The Second Bill of Rights*, is set forth in the Appendix. There are no changes to the text of the original Constitution or the first Bill of Rights (Amendments 1 to 10). Portions of the language in Amendments 13, 14, 15, 16, 19, 23, 24, and 26 are deleted, and shown as strikethrough text—as shown here. The Second Bill of Rights is inserted as Amendments 28 to 38 to the Constitution of the United States of America.

NUMBER 50.
It's the 468 Bi-Annual Seats in Congress! (Not the Presidency)

Wouldn't it be easier if the protection of individual freedom and liberty rights could just be assigned to a single American citizen? With a backup in place, government could rely just on the President and the Vice President. They could assess the national and worldwide situation; ask the advice of experts of their own choosing; decide who would be taxed, for what, and how much; field an army, navy, air force, and marines; and protect the home land. The President, alone, could certainly make a decision and if agreement on everything were needed, the Vice President would be there to provide instant agreement.

It would be easier to leave all of this to others. Most of us are just too busy with our lives, playing the genetic hand we've been dealt, exploring what we can do to make a living while balancing work and family and remaining flexible. We don't know what opportunities lie around the corner.[304] Day-to-day challenges consume us—food, shelter, clothing, and children.

The Founders—with the irrefutable support of history—scream at us across the centuries that reliance on one (or a few individuals) can *never* lead to individual freedom with liberty rights.

Freedom and liberty in matters of everyday life cannot coexist with central planning. The Founders knew this well. They had experienced similar despotism from royal government inspired by divine right.[305] They knew the destructive power of factions, having seen its fruits in the royal governments of London and Paris,[306] and in colonial governments.

---

304 See Number 3, above. *The Humble Logic of Individual Freedom and Liberty Rights.*
305 Divine inspiration ensured that royal decisions were correct. Instead of inspiration of a divinity, modern Presidents are inspired by the experts, preferably from academia, eager and willing to experiment with the freedom and liberty of their fellow citizens.
306 The history of France and England is replete with rivalries, often deadly, among

They knew that factions would adapt over time, learning how to push and pull officials in the exercise of the coercive power of any national government. They knew that men were not angels.

The Founders did not set up an imperial Presidency—far from it. As just a few examples:

- Without a majority vote of the House of Representatives, on a bill originating there, not one single tax dollar may be collected by the President, any of his cabinet secretaries, or any lower level (petty) official. (Article I, Section 7)
- Without a vote of both the House and the Senate, the President has no power to declare War. (Article I, Section 8)
- Without a 2/3 vote of approval by the Senate, no treaty negotiated between the President and any foreign nation can have the force and effect of law in the United States. (Article II, Section 2)
- Without the advice and consent of the Senate, the President cannot complete the appointment of ambassadors, justices, consuls, and other officers of the United States. (Article II, Section 2)[307]

468 Seats in the House and Senate—Every Two Years

In even-numbered years, on the first Tuesday of November, 435 members of the House of Representatives stand for election. At the same time, 33 members of the Senate stand for election (once every six years it is 34). The only choice of incumbents is whether to run. And, on that day, the Founders ensured that elected federal officials are accountable to citizens.

Do the math! In two election cycles, the entirety of the House of Representatives can be replaced twice. In two election cycles, 2/3 of the Senate can be replaced.[308]

The Founders' separated the powers of the national government—locating different powers in the House, the Senate, the President, and the Judiciary, with internal and external controls that provide internal checks

---

competing court factions.

307 There is an exception for recess appointments to fill vacancies in Article II, Section 2, para. 3.

308 Another of the Founders' *internal* controls. George Washington likened the House to hot tea, and the Senate to the saucer that cooled it.

and balances, so that the branches are co-equal and none can dominate the others.

Hamilton believed the House of Representatives would be the "most popular [appreciated] branch of . . . government—a full match, if not an overmatch, for every other [branch] of the government."[309] Madison confirmed that "frequent elections" were "unquestionably" the only policy by which the common interest, "immediate dependence on, and . . . intimate sympathy with the people" could [be] effectually secured.[310]

The controls and precautions the Founders established are there. The presumption of validity in a citizen's exercise of liberty rights is an additional precaution added by *The Second Bill of Rights*. In one election, on one day, the authority to spend money, collect taxes, and prosecute a war can be started or ended—by the House. The Founders put teeth into each of the branches of the national government, so that each could defend itself against the others, none could dominate, and even all three, together, couldn't dominate the people for more than two years.

In today's environment, in which Presidents, parties, and candidates assert they can reach agreement on everything—Einstein's definition of insanity comes to mind.

Hayek's fear that the failures of central planning would be laid at the feet of democratic institutions rather than at their root cause—the self-interest of factions that promote central planning—has also come true.[311] After decades of claims by majority parties in the House or the Senate that they can reach *agreement on everything*—the inevitable failures of central planning have been blamed not on the arrogance of factions and the abuse of the Founders' framework, but rather, and quite conveniently for those who have failed, on the institutions the Founders created.

---

309 Federalist Papers, No. 66, at p. 403.
310 Federalist Papers, No. 32, at p. 327.
311 One recent example is the Super-committee of Senators and Congressmen supposed to come up with a solution to the financial crisis of the nation—a task that is on the one hand too partisan to solve and on the other hand so urgent that an immediate solution without debate is necessary. What utter nonsense! Wouldn't it be refreshing if 535 members of the House and Senate resigned, admitting that because of their fear of being accountable, it is better that other citizens step forward and perform their constitutional function?

As factions fail to reach agreement on matters beyond the enumerated powers listed in the Founders' framework, their rhetoric continues to intensify, and their drums beat ever louder for urgent action on ever more massive central plans that require complete agreement and perfect results to be reached, with details assigned to others, and with no agreement on means, methods or ends. And, of course, urgency is claimed to require that constitutional processes be ignored or by-passed.[312]

Millions of American parents are unable to achieve complete agreement on everything affecting the daily lives of their families. It is not possible to do so. Similarly, and for essentially the same reasons, the Founders never gave the federal government the assignment of reaching agreement on everything. They assigned some enumerated items to the national government, left many more to the States, and left individual freedom and liberty rights to citizens to freely use in developing their own plans for pursuing happiness.

We know that the Founders did not believe the original Constitution was perfect because they not only included the power to amend the Constitution but also used this power to add eleven amendments within the first decade of initial ratification. They were humble in this respect, too.

The Second Bill of Rights isn't perfect either. George Washington's 1787 description of its imperfections is still accurate, two hundred twenty-five years later. Those who come after us can judge, with the advantage of experience, whether further alterations and amendments are appropriate to meet new challenges to individual freedom in the exercise of liberty

---

312 The entire charade is preposterous. Senate and House committees have time to bully professional baseball players, but the Senate has not had time to pass a budget in nearly three years. A baseball player can't fight back—while to a Senator or Representative, taking a clear position has consequences in subsequent elections.
Mel Brooks' movie Blazing Saddles comes to mind, and his role as Governor Le Petomane.
Governor. "Holy underwear! Sheriff murdered! Innocent women and children blown to bits! We've got to protect our phony baloney jobs, gentlemen. We must do something about this, immediately, immediately, immediately! Harrumph! Harrumph! Harrumph! Harrumph! Harrumph!
I didn't get a 'harrumph' out of that guy!
Lamarr. Give the governor a 'harrumph!'
Reporter. Harrumph!

rights. "*[We] do not think we are more inspired, have more wisdom, or possess more virtue, than those who will come after us.*"[313]

We hope the entire package will be understood for what it is: a balanced effort to re-energize the Founders' vision of the Rule of Law under a limited, federal, constitutional republic. Few ideas expressed in *The Second Bill of Rights* do more than tinker with concepts developed and incorporated into the Constitution by the Founders. Even if adopted in full, the amended Constitution will require continued attention, consideration, and care in the future.

The Second Bill of Rights is offered with malice toward none, with charity for all and in the hope of a new birth of freedom in the United States.[314]

Valerius

---

313 See, Editor's Note, *supra*, for the full quotation from George Washington's 1787 letter to his nephew Bushrod Washington.
314 The *Constitution of the United States*, including *The Second Bill of Rights*, is set forth in the Appendix.

Bibliography

Cases

Allen v. Tooley, 80 Eng. Rep. 1055 (K.B. 1614).
Barron v. Baltimore, 32 U.S. 243 (1833)
Brown v. Board of Education, 347 U.S. 483 (1952)
Burns v. Richardson, 384 U.S. 72, 89 (1966).
Dr. Bonham's Case, 8 Co. Rep. 114 (1610)
Chas. Steward Mach. Co. v. Davis, 301 U.S. 548 (1937)
Corfield v. Coryell, 6 Fed. Cases 546 (1823)
Cunningham v. Brown, 265 U.S. 1 (1924)
Davis v. Bandemer, 478 U.S. 109 (1986).
FCC v Beach Communications, Inc., 508 U.S. 307 (1993)
Gary v. Sanders, 372 U.S. 368 (1963).
Griswold v. Connecticut, 391 U.S. 479 (1965)
Helvering v. Davis, 301 U.S. 619 (1937)
Lochner v. New York, 198 U.S. 45 (1905)
McCulloch v. Maryland, 17 U.S. 579 (1819)
Nebbia v. New York, 291 U.S. 502 (1934)
New State Ice Co. v. Liebmann, 285 U.S. 262 (1932)
Norman v. Baltimore & O.R. Co. United States et al v. Bankers Trust Co. et al, 294 U.S. 240 (1935).
People v. Nebbia, 262 N.Y. 259, 186 N.E. 694 (1933)
Plessy v. Ferguson, 163 U.S. 537 (1896)
Pollock v. Farmer's Loan & Trust Co., 158 U.S. 601 (1895)
Roe v Wade, 410 U.S. 113 (1973)
Shaw v. Reno, 509 U.S. 630 (1993).
Slaughterhouse Cases, 83 U.S. 36 (1873)

Dissent of Mr. Justice Field in *Slaughterhouse Cases*, 83 U.S. 36, at 87 (1873)
South Carolina State Highway Department v Barnwell Bros., 303 U.S. 177 (1938)
The Civil Rights Cases, 109 U.S. 3 (1883)
Thornburg v. Gingles, 476 U.S. 30 (1986).
United States v Carolene Products, 304 U.S. 144 (1938)
United States v. Comstock, 560 U.S.   , 130 S.Ct. 1949 (2010)
United States v. Cruikshank, 92 U.S. 542 (1875).
Wesberry v. Sanders, 376 U.S. 1 (1964).
West Coast Hotel Co. v. Parrish, 300 U.S. 379 (1936)
Wickard v. Filburn, 317 U.S. 111 (1942)

Books

The Federalist Papers, Mentor, 1961.

Barnett, Randy E., *Restoring the Lost Constitution*, The Presumption of Liberty, Princeton University Press, 2004, ISBN-13: 978-0-691-12376-9.

Barnett, Randy E., *Constitutional Law, Cases in Context*, 2008, ISBN 978-0-7355-6344-5, Wolters Kluwer Law & Business, Aspen Publishers.

Bowen, Catherine Drinker, *The Lion and the Throne*, Little Brown & Co., 1957.

Dickens, Charles, *Little Dorrit*, (Monthly Serial, December 1855 to June 1857).

Jefferson, Thomas, *The Writings of Thomas Jefferson*, Memorial Edition (Lipscomb and Bergh, editors) 20 Vols., Washington DC, 1903-04.

Ledbetter, Mark David, *America's Forgotten History, Part One, Foundations*, 2011, available at *Smashwords.com*

Lippmann, Walter, *An Inquiry into the Principles of the Good Society*, 1937.

Maddison, Angus, *Monitoring the World Economy, 1820 -1992*, OECD Development Centre, 1995, Paris, France

Hayek, F. A., *The Road to Serfdom*, Text and Documents, The Definitive Edition, Edited by Bruce Caldwell, 2007, The University of Chicago Press.

Hayek, F. A., "Freedom and the Economic System" [1938], Vol. 10 of The Collected Works of F. A. Hayek (1997).

Olson, Mancur, The Logic of Collective Action, 1965

Sandefur, Timothy, *The Right to Earn a Living*: Economic Freedom and the Law, The Cato Institute, 2010

Shlaes, *Amity, The Greedy Hand: How Taxes Drive Americans Crazy and What to Do About* It, Random House, New York, 1999.

Smith, Adam, *Inquiry Into the Nature and Causes of the Wealth of Nations,* 1776.

Constitutions

The 1780 Massachusetts Constitution
The 1776 Virginia Declaration of Rights
The 1787 United States Constitution

Speeches, Hearings, Proclamations

Bingham, John, New York Congressman, speech in Congress regarding the 14th Amendment, February 29, 1866.

Burke, Sen. Edward (Nebraska), Reorganization of the Federal Judiciary, Question Posed in Hearings before the Committee on the Judiciary, U.S. Senate, 75th Cong., 1st Session (Washington: G.P.O., 1937), at 57.

King, Jr., Martin Luther, *"I Have a Dream,"* Speech at the Lincoln Memorial, Aug. 28, 1963.

Lincoln, Abraham, *Second Inaugural Address,* Saturday, March 4, 1865

Lincoln, Abraham, *Gettysburg Address,* November 19, 1963

Lincoln, Abraham, The Emancipation Proclamation, January 1, 1863

Thatcher, Margaret, Prime Minister of Britain, Wiki Answers, television interview for Thames TV This Week, February 5, 1976.

Statutes

The Coinage Act of 1792
The Mississippi Black Codes, 1865.
The Civil Rights Act of 1866
The 1867 Reconstruction Acts, 39th Congress Session II, Chapter 153, and 40th Congress, Session 1, Chapter 30.
March 4, 1923, c. 262, 42 Stat. 1486, 21 U.S.C. §§ 61 63, 21 U.S.C.A. § 61—63.
The Patient Protection and Affordable Care Act, enacted in January 2010
The Dodd-Frank Wall Street Reform and Consumer Protection Act of 2010

The Internal Revenue Code, from http://uscode.house.gov/download/
title_26.shtm

Media

http://www.youtube.com/watch?v=69kr5WpYjgA
http://en.wikipedia.org/wiki/USS_Constitution#Sail_200
http://ssa.gov
http://www.ssa.gov/oact/progdata/fundFAQ.html
Blazing Saddles, movie produced by Mel Brooks.
The Gerrymander Cartoon (1812), http://en.wikipedia.org/wiki/Gerrymandering

Other Sources

The House That Jack Built, 18th Century English Nursery Rhyme.
Notes of Dr. James McHenry, The American Historical Review, vol. 11, 1906,
at p. 618.
GASB Statement No. 34—Basic Financial Statements—and Management's Discussion and Analysis—for State and Local Governments
Miller, Geoff, "The True Story of Carolene Products," Supreme Court
Review (1987), 397-428;
Miller, Geoff, "Public Choice at the Dawn of the Special Interest State:
The Story of Butter and Margarine," California Law Review 77
(1989).
Photograph of William F. Russell [search the web for "Bill Russell Rings."]
National Executive Committee of the Labour Party, Annual Conference,
London, May 25-28, 1942
The Rising Cost of Complying with the Federal Income Tax, Tax Foundation
Special Report No. 138 (January 2006)
Income Mobility in the U.S. from 1996 to 2007, Report of the Department
of the Treasury, November 13, 2007 (Typographical revisions, March
2008).
U.S. Debt Clock 1 January 2012. 1:48 PM.

Appendix

The Constitution of the United States of America, Including *The Second Bill of Rights*

The Constitution of the United States of America is set forth in this Appendix, with *The Second Bill of Rights* incorporated in full.

There are no changes to the text of the original Constitution or the first Bill of Rights (Amendments 1 to 10).

Portions of the language in Amendments 13, 14, 15, 16, 19, 23, 24, and 26 are deleted, and shown as strikethrough text—as shown here. Where appropriate, paragraph numbers are revised. Italicized text explains each deletion by reference to *The Second Bill of Rights*.

The Second Bill of Rights is inserted as Amendments 28 to 38 to the Constitution of the United States of America.

Constitution of the United States of America

We the People of the United States, in Order to form a more perfect Union, establish Justice, insure domestic Tranquility, provide for the common defence, promote the general Welfare, and secure the Blessings of Liberty to ourselves and our Posterity, do ordain and establish this Constitution for the United States of America.

Article 1.

Section 1
All legislative Powers herein granted shall be vested in a Congress of the United States, which shall consist of a Senate and House of Representatives.

Section 2
The House of Representatives shall be composed of Members chosen every second Year by the People of the several States, and the Electors in each State shall have the Qualifications requisite for Electors of the most numerous Branch of the State Legislature.

No Person shall be a Representative who shall not have attained to the Age of twenty five Years, and been seven Years a Citizen of the United States, and who shall not, when elected, be an Inhabitant of that State in which he shall be chosen.

Representatives and direct Taxes shall be apportioned among the several States which may be included within this Union, according to their respective Numbers, which shall be determined by adding to the whole Number of free Persons, including those bound to Service for a Term of Years, and excluding Indians not taxed, three fifths of all other Persons. The actual Enumeration shall be made within three Years after the first Meeting of the Congress of the United States, and within every subsequent Term of ten Years, in such Manner as they shall by Law direct. The Number of Representatives shall not exceed one for every thirty Thousand, but each State shall have at Least one Representative; and until such enumeration shall be made, the State of New Hampshire shall be entitled to choose three, Massachusetts eight, Rhode Island and Providence Plantations one, Connecticut five, New York six, New Jersey four, Pennsylvania eight, Delaware one, Maryland six, Virginia ten, North Carolina five, South Carolina five and Georgia three.

When vacancies happen in the Representation from any State, the Executive Authority thereof shall issue Writs of Election to fill such Vacancies.

The House of Representatives shall choose their Speaker and other Officers; and shall have the sole Power of Impeachment.

Section 3
The Senate of the United States shall be composed of two Senators from each State, chosen by the Legislature thereof, for six Years; and each Senator shall have one Vote.

Immediately after they shall be assembled in Consequence of the first Election, they shall be divided as equally as may be into three Classes. The Seats of the Senators of the first Class shall be vacated at the Expiration of the second Year, of the second Class at the Expiration of the fourth Year, and of the third Class at the Expiration of the sixth Year, so that one third may be chosen every second Year; and if Vacancies happen by Resignation, or otherwise, during the Recess of the Legislature of any State, the Executive thereof may make temporary Appointments until the next Meeting of the Legislature, which shall then fill such Vacancies.

No person shall be a Senator who shall not have attained to the Age of thirty Years, and been nine Years a Citizen of the United States, and who shall not, when elected, be an Inhabitant of that State for which he shall be chosen.

The Vice President of the United States shall be President of the Senate, but shall have no Vote, unless they be equally divided.

The Senate shall choose their other Officers, and also a President pro tempore, in the absence of the Vice President, or when he shall exercise the Office of President of the United States.

The Senate shall have the sole Power to try all Impeachments. When sitting for that Purpose, they shall be on Oath or Affirmation. When the President of the United States is tried, the Chief Justice shall preside: And no Person shall be convicted without the Concurrence of two thirds of the Members present.

Judgment in Cases of Impeachment shall not extend further than to removal from Office, and disqualification to hold and enjoy any Office of honor, Trust or Profit under the United States: but the Party convicted shall nevertheless be liable and subject to Indictment, Trial, Judgment and Punishment, according to Law.

Section 4

The Times, Places and Manner of holding Elections for Senators and Representatives, shall be prescribed in each State by the Legislature thereof; but the Congress may at any time by Law make or alter such Regulations, except as to the Place of Choosing Senators.

The Congress shall assemble at least once in every Year, and such Meeting shall be on the first Monday in December, unless they shall by Law appoint a different Day.

Section 5

Each House shall be the Judge of the Elections, Returns and Qualifications of its own Members, and a Majority of each shall constitute a Quorum to do Business; but a smaller number may adjourn from day to day, and may be authorized to compel the Attendance of absent Members, in such Manner, and under such Penalties as each House may provide.

Each House may determine the Rules of its Proceedings, punish its Members for disorderly Behavior, and, with the Concurrence of two-thirds, expel a Member. Each House shall keep a Journal of its Proceedings, and from time to time publish the same, excepting such Parts as may in their Judgment require Secrecy; and the Yeas and Nays of the Members of either House on any question shall, at the Desire of one fifth of those Present, be entered on the Journal.

Neither House, during the Session of Congress, shall, without the Consent of the other, adjourn for more than three days, nor to any other Place than that in which the two Houses shall be sitting.

Section 6

The Senators and Representatives shall receive a Compensation for their Services, to be ascertained by Law, and paid out of the Treasury of the United States. They shall in all Cases, except Treason, Felony and Breach of the Peace, be privileged from Arrest during their Attendance at the Session of their respective Houses, and in going to and returning from the same; and for any Speech or Debate in either House, they shall not be questioned in any other Place.

No Senator or Representative shall, during the Time for which he was elected, be appointed to any civil Office under the Authority of the United States which shall have been created, or the Emoluments whereof shall have been increased during such time; and no Person holding any Office under the United States, shall be a Member of either House during his Continuance in Office.

Section 7
All bills for raising Revenue shall originate in the House of Representatives; but the Senate may propose or concur with Amendments as on other Bills.

Every Bill which shall have passed the House of Representatives and the Senate, shall, before it become a Law, be presented to the President of the United States; If he approve he shall sign it, but if not he shall return it, with his Objections to that House in which it shall have originated, who shall enter the Objections at large on their Journal, and proceed to reconsider it. If after such Reconsideration two thirds of that House shall agree to pass the Bill, it shall be sent, together with the Objections, to the other House, by which it shall likewise be reconsidered, and if approved by two thirds of that House, it shall become a Law. But in all such Cases the Votes of both Houses shall be determined by Yeas and Nays, and the Names of the Persons voting for and against the Bill shall be entered on the Journal of each House respectively. If any Bill shall not be returned by the President within ten Days (Sundays excepted) after it shall have been presented to him, the Same shall be a Law, in like Manner as if he had signed it, unless the Congress by their Adjournment prevent its Return, in which Case it shall not be a Law.

Every Order, Resolution, or Vote to which the Concurrence of the Senate and House of Representatives may be necessary (except on a question of Adjournment) shall be presented to the President of the United States; and before the Same shall take Effect, shall be approved by him, or being disapproved by him, shall be repassed by two thirds of the Senate and House of Representatives, according to the Rules and Limitations prescribed in the Case of a Bill.

Section 8

The Congress shall have Power To lay and collect Taxes, Duties, Imposts and Excises, to pay the Debts and provide for the common Defence and general Welfare of the United States; but all Duties, Imposts and Excises shall be uniform throughout the United States;

To borrow money on the credit of the United States;

To regulate Commerce with foreign Nations, and among the several States, and with the Indian Tribes;

To establish an uniform Rule of Naturalization, and uniform Laws on the subject of Bankruptcies throughout the United States;

To coin Money, regulate the Value thereof, and of foreign Coin, and fix the Standard of Weights and Measures;

To provide for the Punishment of counterfeiting the Securities and current Coin of the United States;

To establish Post Offices and Post Roads;

To promote the Progress of Science and useful Arts, by securing for limited Times to Authors and Inventors the exclusive Right to their respective Writings and Discoveries;

To constitute Tribunals inferior to the supreme Court;

To define and punish Piracies and Felonies committed on the high Seas, and Offenses against the Law of Nations;

To declare War, grant Letters of Marque and Reprisal, and make Rules concerning Captures on Land and Water;

To raise and support Armies, but no Appropriation of Money to that Use shall be for a longer Term than two Years;

To provide and maintain a Navy;

To make Rules for the Government and Regulation of the land and naval Forces;

To provide for calling forth the Militia to execute the Laws of the Union, suppress Insurrections and repel Invasions;

To provide for organizing, arming, and disciplining the Militia, and for governing such Part of them as may be employed in the Service of the United States, reserving to the States respectively, the Appointment of the Officers, and the Authority of training the Militia according to the discipline prescribed by Congress;

To exercise exclusive Legislation in all Cases whatsoever, over such District (not exceeding ten Miles square) as may, by Cession of particular States, and the acceptance of Congress, become the Seat of the Government of the United States, and to exercise like Authority over all Places purchased by the Consent of the Legislature of the State in which the Same shall be, for the Erection of Forts, Magazines, Arsenals, dock-Yards, and other needful Buildings; And

To make all Laws which shall be necessary and proper for carrying into Execution the foregoing Powers, and all other Powers vested by this Constitution in the Government of the United States, or in any Department or Officer thereof.

Section 9

The Migration or Importation of such Persons as any of the States now existing shall think proper to admit, shall not be prohibited by the Congress prior to the Year one thousand eight hundred and eight, but a tax or duty may be imposed on such Importation, not exceeding ten dollars for each Person.

The privilege of the Writ of Habeas Corpus shall not be suspended, unless when in Cases of Rebellion or Invasion the public Safety may require it.

No Bill of Attainder or ex post facto Law shall be passed.

No capitation, or other direct, Tax shall be laid, unless in Proportion to the Census or Enumeration herein before directed to be taken.

No Tax or Duty shall be laid on Articles exported from any State.

No Preference shall be given by any Regulation of Commerce or Revenue to the Ports of one State over those of another: nor shall Vessels bound to, or from, one State, be obliged to enter, clear, or pay Duties in another.

No Money shall be drawn from the Treasury, but in Consequence of Appropriations made by Law; and a regular Statement and Account of the Receipts and Expenditures of all public Money shall be published from time to time.

No Title of Nobility shall be granted by the United States: And no Person holding any Office of Profit or Trust under them, shall, without the Consent of the Congress, accept of any present, Emolument, Office, or Title, of any kind whatever, from any King, Prince or foreign State.

Section 10
No State shall enter into any Treaty, Alliance, or Confederation; grant Letters of Marque and Reprisal; coin Money; emit Bills of Credit; make any Thing but gold and silver Coin a Tender in Payment of Debts; pass any Bill of Attainder, ex post facto Law, or Law impairing the Obligation of Contracts, or grant any Title of Nobility.

No State shall, without the Consent of the Congress, lay any Imposts or Duties on Imports or Exports, except what may be absolutely necessary for executing its inspection Laws: and the net Produce of all Duties and Imposts, laid by any State on Imports or Exports, shall be for the Use of the Treasury of the United States; and all such Laws shall be subject to the Revision and Control of the Congress.

No State shall, without the Consent of Congress, lay any duty of Tonnage, keep Troops, or Ships of War in time of Peace, enter into any Agreement or Compact with another State, or with a foreign Power, or engage in War, unless actually invaded, or in such imminent Danger as will not admit of delay.

Article 2.

Section 1

The executive Power shall be vested in a President of the United States of America. He shall hold his Office during the Term of four Years, and, together with the Vice-President chosen for the same Term, be elected, as follows:

Each State shall appoint, in such Manner as the Legislature thereof may direct, a Number of Electors, equal to the whole Number of Senators and Representatives to which the State may be entitled in the Congress: but no Senator or Representative, or Person holding an Office of Trust or Profit under the United States, shall be appointed an Elector.

The Electors shall meet in their respective States, and vote by Ballot for two persons, of whom one at least shall not lie an Inhabitant of the same State with themselves. And they shall make a List of all the Persons voted for, and of the Number of Votes for each; which List they shall sign and certify, and transmit sealed to the Seat of the Government of the United States, directed to the President of the Senate. The President of the Senate shall, in the Presence of the Senate and House of Representatives, open all the Certificates, and the Votes shall then be counted. The Person having the greatest Number of Votes shall be the President, if such Number be a Majority of the whole Number of Electors appointed; and if there be more than one who have such Majority, and have an equal Number of Votes, then the House of Representatives shall immediately choose by Ballot one of them for President; and if no Person have a Majority, then from the five highest on the List the said House shall in like Manner choose the President. But in choosing the President, the Votes shall be taken by States, the Representation from each State having one Vote; a quorum for this Purpose shall consist of a Member or Members from two-thirds of the States, and a Majority of all the States shall be necessary to a Choice. In every Case, after the Choice of the President, the Person having the greatest Number of Votes of the Electors shall be the Vice President. But if there should remain two or more who have equal Votes, the Senate shall choose from them by Ballot the Vice-President.

The Congress may determine the Time of choosing the Electors, and the Day on which they shall give their Votes; which Day shall be the same throughout the United States.

No person except a natural born Citizen, or a Citizen of the United States, at the time of the Adoption of this Constitution, shall be eligible to the Office of President; neither shall any Person be eligible to that Office who shall not have attained to the Age of thirty-five Years, and been fourteen Years a Resident within the United States.

In Case of the Removal of the President from Office, or of his Death, Resignation, or Inability to discharge the Powers and Duties of the said Office, the same shall devolve on the Vice President, and the Congress may by Law provide for the Case of Removal, Death, Resignation or Inability, both of the President and Vice President, declaring what Officer shall then act as President, and such Officer shall act accordingly, until the Disability be removed, or a President shall be elected.

The President shall, at stated Times, receive for his Services, a Compensation, which shall neither be increased nor diminished during the Period for which he shall have been elected, and he shall not receive within that Period any other Emolument from the United States, or any of them.

Before he enter on the Execution of his Office, he shall take the following Oath or Affirmation:

"I do solemnly swear (or affirm) that I will faithfully execute the Office of President of the United States, and will to the best of my Ability, preserve, protect and defend the Constitution of the United States."

Section 2
The President shall be Commander in Chief of the Army and Navy of the United States, and of the Militia of the several States, when called into the actual Service of the United States; he may require the Opinion, in writing, of the principal Officer in each of the executive Departments, upon any subject relating to the Duties of their respective Offices, and he shall have Power to Grant Reprieves and Pardons for Offenses against the United States, except in Cases of Impeachment.

He shall have Power, by and with the Advice and Consent of the Senate, to make Treaties, provided two thirds of the Senators present concur; and he shall nominate, and by and with the Advice and Consent of the Senate, shall appoint Ambassadors, other public Ministers and Consuls,

Judges of the supreme Court, and all other Officers of the United States, whose Appointments are not herein otherwise provided for, and which shall be established by Law: but the Congress may by Law vest the Appointment of such inferior Officers, as they think proper, in the President alone, in the Courts of Law, or in the Heads of Departments.

The President shall have Power to fill up all Vacancies that may happen during the Recess of the Senate, by granting Commissions which shall expire at the End of their next Session.

Section 3

He shall from time to time give to the Congress Information of the State of the Union, and recommend to their Consideration such Measures as he shall judge necessary and expedient; he may, on extraordinary Occasions, convene both Houses, or either of them, and in Case of Disagreement between them, with Respect to the Time of Adjournment, he may adjourn them to such Time as he shall think proper; he shall receive Ambassadors and other public Ministers; he shall take Care that the Laws be faithfully executed, and shall Commission all the Officers of the United States.

Section 4

The President, Vice President and all civil Officers of the United States, shall be removed from Office on Impeachment for, and Conviction of, Treason, Bribery, or other high Crimes and Misdemeanors.

Article 3.

Section 1

The judicial Power of the United States, shall be vested in one supreme Court, and in such inferior Courts as the Congress may from time to time ordain and establish. The Judges, both of the supreme and inferior Courts, shall hold their Offices during good Behavior, and shall, at stated Times, receive for their Services a Compensation which shall not be diminished during their Continuance in Office.

Section 2

The judicial Power shall extend to all Cases, in Law and Equity, arising under this Constitution, the Laws of the United States, and Treaties made, or which shall be made, under their Authority; to all Cases affecting Ambassadors, other public Ministers and Consuls; to all Cases of admiralty and maritime Jurisdiction; to Controversies to which the United States shall be a Party; to Controversies between two or more States; between a State and Citizens of another State; between Citizens of different States; between Citizens of the same State claiming Lands under Grants of different States, and between a State, or the Citizens thereof, and foreign States, Citizens or Subjects.

In all Cases affecting Ambassadors, other public Ministers and Consuls, and those in which a State shall be Party, the supreme Court shall have original Jurisdiction. In all the other Cases before mentioned, the supreme Court shall have appellate Jurisdiction, both as to Law and Fact, with such Exceptions, and under such Regulations as the Congress shall make.

The Trial of all Crimes, except in Cases of Impeachment, shall be by Jury; and such Trial shall be held in the State where the said Crimes shall have been committed; but when not committed within any State, the Trial shall be at such Place or Places as the Congress may by Law have directed.

Section 3
Treason against the United States, shall consist only in levying War against them, or in adhering to their Enemies, giving them Aid and Comfort. No Person shall be convicted of Treason unless on the Testimony of two Witnesses to the same overt Act, or on Confession in open Court.

The Congress shall have power to declare the Punishment of Treason, but no Attainder of Treason shall work Corruption of Blood, or Forfeiture except during the Life of the Person attainted.

Article 4.
Section 1
Full Faith and Credit shall be given in each State to the public Acts, Records, and judicial Proceedings of every other State. And the Congress may by general Laws prescribe the Manner in which such Acts, Records and Proceedings shall be proved, and the Effect thereof.

Section 2
The Citizens of each State shall be entitled to all Privileges and Immunities of Citizens in the several States.

A Person charged in any State with Treason, Felony, or other Crime, who shall flee from Justice, and be found in another State, shall on demand of the executive Authority of the State from which he fled, be delivered up, to be removed to the State having Jurisdiction of the Crime.

No Person held to Service or Labour in one State, under the Laws thereof, escaping into another, shall, in Consequence of any Law or Regulation therein, be discharged from such Service or Labour, But shall be delivered up on Claim of the Party to whom such Service or Labour may be due.

Section 3

New States may be admitted by the Congress into this Union; but no new States shall be formed or erected within the Jurisdiction of any other State; nor any State be formed by the Junction of two or more States, or parts of States, without the Consent of the Legislatures of the States concerned as well as of the Congress.

The Congress shall have Power to dispose of and make all needful Rules and Regulations respecting the Territory or other Property belonging to the United States; and nothing in this Constitution shall be so construed as to Prejudice any Claims of the United States, or of any particular State.

Section 4

The United States shall guarantee to every State in this Union a Republican Form of Government, and shall protect each of them against Invasion; and on Application of the Legislature, or of the Executive (when the Legislature cannot be convened) against domestic Violence.

Article 5.

The Congress, whenever two thirds of both Houses shall deem it necessary, shall propose Amendments to this Constitution, or, on the Application of the Legislatures of two thirds of the several States, shall call a Convention for proposing Amendments, which, in either Case, shall be valid to all Intents and Purposes, as part of this Constitution, when ratified by the Legislatures of three fourths of the several States, or by Conventions in three fourths thereof, as the one or the other Mode of Ratification may be proposed by the Congress; Provided that no Amendment which may be made prior to the Year One thousand eight hundred and eight shall in any Manner affect the first and fourth Clauses in the

Ninth Section of the first Article; and that no State, without its Consent, shall be deprived of its equal Suffrage in the Senate.

Article 6.

All Debts contracted and Engagements entered into, before the Adoption of this Constitution, shall be as valid against the United States under this Constitution, as under the Confederation.

This Constitution, and the Laws of the United States which shall be made in Pursuance thereof; and all Treaties made, or which shall be made, under the Authority of the United States, shall be the supreme Law of the Land; and the Judges in every State shall be bound thereby, any Thing in the Constitution or Laws of any State to the Contrary notwithstanding.

The Senators and Representatives before mentioned, and the Members of the several State Legislatures, and all executive and judicial Officers, both of the United States and of the several States, shall be bound by Oath or Affirmation, to support this Constitution; but no religious Test shall ever be required as a Qualification to any Office or public Trust under the United States.

Article 7.

The Ratification of the Conventions of nine States, shall be sufficient for the Establishment of this Constitution between the States so ratifying the Same.

Done in Convention by the Unanimous Consent of the States present the Seventeenth Day of September in the Year of our Lord one thousand seven hundred and Eighty seven and of the Independence of the United States of America the Twelfth.

In Witness whereof We have hereunto subscribed our Names.

George Washington—President and deputy from Virginia
New Hampshire—John Langdon, Nicholas Gilman
Massachusetts—Nathaniel Gorham, Rufus King
Connecticut—William Samuel Johnson, Roger Sherman
New York—Alexander Hamilton
New Jersey—William Livingston, David Brearley, William Paterson, Jonathan Dayton

Pennsylvania—Benjamin Franklin, Thomas Mifflin, Robert Morris, George Clymer, Thomas Fitzsimons, Jared Ingersoll, James Wilson, Gouvernour Morris Delaware—George Read, Gunning Bedford Jr., John Dickinson, Richard Bassett, Jacob Broom
Maryland—James McHenry, Daniel of St Thomas Jenifer, Daniel Carroll
Virginia—John Blair, James Madison Jr.
North Carolina—William Blount, Richard Dobbs Spaight, Hugh Williamson
South Carolina—John Rutledge, Charles Cotesworth Pinckney, Charles Pinckney, Pierce Butler
Georgia—William Few, Abraham Baldwin
Attest: William Jackson, Secretary

[THE BILL OF RIGHTS—Amendments 1 through 10]

Amendment 1
Congress shall make no law respecting an establishment of religion, or prohibiting the free exercise thereof; or abridging the freedom of speech, or of the press; or the right of the people peaceably to assemble, and to petition the Government for a redress of grievances.

Amendment 2
A well regulated Militia, being necessary to the security of a free State, the right of the people to keep and bear Arms, shall not be infringed.

Amendment 3
No Soldier shall, in time of peace be quartered in any house, without the consent of the Owner, nor in time of war, but in a manner to be prescribed by law.

Amendment 4
The right of the people to be secure in their persons, houses, papers, and effects, against unreasonable searches and seizures, shall not be violated, and no Warrants shall issue, but upon probable cause, supported by Oath or affirmation, and particularly describing the place to be searched, and the persons or things to be seized.

Amendment 5

No person shall be held to answer for a capital, or otherwise infamous crime, unless on a presentment or indictment of a Grand Jury, except in cases arising in the land or naval forces, or in the Militia, when in actual service in time of War or public danger; nor shall any person be subject for the same offense to be twice put in jeopardy of life or limb; nor shall be compelled in any criminal case to be a witness against himself, nor be deprived of life, liberty, or property, without due process of law; nor shall private property be taken for public use, without just compensation.

Amendment 6

In all criminal prosecutions, the accused shall enjoy the right to a speedy and public trial, by an impartial jury of the State and district wherein the crime shall have been committed, which district shall have been previously ascertained by law, and to be informed of the nature and cause of the accusation; to be confronted with the witnesses against him; to have compulsory process for obtaining witnesses in his favor, and to have the Assistance of Counsel for his defence.

Amendment 7

In Suits at common law, where the value in controversy shall exceed twenty dollars, the right of trial by jury shall be preserved, and no fact tried by a jury, shall be otherwise re-examined in any Court of the United States, than according to the rules of the common law.

Amendment 8

Excessive bail shall not be required, nor excessive fines imposed, nor cruel and unusual punishments inflicted.

Amendment 9

The enumeration in the Constitution, of certain rights, shall not be construed to deny or disparage others retained by the people.

Amendment 10

The powers not delegated to the United States by the Constitution, nor prohibited by it to the States, are reserved to the States respectively, or to the people.

Amendment 11

The Judicial power of the United States shall not be construed to extend to any suit in law or equity, commenced or prosecuted against one of the United States by Citizens of another State, or by Citizens or Subjects of any Foreign State.

Amendment 12

The Electors shall meet in their respective states, and vote by ballot for President and Vice-President, one of whom, at least, shall not be an inhabitant of the same state with themselves; they shall name in their ballots the person voted for as President, and in distinct ballots the person voted for as Vice-President, and they shall make distinct lists of all persons voted for as President, and of all persons voted for as Vice-President and of the number of votes for each, which lists they shall sign and certify, and transmit sealed to the seat of the government of the United States, directed to the President of the Senate; The President of the Senate shall, in the presence of the Senate and House of Representatives, open all the certificates and the votes shall then be counted; The person having the greatest Number of votes for President, shall be the President, if such number be a majority of the whole number of Electors appointed; and if no person have such majority, then from the persons having the highest numbers not exceeding three on the list of those voted for as President, the House of Representatives shall choose immediately, by ballot, the President. But in choosing the President, the votes shall be taken by states, the representation from each state having one vote; a quorum for this purpose shall consist of a member or members from two-thirds of the states, and a majority of all the states shall be necessary to a choice. And if the House of Representatives shall not choose a President whenever the right of choice shall devolve upon them, before the fourth day of March next following, then the Vice-President shall act as President, as in the case of the death or other constitutional disability of the President.

The person having the greatest number of votes as Vice-President, shall be the Vice-President, if such number be a majority of the whole number of Electors appointed, and if no person have a majority, then from the two highest numbers on the list, the Senate shall choose the Vice-President; a quorum for the purpose shall consist of two-thirds of the whole number of Senators, and a majority of the whole number shall be necessary to a choice. But no person constitutionally ineligible to the office of President shall be eligible to that of Vice-President of the United States.

[THE CIVIL WAR AMENDMENTS— Amendments 13 through 15]

Amendment 13

~~1.~~ Neither slavery nor involuntary servitude, except as a punishment for crime whereof the party shall have been duly convicted, shall exist within the United States, or any place subject to their jurisdiction.

~~2. Congress shall have power to enforce this article by appropriate legislation.~~ *(Repealed Amendment 37.)*

Amendment 14

~~1. All persons born or naturalized in the United States, and subject to the jurisdiction thereof, are citizens of the United States and of the State wherein they reside. No State shall make or enforce any law which shall abridge the privileges or immunities of citizens of the United States; nor shall any State deprive any person of life, liberty, or property, without due process of law; nor deny to any person within its jurisdiction the equal protection of the laws.~~ *(Note Section 1 is replaced by Amendments 29 and 30.)*

~~2~~*1*. Representatives shall be apportioned among the several States according to their respective numbers, counting the whole number of persons in each State, excluding Indians not taxed. But when the right to vote at any election for the choice of electors for President and Vice-President of the United States, Representatives in Congress, the Executive and Judicial officers of a State, or the members of the Legislature thereof, is denied to any of the male inhabitants of such State, being twenty-one years of age, and citizens of the United States, or in any way abridged, except for participation in rebellion, or other crime, the basis of representation therein shall be reduced in the proportion which the number of such male citizens shall bear to the whole number of male citizens twenty-one years of age in such State.

~~3~~*2*. No person shall be a Senator or Representative in Congress, or elector of President and Vice-President, or hold any office, civil or military, under the United States, or under any State, who, having previously taken an oath, as a member of Congress, or as an officer of the United States, or as a member of any State legislature, or as an executive or judicial officer of any State, to support the Constitution of the United States, shall have engaged in insurrection or rebellion against the same, or given aid or comfort to the enemies thereof. But Congress may by a vote of two-thirds of each House, remove such disability.

43. The validity of the public debt of the United States, authorized by law, including debts incurred for payment of pensions and bounties for services in suppressing insurrection or rebellion, shall not be questioned. But neither the United States nor any State shall assume or pay any debt or obligation incurred in aid of insurrection or rebellion against the United States, or any claim for the loss or emancipation of any slave; but all such debts, obligations and claims shall be held illegal and void.

5. ~~The Congress shall have power to enforce, by appropriate legislation, the provisions of this article.~~ *(Repealed: Amendment 37.)*

Amendment 15

1. ~~The~~ right of citizens of the United States to vote shall not be denied or abridged by the United States or by any State on account of race, color, or previous condition of servitude.

2. ~~The Congress shall have power to enforce this article by appropriate legislation.~~ *(Repealed Amdt 37.)*

Amendment 16   *(Repealed by Amendment 33.)*
~~The Congress shall have power to lay and collect taxes on incomes, from whatever source derived, without apportionment among the several States, and without regard to any census or enumeration.~~

Amendment 17
The Senate of the United States shall be composed of two Senators from each State, elected by the people thereof, for six years; and each Senator shall have one vote. The electors in each State shall have the qualifications requisite for electors of the most numerous branch of the State legislatures.

When vacancies happen in the representation of any State in the Senate, the executive authority of such State shall issue writs of election to fill such vacancies: Provided, That the legislature of any State may empower the executive thereof to make temporary appointments until the people fill the vacancies by election as the legislature may direct.

This amendment shall not be so construed as to affect the election or term of any Senator chosen before it becomes valid as part of the Constitution.

Amendment 18

1. After one year from the ratification of this article the manufacture, sale, or transportation of intoxicating liquors within, the importation thereof into, or the exportation thereof from the United States and all territory subject to the jurisdiction thereof for beverage purposes is hereby prohibited.

2. The Congress and the several States shall have concurrent power to enforce this article by appropriate legislation.

3. This article shall be inoperative unless it shall have been ratified as an amendment to the Constitution by the legislatures of the several States, as provided in the Constitution, within seven years from the date of the submission hereof to the States by the Congress.

Amendment 19

The right of citizens of the United States to vote shall not be denied or abridged by the United States or by any State on account of sex.

~~Congress shall have power to enforce this article by appropriate legislation.~~ *(Repealed Amendment 37.)*

Amendment 20

1. The terms of the President and Vice President shall end at noon on the 20th day of January, and the terms of Senators and Representatives at noon on the 3d day of January, of the years in which such terms would have ended if this article had not been ratified; and the terms of their successors shall then begin.

2.   The Congress shall assemble at least once in every year, and such meeting shall begin at noon on the 3d day of January, unless they shall by law appoint a different day.

3.   If, at the time fixed for the beginning of the term of the President, the President elect shall have died, the Vice President elect shall become President. If a President shall not have been chosen before the time fixed for the beginning of his term, or if the President elect shall have failed to qualify, then the Vice President elect shall act as President until a President shall have qualified; and the Congress may by law provide for the case wherein neither a President elect nor a Vice President elect shall have qualified, declaring who shall then act as President, or the manner in which one who is to act shall be selected, and such person shall act accordingly until a President or Vice President shall have qualified.

4.   The Congress may by law provide for the case of the death of any of the persons from whom the House of Representatives may choose a President whenever the right of choice shall have devolved upon them, and for the case of the death of any of the persons from whom the Senate may choose a Vice President whenever the right of choice shall have devolved upon them.

5.   Sections 1 and 2 shall take effect on the 15th day of October following the ratification of this article.

6.   This article shall be inoperative unless it shall have been ratified as an amendment to the Constitution by the legislatures of three-fourths of the several States within seven years from the date of its submission.

Amendment 21

1.   The eighteenth article of amendment to the Constitution of the United States is hereby repealed.

2.   The transportation or importation into any State, Territory, or possession of the United States for delivery or use therein of intoxicating liquors, in violation of the laws thereof, is hereby prohibited.

3.   The article shall be inoperative unless it shall have been ratified as an amendment to the Constitution by conventions in the several States,

as provided in the Constitution, within seven years from the date of the submission hereof to the States by the Congress.

Amendment 22

1. No person shall be elected to the office of the President more than twice, and no person who has held the office of President, or acted as President, for more than two years of a term to which some other person was elected President shall be elected to the office of the President more than once. But this Article shall not apply to any person holding the office of President, when this Article was proposed by the Congress, and shall not prevent any person who may be holding the office of President, or acting as President, during the term within which this Article becomes operative from holding the office of President or acting as President during the remainder of such term.

2. This article shall be inoperative unless it shall have been ratified as an amendment to the Constitution by the legislatures of three-fourths of the several States within seven years from the date of its submission to the States by the Congress.

Amendment 23 *(Repealed and Replaced by Amendment 35, Section 2.)*

1. ~~The District constituting the seat of Government of the United States shall appoint in such manner as the Congress may direct: A number of electors of President and Vice President equal to the whole number of Senators and Representatives in Congress to which the District would be entitled if it were a State, but in no event more than the least populous State; they shall be in addition to those appointed by the States, but they shall be considered, for the purposes of the election of President and Vice President, to be electors appointed by a State; and they shall meet in the District and perform such duties as provided by the twelfth article of amendment.~~

2. ~~The Congress shall have power to enforce this article by appropriate legislation.~~

Amendment 24

~~1.~~ The right of citizens of the United States to vote in any primary or other election for President or Vice President, for electors for President or Vice President, or for Senator or Representative in Congress, shall not be denied or abridged by the United States or any State by reason of failure to pay any poll tax or other tax.

2. ~~The Congress shall have power to enforce this article by appropriate legislation.~~ *(Repealed Amdt. 37.)*

Amendment 25

1. In case of the removal of the President from office or of his death or resignation, the Vice President shall become President.

2. Whenever there is a vacancy in the office of the Vice President, the President shall nominate a Vice President who shall take office upon confirmation by a majority vote of both Houses of Congress.

3. Whenever the President transmits to the President pro tempore of the Senate and the Speaker of the House of Representatives his written declaration that he is unable to discharge the powers and duties of his office, and until he transmits to them a written declaration to the contrary, such powers and duties shall be discharged by the Vice President as Acting President.

4. Whenever the Vice President and a majority of either the principal officers of the executive departments or of such other body as Congress may by law provide, transmit to the President pro tempore of the Senate and the Speaker of the House of Representatives their written declaration that the President is unable to discharge the powers and duties of his office, the Vice President shall immediately assume the powers and duties of the office as Acting President.

Thereafter, when the President transmits to the President pro tempore of the Senate and the Speaker of the House of Representatives his written declaration that no inability exists, he shall resume the powers and duties of his office unless the Vice President and a majority of either the principal officers of the executive department or of such other body as Congress may by law provide, transmit within four days to the President pro tempore of the Senate and the Speaker of the House of Representatives their written declaration that the President is unable to discharge the powers and duties of his office. Thereupon Congress shall decide the issue, assembling within forty eight hours for that purpose if not in session. If the Congress, within twenty one days after receipt of the latter written declaration, or, if Congress is not in session, within twenty one days after Congress is required to assemble, determines by two thirds vote of both Houses that the President is unable to discharge the powers and duties of his office, the Vice President shall continue to discharge the same as Acting President; otherwise, the President shall resume the powers and duties of his office.

Amendment 26

1. The right of citizens of the United States, who are eighteen years of age or older, to vote shall not be denied or abridged by the United States or by any State on account of age.

2. The Congress shall have power to enforce this article by appropriate legislation. *(Repealed Amendment 37.)*

Amendment 27

No law, varying the compensation for the services of the Senators and Representatives, shall take effect, until an election of Representatives shall have intervened.

[THE SECOND BILL OF RIGHTS— Amendments 28 through 38]

Amendment 28 [1.]

1. The Rule of Law in the United States shall forever be comprised of: allocated powers among the people, the states, and the national government under this Constitution; broad liberty rights retained by the people; the police power retained by each State to preserve the common exercise of liberty rights; limited, enumerated legislative powers vested in and exercisable only by an elected Congress; separation of national powers among Congress, the Executive, and the Judiciary; and development of the common law consistent therewith by an independent state and federal judiciary.

2. The Preamble to this Constitution is a statement of general purpose, and not a grant of powers to the government. The language in Article I, Section 8 "to pay the Debts and provide for the common Defence and general Welfare of the United States" is a limitation on the power

of Congress to lay and collect taxes, duties, imposts, and excises, not an independent grant of power in addition to those otherwise set forth in Section 8. The Judiciary shall rely, when interpreting this Constitution, on the publicly known meaning of the words contained in the Constitution at the time such words were adopted.

Amendment 29 [2.]

1. All persons born or naturalized in the United States and subject to the jurisdiction thereof are citizens of the United States. Section 1 of Amendment XIV is repealed.

2. The freedoms, privileges, and immunities—together, the liberty rights—held by citizens at the adoption of this Constitution are retained by the people, are not surrendered to government, and shall not be abridged by the United States. Citizens are endowed with inalienable power to exercise their liberty rights under the Rule of Law. Neither Congress, nor the Executive, nor the Judiciary shall have power to create or grant liberty rights.

3. Liberty rights include, but are not limited to, the rights to life, liberty, and pursuit of happiness; to property in one's own labor and industry; to preserve and secure personal health and safety; to keep and bear arms; to acquire, inherit, purchase, lease, sell, hold, convey, and enjoy real and personal property; to religious liberty; to freedom in matters of conscience; to freedom in making and enforcing lawful contracts of all kinds (including freedom not to contract); to establish a family, to care for and to raise children, and to secure the health, education, and safety thereof; to freedom of press, speech, assemblage, and petition; to pursue any lawful livelihood or avocation; to engage in a profession, trade, business, or calling; and to privacy in one's person, effects, papers, preferences, and affairs.

4. The exercise by a citizen of liberty rights shall be presumed valid by the Judiciary against any law made by Congress and any rule or order made by the Executive that denies or abridges such rights; Provided, that this presumption shall not prevail with respect to laws made pursuant to an enumerated power; and Provided Further, that where Congress relies in part upon the necessary and proper clause of Article 1 Section 8 to make any such law, this presumption may be rebutted upon a showing by the Executive that such law: (i) is plainly necessary in the

exercise of an enumerated power; (ii) could not achieve the purpose of an enumerated power by other means not so restrictive of liberty rights, and (iii) is consistent with the Rule of Law.

Amendment 30 [3.]

Neither Congress nor the Executive, and no State shall deprive any citizen of life, liberty, or property without due process in accord with the Rule of Law; nor deny to any citizen the equal protection of the laws; nor discriminate for or against any citizen on the basis of race, color, national origin, or gender, or on the basis of belief or non-belief in any creed or religion.

Amendment 31 [4.]

1. The police power is reserved to each of the States under Amendment 10 and includes the power to promote the health, good order, morals, peace, and safety of citizens residing therein through laws of general application that preserve the common exercise of liberty rights.

2. The exercise by a citizen of liberty rights shall be presumed valid against any state law that denies or abridges such rights; Provided, that this presumption may be rebutted upon a showing by the state that such law could not achieve the purpose of the police power by other means not so restrictive of liberty rights.

3. Neither Congress nor the Executive shall make any law, rule, or order requiring a State to exercise the police power in a specific manner as a condition of receiving grants, appropriations, funds, or benefits from, or avoiding penalties imposed by, the federal government. All such conditions shall be held illegal and void.

4. All cases, in law and equity, arising under this amendment shall be heard in the courts of the several States. The Supreme Court may review such cases, with due deference to each State's exercise of the police power.

Amendment 32 [5.]

1. The fiscal year for the federal government shall begin on April 1 and end on the following March 31. Before October 1, the President shall present to Congress government-wide financial statements in accord with generally accepted government accounting principles for the

previous fiscal year with comparisons to the prior two fiscal years, and which shall: include a statement of net assets and a statement of activities; report all of the assets, the condition thereof, current and future liabilities, revenues, expenses, gains and losses of government; distinguish between governmental and business-type activities; and include discussion and analysis. Before October 1, the President shall present to Congress his recommended budget for the next fiscal year, in a format consistent with the government-wide financial statements, with projected revenues, expenses, gains, and losses, changes in assets and the condition thereof, current and future liabilities, along with discussion and analysis.

2. Congress shall by law establish the number of grains of gold nine-tenths fine that shall be the standard unit of value equivalent to the U.S. dollar, which standard shall thereafter be adjusted only through legislation originating in the House of Representatives, and passed by three fifths of both the House of Representatives and the Senate. All forms of money issued or coined by the United States shall be in parity with this standard. Congress shall not delegate the setting or adjustment of this standard to anyone, including the Executive.

Amendment 33 [6.]

1. Congress shall have the power to lay and the States to collect on its behalf, a uniform consumption tax on all retail sales of new goods and services to all purchasers, including local, state, and federal government purchasers; Provided, that Congress shall at the same time establish uniform rebates for adults and for children, indexed for inflation and deflation, to shield basic household necessities from such consumption tax, paid monthly to each citizen, legal resident, or the guardian thereof, by the State in which they then reside.

2. Congress shall have no power to levy federal taxes on income, estates, and gifts; no power to lay or collect a Value Added Tax; and no power to levy any excise tax measured by wages. The sixteenth article of amendment to this constitution is repealed.

ALTERNATE Amendment 33 [Alt. 6.]

1. Congress shall have no power to levy other than a single tax on the income of individuals, and a single tax on the net income of business

entities determined in accordance with generally accepted accounting principles under the common law. The highest rate of tax imposed on ordinary income shall not exceed thirty percent and shall not exceed two times the lowest rate so imposed. The rate of tax imposed on income from (i) property held for one year or more, including property so held by or on behalf of individuals for retirement; (ii) the domestic manufacture of durable goods for sale; and (iii) the design, construction, repair, maintenance and operation of domestic infrastructure facilities (including water supply and treatment, energy supply and generation, road, port, airport, rail, transit, and such other facilities as may be identified by Congress) shall not exceed one-half of the lowest rate of tax imposed on ordinary income.

2. Congress shall establish for individuals: (i) separate personal exemptions from gross income uniformly applicable to each adult and dependent child; (ii) a separate maximum exemption uniformly applicable to each adult deferring from gross income funds actually set aside by the taxpayer during the year for retirement, but not in excess of 20% of gross income; (iii) separate exemptions from gross income uniformly applicable to each adult and dependent child who has contracted for basic health care coverage, as defined by the state in which the taxpayer resides; and (iv) an annual deduction not in excess of 20% of adjusted gross income uniformly applicable to each taxpayer for funds actually contributed to charitable organizations during the year. Exemptions shall be indexed for inflation and deflation. No other adjustment to income or to tax on income shall depend on a taxpayer's level of income, value of assets held, or applicable rate of tax.

3. Congress shall have no power to levy any excise tax on employers measured by wages and no power to levy any tax on the estates of, or on gifts made by, citizens and residents of the United States. Gifts and bequests shall not be income to recipients.

4. Congress shall have no power to lay or collect a Value Added Tax or a Consumption Tax.

Amendment 34 [7.]

As part of a uniform Rule of Naturalization, Congress shall provide a process in law: (i) for any person not a citizen to make application for residence or for naturalization (that is, citizenship) in the United States,

(ii) for clear standards for approval and prompt review of each such application; and (iii) if approved, for an applicant to thereby become subject to the jurisdiction of the United States as a citizen or as a resident.

Amendment 35 [8.]

1. No decennial Enumeration shall be other than an actual count of citizens, and shall in no event include estimates. Based upon each Enumeration, every State with more than one district shall establish district boundaries for the House of Representatives that are substantially different from the preceding Enumeration, without regard to race, color, gender, creed, religion, or party affiliation of persons therein. Each district shall comprise an area that is contiguous and not of unusually irregular shape. The quotient obtained from dividing the sum of the outer circumference of each district by the square root of the area of the district shall be as close as reasonably practicable to that obtained for all other districts and as close as reasonably practical to four—that of a square. Boundaries with other States and with navigable waters may be approximated by straight lines. The cognizant United States Court of Appeals shall have original trial jurisdiction in an action by a citizen to enforce this Amendment for a district in which the citizen resides.

2. One year after the effective date of this amendment, the Seat of Government—Washington DC—shall be limited to the land, as Congress shall identify prior to such date by legislation, now comprising the National Mall with its museums and libraries, the Lincoln and Jefferson Memorials, the Houses of Congress and their existing office buildings, the Supreme Court, Lafayette Park and its existing office structures, the White House, and such other immediately adjacent facilities. The rest of the District of Columbia shall return to Maryland as Washington City, and its citizens included in the enumeration for Maryland. Amendment XXIII is repealed.

Amendment 36 [9.]

Congress' power to regulate Commerce among the several States shall only extend to transportation, trade, or exchange of goods and services in such Commerce. Congress shall have no power to require any citizen, resident, or legal entity to engage in such commerce. Congress shall have no power to require any citizen, resident, or legal entity to participate in or contribute to any retirement, annuity, insurance, medical, disability, or similar plan established, managed, or controlled by the United States.

Amendment 37 [10.]

1. The Judicial power shall be exercised to preserve liberty rights, the Rule of Law, the police power of each of the several States, and the republican form of government. Section 2 of Amendments XIII, XV, XXIV, and XXVI; Sections 1 and 5 of Amendment XIV; and the second paragraph of Amendment XIX are repealed.

2. The President in nominating, and the Senate in advice and consent, shall consider the experience of each judicial nominee in the practice of the common law.

3. In all Cases before the Courts of the United States between Citizens of different States, the prevailing party or parties shall be awarded reasonable attorneys' fees, costs, and expenses.

4. No inferior court of the United States shall have jurisdiction over: (i) any matter involving a uniformed military service, its policies and regulations, its personnel, its code of military justice, or the conduct of such personnel in military service; or (ii) any case or controversy which the President declares in writing involves terrorism with some foreign element. The President need not disclose specifics of such elements in the notice.

5. Citizens accused of terrorism against the United States may be tried for treason in the Courts of the United States in accord with the Rule of Law.

Amendment 38 [11.]

1. From the effective date of Amendments 28 to 38 (the Second Bill of Rights), the Executive shall not execute or enforce any law, rule, or order, or make any new rule or order inconsistent with the Constitution, as amended. Congress shall promptly modify the statutes of the United States for an orderly transition to conform herewith.

2. Congress may enact legislation that: (i) preserves social security payments and medicare benefits under current law, but free of income tax, for persons who at the date of this amendment are 65 years of age and

older; (ii) gives the option to persons then between 45 and 64 years of age (a) to contribute to social security and medicare under current law and (b) at age 65 to receive such payments and benefits, free of income tax; and (iii) establishes a means test of general application to all persons for reductions, in whole or part, and in amount or time, with respect to one or more of these payments and benefits.

Made in the USA
Lexington, KY
26 March 2012